HONED

A TWIN BROTHER'S BIOGRAPHY OF THE UNFORGETTABLE ROB SLATER

Rich Slater

This story is written from my memories of Rob, many of
which still make me laugh out loud whenever I think of them,
or when I retell them anytime to anyone who will listen. It is
also from the tales of those who knew him best and whose
lives he similarly touched with his unique brand of
determination, forthrightness and his spirit of the wild.

Rob's tale is not meant to be some highbrow treatise or expose
on anything. Those not consulted for this book, or others who
may have witnessed or been involved in events described
herein may have a different memory. That's fine-if you don't
like my version you are, with all respect, free to read
something else. I didn't change any names, but I did leave
some out for obvious reasons. No serious attempt has been
made to protect the sacredness of anything because that
wasn't Rob's style and it's not mine either.

> Yours in sheep,
> Rich Slater

March, 2012

*In Rob's memory, dedicated to the Mary Slaters of my life,
my Family, the Team and the Mountain Gods...*

For Kyle,

My Honed old buddy, roommate, fellow member of the Clan, drinkin' buddy + everything else!

Stay Honed!

Cheers, Rich

Acknowledgements

This has been an epic undertaking for a lot of reasons and I owe many thanks to many people for their encouragement, support and assistance. Thanks to Mary for listening to all the Robbie stories (over and over), the reads and rereads and unwavering love and support. Thanks also to Sis and Dave Jasper and Dr. Delbert and Beverly Fisher for their patient reads and rereads and to Dad, Tommy and Paul for input and encouragement. Thanks to John "Verm" Sherman, Chris "Nick Cafe" Archer, Al "Poncho" Torissi, Dr. Jim Bodenhamer, Mike O'Donnell, John Barbella, Greg Child, Richard Celsi, Dr. Geoff Tabin, Peter and Amy Sherman, Mark Daly, David Williams, the FBI, Bob and Joan Heid, The Chief Ken Bull, the Lynch Mob, Dr. Brent Weigner and Roger Gill for great input, memories and inspiration. Thanks to Bob Birkby for help with the basic mechanics and to Randy "RSL" Leavitt and especially Robin "Black Death" Heid for helping turn a great tale into hopefully a great book. You guys are honed.

TABLE OF CONTENTS

FOREWORD

We all meet unforgettable people during our lives, sometimes in person, sometimes through books, films or folk tales. However we meet them, these unforgettables shape our lives through either positive inspiration or example – or as case studies in how not to be.

Through the pages of *Honed* you are about to meet two such unforgettable people who embody the example that life should be not measured by the number of breaths we take but by the moments that take our breath away.

Richard and Robert Slater were born about two minutes apart on December 6, 1960, and grew up together mostly in Wyoming with their parents Paul and Mary, and their siblings Tom, Paul and Sissy. Like most identical twins, they were closer to each other than ordinary brothers and shared a kind of secret twins language – in their case, a sense of humor the people around them found often impenetrable and usually obnoxious.

Both were also bold and daring, having grown up in the outdoors and learned early that life was to be lived at full throttle, not at idle.

Still, they took different paths as they grew up. Rob fell in love early with the wild, and with rock climbing in particular, while Rich took the more conventional testosterone-releasing path of raising hell and chasing hot chicks.

It was during their college years that I met Rich and Rob, mostly because Rob had decided to learn how to BASE jump after watching a jumper zoom by him like a jet fighter as he hung one day on ropes and steel far up on the vertical granite face of Yosemite's El Capitan Mountain – after which he resolved to never walk down from its summit again.

I met Rob one sunny day in Eldorado Canyon, a climbing Mecca south of Boulder, Colorado, where Rob attended the University of Colorado along with renowned climber Randy Leavitt. Leavitt knew us both and had taught Rob to skydive through a rather unconventional training method, then brought him to me to further his parachuting skills in preparation for what would be a short but notable BASE jumping career.

It's no stretch to say that Rob is one of the most unforgettable people I've had the pleasure to personally meet – and believe me, I've met several, as well as a good friend and a person I admired greatly.

I had both the privilege and pleasure of helping Rob learn to BASE jump as he taught me to climb, and shared in many of his BASE jumping adventures, then had the continuing privilege and pleasure of watching him from near and far as he sought and reached new climbing goals in the rocks around Boulder, the mud walls of Moab and Monument Valley, and in the icy wilds of Canada and the Karakoram. Rob was, in fact, not only one of the most unforgettable people I've known but unequivocally the most vibrantly alive.

So it's no coincidence that, as almost all Americans remember precisely where they were and what they were doing on 9/11 or the day John F. Kennedy was shot, I still remember as if it was yesterday where I was and what I was doing when I learned that K2 had killed Rob Slater.

I was sitting in southern California at a friend's kitchen breakfast bar, skimming through the *Orange County Register* when I came across a small item about six climbers missing on K2 after a storm.

"Dammit!" I said out loud, because I knew enough about K2 and 8,000-meter peak climbing to know even Rob Slater would need a miracle to live through a storm on Earth's most heinous dangerous mountain.

I quickly called Randy Leavitt, who had already been in touch with "the community," and from him I learned that there was conflicting information and the slim hope that Rob and the other climbers may have lived through the tempest.

Then we all became momentary victims of a world media unfamiliar with K2 climbing that reported Rob's team as having left for the summit after noon on August 13 – 12 hours late and thus utterly suicidal. Suddenly, we all felt some anger and much bewilderment that he and the others would succumb so mightily to summit fever to make a doomed-from-the-start sortie for the top.

Several urgent satellite calls to the Karakoram later, we learned to our relief though not joy that Rob's party had left at midnight, an hour earlier than the generally recognized departure deadline of 1 a.m. – and that the most formidable K2 storm in living memory or known history had given little sign of its coming until they approached the summit.

"Rob didn't make any mistakes," Leavitt concluded after talking with climbers who had been high up on nearby Broad Peak as the storm engulfed the Karakoram and climbed K2's icy flanks until it reached Rob and his companions as they descended the completely exposed summit ridge toward the relative safety of the mountain's flanks. "Sometimes you do everything right and you still die."

By then, however, two or three days had passed and we knew that Rob had taken his last breath somewhere in the ice and snow and stone at the top of the world. We were all sad that he had passed, and some of the less adventurous among us were shaken that a superman like Rob could die at all during any kind of adventure, but eventually we all moved on with our lives.

We never forgot Rob Slater, though, and he continues to be a bond between those of us who knew him, and even those who knew him only through tales of his exploits. A case in point; one day I was at a southern California climbing gym, wearing Rob's swami belt with his name written on it in black marker when a young man approached me, eyes wide open and a look of wonder on his face.

"That's Rob Slater's swami belt?" he asked. I nodded and he said, "You knew him?" And when I nodded again, he immediately recited all the unforgettable stories he remembered about Rob – and I knew that from that day forward, he would add to his Rob Slater repertoire the day he saw and touched with his own hands one of the very climbing harnesses Rob wore during several of his El Cap and desert exploits.

I still have that swami belt, despite Randy Leavitt's efforts to talk me out of it, and several of Rob's El Cap etriers too. I keep them as tokens of one of the most unforgettable people I've known, and because I still use them, the swami belt for climbing and the etriers for various projects where some bulletproof tubular nylon is needed.

That gear remained my closest connection to Rob until one day in late 2009 when Randy called to say that Rich Slater was writing a book about his twin brother and that, given my knowledge of Rob and his life, and my professional skillset as a writer and editor, it might be good for Rich and me to hook up.

As I mentioned earlier, I met Rich about the same time I met Rob, during a couple of Rob's BASE jumping adventures. We didn't spend much time together, but he came across as a solid guy in the commando-style environment of illegal BASE jumping – and, of course, Rob always spoke highly of his twin.

Soon after we started working on *Honed* together, however, I discovered that Rich had picked up the unforgettable mantle his brother first wore and ran with it – literally. Let me bottom-line it for you this way: Just as 8,000-meter climbers are the most elite of the world's mountaineers, "ultra runners" are the most elite of the world's long-distance runners.

Ultra runners don't just run marathons; they run marathons to train for their "real" races, which range in distance from about 31 miles (five miles longer than a marathon) to 100 miles. Ultra runners don't just get blisters and shin splints; they get hallucinations and their kidneys shut down.

Rich isn't into organized racing much; he prefers to just go out alone in the mountains and run as far as he can. At first he did it to escape the rage and despair he felt over his twin's death; now he does it to embrace his brother's memory – and because Rich Slater now wills himself on to ever greater extremes along his own wild path in precisely the same way Rob Slater did on his.

So as *Honed* takes you on an journey to meet two unforgettable people whose lives will take your breath away, you may find that they inspire you to get honed and do something breathtaking yourself.

– Robin "Black Death" Heid
Crawford, Colorado, December 2011

Preface

Honed: adj. impressive, attractive, praiseworthy, worthy of emulation

–The Rob Slater Dictionary

Before there was Tony Hawk skateboarding in empty swimming pools there was Robbie Slater screaming down the Cheyenne Frontier Days arena ramps and launching himself on his old green Schwinn. Before there was Fear Factor contestants climbing scaffolding with safety lines and eating worms there was Robbie Slater topping out on the hardest routes in Yosemite having subsisted for five days on Sara Lee coffee cakes and Mint Milanos, three days on water alone and the last two days on nothing. Before there was the X Games and its generation of pop culture daredevils there was Robbie Slater diving off antennae, bridges, skyscrapers, mountain cliffs and canyon walls with a parachute, mostly at night. Before climbers wore Lycra there was Robbie Slater wielding the Lovetron on previously inconceivable, death-defying aid moves on El Capitan. Long before "crazy" became cool and popular on TV there was Robbie Slater.

If there had been X Games, Fear Factor, skateboard parks and the like, Robbie might have found all the danger he needed to satisfy his drive to do what no one else would even dare. Maybe he could have done without skydiving and BASE jumping. Maybe he wouldn't have been so hell-bent on risking everything time after time putting up the toughest new routes on sheer granite walls. Most of all, he might have been able to do without K2, the world's deadliest mountain that became his obsession and drew him far too soon to his demise.

But I doubt it. I know about Robbie because I am his identical twin brother. I called him Robbie and he called me Richie. As we got older, we were called Rob and Rich by others, but between us it was always Robbie and Richie. We were in many ways as similar as two human beings could be. We looked alike, talked alike and even liked the same kind of Pop Tarts. But when it came to living life, Robbie went much further out on that razor's edge, staring down The Reaper and thumbing his nose at disaster than I ever had the courage for. I have never been afraid of dying, but my twin brother had a much greater need for adrenaline and danger than I've ever felt. Quoting the infamous Charles Manson, Robbie used to joke he "was crazy back when being crazy meant something." But it was much more than that.

Looking back, I wonder how, as twins, we could be so different. By telling his tale and sharing with you his accomplishments and personality, I hope to understand him better. I know what he loved, but I am also compelled to seek out what motivated him and what he feared. I want to be with my brother again, but not just in spirit. Perhaps if I can understand him – and therefore, myself – better through this memoir, we'll grow closer. Perhaps I'll discover we weren't so different after all.

Rob grinning down on El Cap

Prologue

"…nothing but dogshit here, Mikey."
—Rob Slater
"You're under arrest. Stop."
—Unknown ranger

El Capitan is horrendous. It's hideous and heinous. It's a horrifically terrifying cliff. Unsurprisingly, it's also a rock climbing Mecca. Towering more than 3,000 feet from the valley floor in Yosemite National Park in central California, you can hike to its base, look up and barely be able to see the top. It's a huge overhang, steeper than vertical. If you look really hard, you may be able to discern tiny spots clinging high above to the smooth granite walls. They're aid climbers, fearless souls who use ropes and an array of small gadgetry to ascend the huge, glassy face that's impossible to climb otherwise.

One summer day in June, 1982, Mike O'Donnell of Boulder, Colorado, looked up from his spot on a tiny ledge on an upper portion of Sea of Dreams, one of "El Cap's" toughest routes. Mike could barely see his friend and climbing partner Rob Slater on the immense rock overhang above – though he could easily hear Rob's nonstop monologue about Danny Thomas, Phil Donahue, Tony Curtis, pop culture and junior high girls on swim teams. However, when Rob occasionally looked down, Mike could clearly see a speck of white which he recognized as Rob's maniacal grin.

Later on, on a particularly dicey section, Mike became uncharacteristically concerned because the rock – and the risk – was way beyond heinous. It was "weinous" as Rob would say – and way past any reasonable definition of "the edge." But then Mike remembered that Rob's "edge" was way further out than pretty much everyone.

"Throughout, Slater displayed astonishing cockiness in the face of death. He'd be looking down at a pinnacle 100 feet below that he'd impale himself on, and yell down, 'This is nothing but dogshit here, Mikey,'" O'Donnell recalled, shaking his head at Rob's uncanny ability to remain incredibly focused on the climb and maintain a razor-thin balance to stay on the rock.

The weinous route slowed them down more than they had planned and for the last three days, they had no food. On the final day, to lighten their load, they jettisoned all nonessential gear, including sleeping bags and coats. At the end, Rob was so weak he could manage only one swing of his hammer at each pin as he cleaned the hardware from the last pitch. They finally reached the top, triumphant because they were alive, successful and they were still friends. Pounded by a wind-driven rain, they huddled under their remaining haul bags to face a long, grim night.

Rob had one thing left to do. The wind and rain abated before dawn, leaving conditions perfect for Rob's final "pitch" on Sea of Dreams. Rob strapped on a parachute rig a friend had stashed at the top for him then dove off the edge. In seconds, he hurtled past the rock on which he and "Mikey" had just spent a week and a half clawing their way up. In the silent blackness he pitched his pilot chute, deployed his main parachute and sailed towards El Cap Meadow below. During his final approach to landing, two headlights appeared. Rob swooped through their beams, hitting the ground 30 feet from… a National Park Service patrol car. He heard doors slam.

"You're under arrest. Stop."

But Rob didn't stop. Instead, he ran off across the meadow, gathering his parachute as he went. Even in his weakened condition, burdened with a parachute, Rob easily outran the first of the two pursuing park rangers, who apparently suffered from Krispy Kreme Syndrome and who quickly gave up the chase. The other, more physically fit from hours spent polishing his badge, started gaining on Rob, who up to then had a clean police record, but now faced arrest and incarceration for trespassing, attempting to elude and resisting arrest.

The gig was almost up, but not quite. Rob dumped his rig and dove into the icy waters of the Merced River, hoping the current would carry him to freedom. The remaining ranger ran along the bank waving his pistol and screaming at Rob. Eventually, he too abandoned the pursuit, apparently concluding the situation didn't warrant gunfire and all the extra paperwork.

Rob floated down the Merced about three miles before dragging himself out and running into the forest to hide. Two days later, he emerged from the woods and casually rode the bus back to camp, completing his escape.

Rob kept his freedom but lost about three grand in confiscated gear, an amount he laughed off as "worth every penny." When he told me the tale, I wondered if the chase and dive into the river was more exciting for him than the parachute dive off the cliff. It certainly added to the story – but it also gave me at least a glimpse of part of my twin's underlying motivation…

Rob diving into the Black Canyon

Chapter I

The Leavitt Accelerated Free Fall School and the Black Death School of BASE

The Leavitt Accelerated Free Fall School did not have a dean's office, much less a campus. It had no phone listing in the Yellow Pages and its proprietor didn't have a business license, insurance bond, or even a sign on the side of his car. There was no alumni booster club and, unfortunately, no cheerleaders. In fact, it only had one student that day in the spring of 1981. The tuition was entirely reasonable.

"Go buy a rig so I know you're serious – and pay for my jump," said Randy Leavitt to Rob Slater, who readily agreed.

The summer before, while making his first ascent of El Cap, Rob's concentration on climbing a tiny crack thousands of feet above the ground was interrupted by a skydiver whizzing past, flashing toward the valley floor at 100 miles per hour before popping his parachute and floating effortlessly to a soft landing in the meadow below. In a matter of seconds he had descended a distance that would take Rob nearly two weeks to climb – and hours to descend. Turning back to the strenuous task of setting protection and working his way upward, Rob vowed that he, too, would someday fly.

"I'm never going to walk down from the top of El Cap again," Rob declared.

Sometime later, Rob found his way to a parachute center, whose name he never mentioned to me. There, he made four military-style "static line" jumps, where he leapt out of the plane and had his parachute automatically opened at the end of a ten-foot line attached at one end to the airplane and at the other end to his parachute.

There was no freefall involved in those first jumps and, according the conventional static line training method of the time, it would take Rob another 30-50 freefall jumps of progressively longer "delays" to learn the freefall skills necessary for him to competently parachute off El Capitan.

"This is going to take forever,'" Rob realized, frustrated he couldn't learn to skydive in a few weeks or months. An opportunity, however, arose by chance one evening on Boulder's Pearl Street Mall.

Rob ran into his climbing friend Leonard Coyne, who was hanging out with well-known climber and fellow Colorado University student Randy Leavitt. In 1979, Randy became the first person in the world to climb and then parachute from the same cliff. Randy had climbed El Capitan's Excalibur route and then dove from the top of the Dawn Wall route made famous in Warren Harding's book, *Downward Bound*. Several months later, Randy climbed the Shield route and jumped again from the Dawn Wall. This time, though, he met a greeting party of park rangers when he landed in the meadow.

"There was legal jumping there for six weeks in 1980," Randy said, "and I got ratted out by some skydivers there eager to show the rangers that they could police themselves." Randy paid the price of the skydivers' pathetic appeasement with a few days in the "John Muir Hotel," as the Yosemite jail was called, followed by a lengthy probation.

Rob knew of Randy's exploits and immediately proclaimed how cool he thought it was and that he wanted to do the same thing. There was something different in Rob's gung-ho demeanor that made Randy think Rob might be serious, but he wanted to test his new acquaintance's mettle. Randy invited Rob to go climbing and the two quickly became friends. Rob referred to his new buddy as "RSL," short for Randall Stephen Leavitt, "The Leavittator," or simply as "Randall," being one of the few to call him by his official moniker.

RSL, with more than 200 jumps at the time, had gone through conventional static line training school in Elsinore, California, but he believed Rob could learn at a much faster pace. As a honed climber, The Leavittator reasoned, Rob already knew how to perform under threat-of-death stress and knew and had confidence in the nylon and high-grade steel components that climbing and parachuting gear shared.

"I gained a lot of respect for Rob through his climbing," RSL said, "and for more than just his skill. I'd climbed with other guys who were as good or better, and some who were faster learners, but with Rob, more than anything, it was his determination that stuck out in my mind. I saw the mental determination that he would accomplish whatever he wanted to do, that when he set a goal, it was not question of could he do it but how fast. When it came to jumping off cliffs, he *was* going to do it. It was only a question of when."

Unlike ski areas or scuba schools, which tailor training programs to fit the learning pace, physical ability and financial means of individual customers, essentially all U.S. parachute centers use a "one size fits all" approach to training. If Rob went the conventional route to parachuting competency, it would take a lot of time and money.

But it wasn't Rob's style to follow the traditional path and, fortunately for him, RSL had a better idea. From their mutual belief in the inadequacies of convention, the Leavitt Accelerated Free Fall School (LAFFS) was born. Simply put, RSL would teach Rob how to jump the same way people learned how to climb. The Leavittator would lay out the basics of technique and equipment and proceed at whatever pace Rob could handle physically and mentally.

The final piece was Rob getting a complete parachute system, consisting of a main parachute, reserve parachute and harness-container system before the training started. This would confirm to RSL that his new student was indeed committed to seeing the process through and not acting on some short-term "Gumby" whim. With purchasing guidance from RSL, preceded by a serious dip into his sacred climbing fund, Rob soon acquired a decent parachute rig that met RSL's requirements. The LAFFS was thus set to commence.

The Leavittator started with the basics: "Get a properly open parachute over your head before you land or you die."

"Cause of death – impact," they both laughed.

RSL showed Rob how the gear worked and how similar it was to climbing equipment in terms of materials, strength and manufacturing standards. He showed him how to correctly pack the chute and get "rigged up" in his parachuting apparatus. Basic aerodynamics were explained so Rob understood how his wing-like "square" parachute moved through the sky and how he could control its direction, rate of descent and landing force by using the toggles at the end of the control line on each side.

"Without the chute you bounce," RSL told Rob, "but do it my way and landing will be like stepping off a phonebook."

Next, RSL had Rob lie on the hood of a car and assume the basic "arch" position used by all parachutists to stay stable in freefall. With arms and legs spread a comfortable distance apart, back arched, head high, hips thrust downward, the arch allows for the unimpeded and all-important proper deployment of the parachute when it came time to "pull."

"Skydiving's pretty easy compared to climbing," RSL told Rob, "but you can't screw up any of the four or five things you have to do right. It really is pretty basic: Arch your back, if you start spinning, dive out of it and re-arch." If something went wrong, he could correct a problem before bouncing.

Under RSL's watchful eye, Rob practiced his arch until he'd developed enough muscle memory for it to feel reasonably natural and comfortable. He also practiced putting his gear on and off, "checking his handles," and doing all the other things an experienced jumper would know and do by heart. Satisfied Rob at least acted like he knew what he was doing; RSL matriculated him from the LAFFS ground school and began outlining his first-jump dive plan.

Rob would jump out and assume the arch position, followed shortly thereafter by RSL. Rob would try to maintain the arch position, hold a heading and check his altimeter until he reached an altitude about 3,500 feet above the ground, the standard pull altitude for less experienced jumpers. It provided several more seconds to open the parachute or, if there was a problem, jettison the main parachute and deploy the reserve.

Pulling at 3,500 feet would also give Rob a longer parachute ride and more time to figure out how to control it, get it aimed in the right direction and have plenty of time to line up and otherwise prepare for landing.

RSL stressed the importance of staying stable – but also the even greater importance of pulling at 3,500 feet no matter what.

"Even if your parachute malfunctions because you're not stable when you pull," counseled RSL, "you still slow things down and that's better than trying to get stable all the way to cause of death – impact."

"Cause of death: panic and impact-and being a pussy," Rob added, laughing.

Then he had Rob mentally practice his landing approach and "flare" – simultaneously pulling down both toggles to slow the parachute's forward and vertical speed. Rob practiced his landing procedures and even stepped off the curb and a phone book to cement the visualization in his mind.

When RSL deemed Rob ready to jump, he presented him with a blank skydiver logbook, used by jumpers to faithfully and honestly record the dates, locations, altitudes, and free fall times of their jumps. Like pilot flight logs, they are sworn records of accomplishment that are not to be trifled with lightly, used by parachutists to officially document their skills and experience when they go to commercial parachute centers.

Of course, no parachute center would allow Rob, with his four static line jumps and no freefall experience, to get on a plane and jump out of it at 10,500 feet. A paper record was needed to match what RSL considered to be his actual ability. That little technicality seemed a not insurmountable problem for persons of intelligence and ingenuity, which Rob and RSL certainly believed themselves to be. Rob sat down, logbook and pen in hand, and forged entry after entry of bogus jumps he would claim to have completed.

When his list topped 50 jumps, he tucked the log book in his pocket, loaded his chute in the car and set off with his friend The Leavittator to the jump site at the Loveland-Fort Collins Airport 40 miles northeast of Boulder to the Sky's West Parachute Center. Rob's bogus logbook passed muster at the manifest counter and RSL and he soon found themselves climbing aboard a Cessna 206 jump plane with four other jumpers.

About 20 minutes later and 10,500 feet higher, the first jumper slid open the segmented Lexan jump door and looked out to "spot" the aircraft. At the appropriate moment, the sky divers would jump out where they had the best chance to land on target.

When the blast of air hit him, Rob knew he was about to literally plunge into a new and exciting part of his life. But the thought passed quickly. It was time to do exactly what he had learned at the LAFFS, all ending with a "...step off a phone book."

The first step was a lot higher. After flashing a big grin at RSL, Rob dove from the airplane and instantly found a freedom and exhilaration he had never before known.

It didn't seem like Rob was falling as the plane floated up and away from him like a balloon, quickly becoming a small dot against the sky. As he hurtled toward the earth at terminal velocity of 120 miles per hour, Rob felt the wind against his body. In his peripheral vision loomed the square summit block of Long's Peak and the other great mountains of Colorado's Front Range. Rob was suspended in space and time, centered, and totally happy. He felt free.

Rob also felt stable and didn't tumble or spin. When it was time to pull, he was in a good body position to allow the parachute to open properly.

Reluctantly, Rob reached for his main parachute's pilot chute, a 30-inch diameter round mini-chute that begins the main parachute deployment process. He had already learned the only "ripcord" on modern parachute systems is on the reserve parachute.

Rob threw the pilot chute into the airflow, where it inflated and served as a portable, in-air anchor for the parachute that stretched out below it as Rob fell earthward. When the main parachute reached "line stretch," Rob felt the hard, comforting jolt of a parachute that opened perfectly.

"It's hellacious," he said later, "to look up and see that it's open the way it's supposed to be."

Rob grabbed the toggles and steered his parachute through the sky toward the drop zone landing area at about 25 miles per hour. Sometimes he turned left, other times right, to compensate for the wind and stay aimed at his target. He also practiced his flare several times by pulling the toggles down until the wind noise stopped as he momentarily floated motionless in the sky.

After a final practice flare, Rob let up on the toggles. The parachute resumed its normal speed as he lined it up for a landing into the wind to give himself the lowest possible groundspeed at touchdown.

Rob flared at just the right time and successfully concluded his first-ever freefall jump and airfoil parachute landing. Moments later, RSL touched down beside him.

"You were right Randall," Rob grinned. "It was just like stepping off a phone book."

As they gathered up their parachutes, Rob couldn't help but to look back up at the blue of the empty sky and think back to the El Cap jumper who had flown past him, sparking his immediate vow to someday fly. Now he had flown too. It had been an indescribable rush – but it wasn't the end of his parachuting road. Rob didn't want to just jump out of airplanes at commercial parachute centers. He had much more in mind.

Rob made nine more jumps with RSL, after which RSL pronounced Rob to be the first graduate of the Leavitt Accelerated Free Fall School. Rob was now good enough to load onto an airplane at any drop zone and competently handle himself in the wide-open skies above. But to successfully jump El Capitan, he needed to learn more than RSL could offer.

"I was more into climbing than jumping," RSL recounted, "and I was still on probation from my El Cap jump, so I couldn't take Rob all the way through his first BASE jumps. I thought it would be better to hook Rob up with someone who was a better fit for that part."

RSL introduced Rob to Robin Heid, an experienced skydiver, skydiving instructor and pioneering BASE jumper – a parachutist who jumps from Buildings, Antennae, Spans (bridges) and Earth (cliffs). Robin was one of the first 50 people in the world to jump with a parachute from a fixed object and had already jumped El Capitan twice. Most recently, Robin had been part of a six-jumper group that made the first-ever descent into Colorado's notoriously dangerous Black Canyon of the Gunnison, a 2,000-foot-deep chasm that contained some of the most hideous big-wall climbing in North America.

"I'd met a jumper at Elsinore named Larry Yohn who had moved to Colorado," RSL recounted, "and I was teaching him how to climb because he wanted to be the first person to climb El Capitan with a peg leg. Larry knew Robin and thought he'd be the perfect choice to take Rob to the next level, so one day we all got together at Eldo."

"When Randy introduced us," said Robin, "I remember this strong, vibrant, grinning guy, confident but not cocky, ready to learn, who knew he could handle what came at him."

Rob looked up to Robin as a renowned adventurer in a honed new sport that he himself wanted to enter. Robin was also a writer with an extensive, colorful vocabulary and way with words – including the use of "black death" to describe any endeavor where the threat of fatal or serious injury laid in wait for the incompetent and the unlucky.

It wasn't long before Rob, who liked giving nicknames to his friends, although he didn't have one of his own, began affectionately referring to his new friend as "Black Death Heid" or "BD" for short. In Rob's mind, a good nickname immortalized in a good-natured way some aspect of the person which Rob admired or found amusing.

Before they could commence, though, they had to agree on a fee. Like the Leavitt Accelerated Free Fall School, tuition at the Black Death Heid School of BASE (BDSB) was entirely reasonable.

"You teach me to climb, I teach you to jump," said Robin Heid to Rob Slater, "*and* pay for my jumps." The tuition was higher because, after all, it was graduate school.

Rob readily agreed and thus began what Black Death Heid calls his "most amazing learning experience." On Saturdays, they jumped and on Sundays they climbed. On Saturdays, BD pushed Rob so hard he gritted his super-white teeth in frustration. On

Sundays, Rob made BD beg for mercy as he took him on routes no one with a month's worth of technical climbing would even consider – even someone named Black Death.

"I don't do anything that easy unless I'm with a *girl*," Rob would laugh as BD protested a particularly featureless or overhanging section he wasn't sure he could surmount. Black Death then usually did, though on the times when he couldn't, Rob's nickname for him temporarily became "Haul Bag Heid".

The net result was "a lifelong friendship and a fast learning curve for both of us," said BD.

Rob and Black Death Heid made a dozen climbs and 15 skydives together. On the rock, BD became a pretty good climber who could lead some respectably difficult routes "if they're not too strenuous," as Rob would add in reference to BD's technique-to-fitness ratio. In the sky, Rob became more than respectable in the skills he needed to jump off El Capitan, fly his body away from the cliff, open his parachute at the right time and land decently on target.

They started with basic forward movement in freefall, then simple turns, then front and back loops, all with an eye toward making Rob feel comfortable and to gain, maintain and regain body stability at will. After opening, there was in-air parachute flight coaching followed by detailed debriefs after landing. As expected, what BD called Rob's "equivalent-risk experience" as a climber allowed him to progress as quickly as RSL had envisioned.

When BD was satisfied with Rob's basic proficiency, he added the element for which Rob had long waited – "tracking." Configured like a ski jumper, Rob learned to fly forward one foot for every foot of fall. Tracking was a must-know skill for Rob if he was to realize his El Cap BASE jump dream. Tracking on an El Cap jump was critical to get him the 200-300 feet of separation from the wall he needed to safely deploy his parachute.

"I'd have him fly to me in freefall and we'd hold hands, or 'dock,'" said Black Death. "Then I would turn 90 degrees and slowly assume the track position and have Rob follow. At first, he flailed all over the sky, but in short order he started holding a heading and moving horizontally."

BD showed Rob no pity and cut him no slack as he left Rob in his skydiver dust for several jumps. Then Rob could stay with him for a while before falling back at the end of their track. But it wasn't long before Rob mastered the track to the point that BD had to work at it to stay ahead.

"Pink steel!" Rob proclaimed of his newfound prowess as a human torpedo, shooting across the sky exactly where he wanted to go. Sometimes it included aiming directly toward the not-too-distant Long's Peak.

"You know everything you need to BASE jump," Black Death Heid proclaimed when they landed on jump number 25. "Next stop, the Black."

Not long after, they found themselves on the North Rim of the Black Canyon at Serpent's Point atop the Painted Wall, looking down at the spring runoff-gorged Gunnison River almost a half-mile below in the central Colorado Mountains.

That day, though, it was only BD who wore a parachute. BD wanted Rob to watch without the distraction of having to jump immediately thereafter, by himself, without his trusty jumpmaster. They stood on the edge as BD "dirt dived" the jump. Black Death would launch, track, open and navigate his way through the formidable canyon to his designated landing spot on a small sandbar on the north bank of the river opposite a much bigger one on the south bank.

"North side takes the river out of play," BD explained to Rob, "but way tighter. South side's bigger but then you have to cross the river. I'll probably end up on the north side, but if for some reason I have to bail, I can divert to the south side."

"Like you said," Rob replied, "have a Plan B, C and D too!"

Rob then took his place slightly downstream on a rock cropping where he could see the whole jump – and get a good launch photo, of course.

Black Death Heid's jump went just like the dirt dive: relaxed arch launch with a fast, smooth transition to an eight-second track followed by parachute opening and a leisurely 45-second "S-turning" approach and center-punch landing on the north-shore sandbar.

"Black Death Heid!" Rob shouted, clapping his hands and grinning broadly, "All right, Black Death!"

Rob was totally enthralled by what he'd just seen – and more confident than ever that he could duplicate BD's feat the next day.

With Black Death Heid and his mother Joan watching and taking pictures, Rob did just that. BD called Rob's first BASE jump "technically and judgmentally perfect. He did it exactly the way I did except he chose at the end to land on the big sandbar, which was the smartest thing he could do because he literally hit the middle of his envelope."

As Rob explained it, "I wasn't worried about crossing the river, but I was a little worried about hitting the small landing area, so it was an easy choice."

After Rob landed, he used a pre-arranged signal to let BD and Joan know he was okay, running several circles around his parachute. Then, he stuffed his chute into a backpack, made an effortless, completely dry crossing by jumping over the raging roiling water from one boulder to another and trotted up the heinous, tick- and poison ivy-infested SOB Gully in two hours. Rob rendezvoused with Joan and BD, who pronounced him to be the first graduate of the Black Death School of BASE.

The next day, Rob jumped again – and nailed it again. Afterward, as he drove back to Denver with Black Death, Rob knew for sure that someday soon his El Capitan jump would happen. He also knew that he had found another mistress, at least for a while.

Meanwhile, the innovative wheels in BD's mind had been turning as he watched over and shared in Rob's BASE jumping exploits. Rob had quickly gone through the 10-jump Leavitt Accelerated Free Fall School and BD's 15-jump Black Death School of BASE. BD saw no reason why the traditional parachute training courses couldn't be dispensed with for others of the similar honed persuasion. There was even a new parachute training technique he could use to eliminate the need for an airplane.

"A major parachute manufacturer had come up with a towing method by which you could learn to fly an airfoil parachute without first jumping from a plane," BD explained later. "It was a great idea in theory, because you could give your students a lot of low-cost reps without the cost, gear and fear of a real parachute jump. They could get ready and confident more quickly." It seemed to be the perfect addition to what RSL and BD had done with Rob.

Unfortunately, the system was still in the test phase and suffered from what turned out to be a fatal flaw: catastrophic results from too much tow line tension and no way to see it coming. If the tow vehicle drove faster than the parachute could fly, or atmospheric conditions added tension to the tow line, the parachute would "lock out" and dive into the ground like a kite with no tail in a high wind. In other words, the situation would go critical before anyone could react to it – even when a "tensiometer" was installed to monitor tow line tension. More unfortunately, the lockout accidents to date had been few and almost exclusively attributed to pilot or tow vehicle driver error.

One warm day in May, 1982, BD, Rob, Leonard Coyne and The Great Matt, another of Rob's climbing partners, all assembled in a wide-open field on the east edge of the Rocky Mountains foothills near the infamous Rocky Flats nuclear weapons plant. The plan was to put Verm Sherman, yet another of Rob's climbing partners, under the towed parachute and teach him how to fly it. Naturally, BD would test the system to make sure everything would work right before putting a noob, or rookie, under the nylon.

A climbing rope was hooked on one end to a car, with the other to a carabiner attached to BD's parachute harness. Then, with Leonard and The Great Matt alongside, the three of them ran down a road until the canopy filled with air and lifted off. BD was soon soaring more than 50 feet above the ground. Everything looked great until the tow car turned through a curve in the road, increasing the tension on the tow line. The canopy started bucking, locked out, tipped over and slammed BD to the ground.

"He hit so hard, we all thought he was dead," Leonard Coyne said later. "When the parachute covered him and he didn't move, we were sure of it."

But BD was honed and he survived, though he spent a month in the hospital and another month in a body cast recovering from a broken back, shattered ankle, broken foot and separated shoulder. For Verm, watching BD crash and burn closed the door on any further thoughts of "non-traditional" parachuting schools – or parachuting at all.

"The only way you're getting a chute on me is if the plane's going down," Verm concluded.

For Rob, thinking his friend BD was dead made his heart sink, but his spirit quickly soared when they raised BD's impromptu parachute shroud to find that conclusions about his death were premature. A still-breathing though not-bleeding Black Death Heid blinked his eyes at them and said, "Okay, what happened?"

Rob spent hours at BD's hospital bedside. Together they recounted the ill-fated events of that day with irreverent laughter. BD had taken it to another level and Rob had been there. They also discussed that, although BD hadn't died that day, the towed-parachute training concept had. When news of BD's accident reached the manufacturer, it immediately canceled the project.

"No reason to stop jumping, though," said BD, with Rob, of course, concurring. Neither of them considered giving up skydiving or BASE jumping just because one parachute ride didn't work out. Rob greatly admired BD and his renegade mentality and, while some members of Rob's climbing team may have acted only in support of Rob's periodic feats of apparent insanity, BD was brave enough to dance on the edge himself. For Rob to renounce this mindset while one of its most esteemed adherents lay in a hospital would have been an unconscionable act of betrayal. Rob and BD knew the risks and accepted the possible negative outcomes as a requirement of getting to that special place they both craved so much. Neither wanted or needed accolades, critique or sympathy. As Black Death Heid told me later, "People like Rob and I are more afraid of not living than we are of dying."

While Black Death Heid cooled his heels in the hospital, Rob and RSL continued climbing together locally in preparation for their upcoming summer trip to Yosemite Valley, or "the Valley" as they called it, checking off route after route on their respective lists of Eldorado and Boulder Canyon climbs. During one of those climbs, Rob told RSL that the Black Canyon was a "Gumby jump" that hadn't been nearly as challenging as he'd expected.

"Okay, then," RSL riposted, "if that's a Gumby jump, let's raise the bar and make it more interesting. We'll do a two-way – and then climb the wall instead of hiking out."

Rob instantly agreed.

"That'll make a great picture!" he declared, then added, "Plus it will be the world's first jump-climb!"

Though the previous solo jumps RSL and Rob had made into the Black Canyon had gone off without a hitch, things went wrong fast soon after they stepped off the edge.

"We launched from the little ledge on Serpent's Point that

BD calls 'The Serpent's Tooth,'" RSL recounted. "I took the grip on Rob's wrist because I had more experience and wanted the control in case something happened. I did the countdown and when we went off, Rob went head-low, so I let go."

RSL started tracking and watched as Rob dove head-first down the cliff for a few seconds before he started tracking away.

"It was maybe the most vivid moment of my entire life," said RSL, "watching the pegmatite stripes going by me, watching my buddy in freefall going past the stripes and the canyon just swallowing him up. I gotta hand it to Rob; I was really impressed by his ability there. He was totally under control the whole time, and totally aware of where he was and what he needed to do. Even as he tracked away, he kept looking over his shoulder to find me to make sure that we had enough separation to not hit each other on opening."

Once Rob assured himself of good separation, he "dumped," or deployed his chute, at 300 feet – way lower than he'd planned. Rob's parachute opened facing back toward the wall. Because he opened too low to reach either sandbar, Rob now faced landing options that were only slightly less heinous than hitting the wall and experiencing a first-hand taste of the "Pinball Effect."

Splashing down in the Grade 6 rapids was sure death by drowning. Crashing into a boulder-and tree-strewn hillside across the Gunnison River was just as sure a visit to the emergency room. Rob chose the least horrendous option of landing downwind at high speed on the south-shore sand bar covered with ankle-breaker rocks. Rob hammered in, badly mauling his foot, but was otherwise not seriously injured.

Maintaining his focus during those imminent-death moments as he plummeted toward the bottom of the canyon slowed down time for Rob. It enabled him to coolly process the situation and extricate himself from danger, all the while getting to savor the experience. Those moments were all his, in a special place and state that risk, determination, courage and focus allowed him to reach.

There would, however, be no effortless dry crossing of the rapids this time. Rob couldn't even walk on the damaged foot, much less climb and jump between house-sized boulders. Rob was a strong swimmer and at first thought about just swimming across the Grade

1 rapids. After the battering he'd taken, though, he decided against it. Fortunately, they had stashed gear for their planned triumphant free climb up the previously aid-only 5.9/A3 Journey through Mirkwood route. RSL retrieved a rope and flung one end to the "madman across the water."

But there was nothing mad about Rob crossing an icy, fast-moving mountain river with a bum foot – as long as he had a rope. After all, he'd been a captain of the high school swim team. It would be a piece of cake.

Rob pulled the rope tight across the river, then waded in, but was immediately swept straight downstream and across the strong current. He and RSL drew on individual strength and climber teamwork to get Rob to the north shore with no further damage. A piece of cake, just like he figured. Safely on the right side of the river, they then planned the rest of the trip out of the Black.

Free climbing Journey through Mirkwood, of course, was out of the question. They would have to get out of the Black Canyon through the SOB Gully, a two- to three-hour hike for strong young men with two good feet but a hideous, heinous, horrendous crawl through poison ivy, ticks and gnarly boulders if one is either figuratively or literally lame.

It took two days for them to get to the top. RSL could have hiked out and been back the same day with rescuers, but to Rob, that would have been poor style that not only detracted from but ruined an otherwise seminal event. Calling for help when they were both still alive and mostly ambulatory was unthinkable.

Afterwards, Rob didn't dwell on the event as a near-death experience so much as a nearly perfect one. So he hurt his foot and got banged up on the landing. Rob and RSL made a spectacular jump together and survived some adversity in freefall with good style. The epic crawl out of the canyon afterwards just added to the experience. It made the satisfaction of successfully meeting the challenge that much better. As Rob told me the story afterwards, though, I wondered what challenge Rob really meant and what was he really trying to overcome?

Whatever it was, Rob healed fast from his Black Canyon adventure and soon he and RSL were in Yosemite, where Rob realized his dream of climbing, then jumping, from El Cap.

The winter before, Rob had shared a house in Boulder with

some fellow CU students. On his bedroom wall he'd hung a topographical chart of the Pacific Ocean Wall, a death-defying sustained overhang of aid climbing more than 2,000 feet high and one of the toughest routes on El Cap. At the top of the topo, Rob had written "SOLO THIS ROUTE."

The P.O. Wall had never been soloed. Rob had never done a solo aid pitch more than 50 feet long. Throughout that winter, Rob often sat in his room, with his coat on and the windows open, staring at the topo and his scrawled protestation to himself.

The summer after he learned to skydive and made his first BASE jumps into the Black Canyon, Rob was back in the Valley where the dream had started. Rob proceeded to solo the P.O. Wall in five days and then parachuted off, just like the anonymous diver who had inspired him years before.

"Right then I knew I'd keep jumping off El Cap until I got caught," Rob said. A short time later, he almost did. As I previously mentioned, Rob repeated his climb-jump feat by climbing the Sea of Dreams with RSL and Mike O'Donnell, then jumping off. He may have got more excitement than he bargained for after he landed, but getting chased by rangers didn't deter him from wanting to jump again.

When Rob returned to Colorado in the fall of 1982, he no longer had a parachute system. But Black Death Heid wasn't yet using his, so Rob borrowed BD's gear and set his sights on the Denver skyline, crowned by the 700-foot-high, still-under-construction City Center tower. I was a student at the University of Wyoming while Rob was attending CU, and one weekend our respective schools played a football game in Boulder.

"Saturday night after the UW-CU football game my twin brother Robbie's going to parachute off the tallest building in Denver," I announced to my beer buddies. "We should go watch."

"I'll drive!" responded Ken Bull, aka "The Chief," my childhood friend with a proclivity to tack on a specific descriptor to anything of which he greatly approved. "That'll be fuckin' righteous," The Chief added, true to form.

After the game my friends and I, along Rob and his friend Tom Kaplan, piled into the Chiefmobile, a humongous 1972 Olds Delta 88 complete with bondo spots and a four-foot skull and crossbones covering the hood, for the midnight journey to Denver. We linked up with Black Death Heid, who had started jumping and climbing again the month before but wasn't yet ready to BASE jump.

City Center was Denver's newest and tallest building and, being still under construction, sported a huge crane on its top. The crane would make Rob's jump safer because jumping from its end put him 30 feet away from the building before he even started.

Before taking his official photographer position, BD stashed my friends in a good spot to watch, though they would have preferred to wait in the bar instead of in the darkness of a deserted downtown street. Kaplan, Rob and I headed for the building and scaled the ten-foot chain link fence surrounding the construction site. We knew we'd be sitting in the city jail if we were caught – but I didn't care because I was with my brother.

We made it inside without being seen and began to climb the 54 flights of metal stairs to the roof. I offered to carry Rob's parachute as a gesture of brotherly affection and because I wanted to be involved as much as possible. For those reasons and, in a gesture of common sense, Rob graciously agreed.

We emerged on the roof to a spectacular view of downtown Denver and the dark nearby mountains. The crane was far bigger up close than it seemed to be from the ground and we discovered in short order that the interior shaft containing the ladder up the crane tower was locked.

"Why would they lock this? Do they think someone's gonna climb up here in the middle of the night?" Rob asked mockingly.

Rob rigged up and got ready to go, then the three of us climbed the first 20 feet on the outside of the crane's skeleton before we could wedge ourselves through the steel lattice inside to the ladder. We hoped we wouldn't have to do the same thing at the top. After all, I joked to Rob, "that would be dangerous."

Luckily, there were no locks at the top and we gathered ourselves at the intersection of the crane's tower and arm. We were literally on the summit of Denver. Looking out to the end of the crane's arm to where Rob would launch was like looking at the edge of space.

"Richie, want to go out there with me? It would be a cool picture," Rob asked.

"Sure," I replied without hesitation. While Kaplan remained at the intersection, I followed Rob out to the end of the crane arm. When we got there, we looked back, each releasing one handhold on the crane to display a clenched fist for Kaplan's camera. Rob then explained his flight plan:

"I'll circle to the right in front of that building and then back to the left over those power lines and land in the parking lot."

Seven hundred feet below, the skull and crossbones of the Chiefmobile were barely visible. Rob and I looked at each other.

"I love you," he said.

"I love you, too," I replied. The "L" word wasn't regularly used between us – it didn't need to be. We also both felt that using it with girls was weak and extremely poor style. But there at the end of the crane arm, it seemed like the right thing to say.

Rob grinned at me and stated confidently, "I'm taking the easy way down."

"See you at the bottom," I grinned back, confident of what he was about to do. In truth, climbing out on the end of the crane with no form of protection was extremely foolhardy – but I did it without hesitation because I was with Rob. With Rob I always felt safe. I believed the feeling was mutual and tried to validate his belief in me. I also knew if something went wrong and Rob met his demise, I would follow. To stay behind in safety and in fear would be an abandonment of my brother as he went into the unknown alone. But I was sure he would make it and the thought quickly passed.

Rob launched and I listened as he counted patiently before throwing out his pilot chute. True to his word, when the canopy cracked open, Rob swooped to the right in front of the building across the street, cranked to the left over the power lines far below and landed near his cheering crew and the getaway car.

On top of the crane, Kaplan and I were no less ecstatic. Boy, did we have great seats. Once we knew Rob was safe, however, the adrenaline began to dissipate and we realized where we were.

"Let's get the hell off here."

On the Denver television news the next evening, the anchor reported that "an unidentified maniac was seen parachuting off the crane on the top of the City Center late last night." They didn't mention another unidentified maniac on the crane without a parachute and they failed to report the real story; that Rob was now one object closer to earning his BASE number.

Earlier, during their mutual quest for BASE numbers, Rob and RSL agreed that BASE numbers were actually rather silly. Skydivers assigned themselves many different numbers, such as when they completed certain formations during group jumps. Nevertheless, Rob and RSL also agreed they should get their BASE numbers. In truth, they realized that BASE jumping was simply too risky to continue long-term and both planned to retire to adjoining 40-acre tracts on the north rim of the Black Canyon, even though neither had the parcels yet nor the money to buy them. But they wouldn't be able to do that if they were both dead.

After the City Center jump, Rob was halfway there. He had an "E" for earth and a "B" for building, but he still needed an "A" for antenna and an "S" for span, which could be a bridge or a domed stadium. Fortunately for Rob, both were within easy reach in the state of Colorado.

Most accessible was a 750-foot-high TV antenna at the summit of Lookout Mountain, guardian of the canyon entrance through which Interstate 70 winds its way into the Rocky Mountains. At night its lights, save for the blinking red one on top, shine indistinguishable from the stars bright enough to be seen over the glow of the city.

"BASE jumping is a great spectator sport," Rob told me more than once, not because he wanted to show off, but because he liked sharing his exhilarating, adrenaline-fueled adventures. To that end, Rob invited a couple of his friends to join Black Death Heid and him for a planned jump from the antenna. Unfortunately, their first two trips to the base of the mountain were greeted by raging winds, which prompted Rob and BD to matter-of-factly abort the "mission."

The second stand-down brought howls of dismay from Rob's friends, who were sick of 4:00 a.m. wakeup calls for nothing. They urged him in profane and insulting terms to jump anyway. Ever the diplomat, Rob told them his decision to launch would not, with all due respect, be swayed by their impatience, inconveniences or unkind references.

"The mistletoe hangs from my coattail; you can begin from there…"

Despite his willingness to share the fun with friends, Rob

never lost track of the fact that BASE jumping was not only incredibly dangerous, but intensely personal, with challenge, achievement and validation playing itself out in the deepest reaches of his soul. When Rob got to go to that special place, it really didn't matter to him if anyone watched or not. Rob and BD eventually jumped the Lookout Mountain antenna in good conditions on another night.

"Perfect form again," said Black Death Heid, "although there was one wild moment for both of us when his pilot chute towed until he had enough speed that the drag overcame the friction of the too-tight pack job I'd done for him. By staying cool, he got a clean, straight opening and it ended up as a routine jump with a little spice in the middle."

After getting his "A," Rob needed only the "S" – not just to get a two-digit BASE number but to become the first-ever Colorado BASE.

Soon thereafter, BD and Rob made a midnight drive two hours south of Denver to the small town of Canon City, best known as the location of the state penitentiary. Nearby, over eons of time, the Arkansas River has gouged through the Sangre de Cristo Range to carve what is now known as the Royal Gorge. If the Black Canyon can be compared to a 2,000-foot funnel, the Royal Gorge must be likened to a 1,000-foot eyedropper. Spanning the gorge, the world's highest suspension bridge hangs 1,055 feet above the river and single railroad track occupying the narrow canyon floor. The Royal Gorge below the bridge is only 100 feet wide, which makes for trickier wind conditions and demands much greater parachute handling skills.

Distinguishing the Royal Gorge from the Black Canyon is the fact that one is wilderness and the other one is a tourist attraction. The Royal Gorge Bridge goes nowhere except to the other side, as it was built in 1929 solely to generate revenue for Canon City. Also distinguishing the Royal Gorge from the Black Canyon is its ease of access and popularity with regular tourist-type folk. Royal Gorge Park offers ample paved parking, a Visitors Center, an inclined railway to the bottom and an aerial tram across the top.

Naturally, it was too windy to jump when they arrived that first night, so they camped out in Rob's car. As the winds blew so strong they rocked the car, Rob and BD catnapped between wind checks, hoping it calmed enough to allow a jump.

"At least they're strong enough that there's no doubt about the decision," Rob said when they finally gave up just before dawn and drove back to Boulder.

Not long after, Rob and BD went south again, this time with me along for the ride, and this time during daylight. The plan was simple: just pay the entrance fee, drive in, walk out onto the bridge and jump off-in broad daylight. We paid our entrance fee at the gate, parked in the lot and headed for the bridge. Strolling along in jeans and light jackets, we stared over the edge into the abyss like everyone else, as the narrow bridge swayed slightly in the breeze.

I proudly strode to the middle of the bridge with my twin, BD trailing with his camera. We blended in just fine except for the fact Rob was wearing a parachute. BD had cameras, but so did every other sightseer at the park, and most of them wore or carried backpacks similar in size to Rob's parachute rig. No one even noticed us – until Rob tossed a roll of toilet paper into the abyss to check the wind.

As we raptly watched it snake its way downward, people suddenly became aware of what was really going on. They rushed to the rail on our side of the bridge to investigate and started snapping pictures.

Rob decided the winds were good enough for jumping and, with the concurrence of the eminent Mr. Black Death, decided it was time to launch. He climbed the railing and stepped onto the foot-thick main suspension cable with agility and ease, pilot chute in hand, his mop of curly brown hair waving in the wind. He steadied himself for a moment and then looked back over his shoulder to me with the same fierce determination and kind of wide-eyed grin I saw on the City Center crane.

"This is the ultimate sport," he proclaimed.

"Go for it," was as profound a reply as I could muster.

With that, he turned and leaped into space. The crowd that had grown instantly larger when Rob stepped up onto the cable let out a collective gasp, then held its breath. They didn't know if they were watching some poor soul commit suicide – or just somebody honed having fun. My eyes widened and my mouth opened. We all leaned over the railing to watch as Rob quickly shrank in size to a fast-moving speck.

"One, two, three, four..." I could hear Rob count before he threw his pilot chute. With a crack muffled by wind and space, the canopy opened several hundred feet below and the crowd cheered loudly as Rob began spiraling into the depths of the gorge.

Once I saw Rob's chute open, I relaxed somewhat. I knew he was enjoying the ride and I did the same. Otherwise the ride was silent but for the commotion on the bridge by the spectators.

"Did you *see* that?" was asked repeatedly in the first five seconds after Rob's parachute opened. BD and I looked at each other, nodding. Yeah, we most certainly had.

As Rob neared the canyon floor, the crowd kept oohing and ahhing but I tensed as I flashed back to Rob's Black Canyon crash landing. What if he landed in the river or got caught in a wind shear and pinballed into the jagged cliffs? If I had to watch him die, I would probably go right off the bridge after him. But again, the thought quickly passed as another cheer went up, this one louder, when Rob made a stand-up landing on the railroad track and could be seen scampering to gather his chute. It was easy for me to see the excitement in his step and feel his exhilaration rise up to me at my place on the bridge.

As we walked back to the car, the excitement and pleasure on our faces was no different from that of the dozens of people who got way more than they paid for that day at the Royal Gorge Bridge.

Meanwhile, a couple of Royal Gorge security guys at the bottom briefly gave chase, but they were clearly unenthusiastic about catching someone who moved so fast and probably equally unmotivated to nab someone who had just done something so cool. As BD said to me with a grin as we watched the unsuccessful chase play out, "Would *you* want to try to chase down someone who was crazy enough to jump off a 1,000-foot bridge?"

"Only to give him a high-five," I replied.

Rob ran down the tracks until he was out of the bridge sightline and then climbed straight up out of the canyon at a speed no one on the bridge company staff or the local police anticipated. We picked up Rob on the entrance road while the authorities were still looking for him at the bottom.

"Richie, that was so great!" he said to me, his eyes still wild with excitement. I told him I knew. Black Death Heid just smiled and held out his hand to Rob.

"Congratulations," he said to my twin as they shook hands. "You are now Colorado BASE Number One." After submitting his information to the U.S. BASE Association, Rob also learned that he was "world" BASE number 43, four numbers behind RSL's number 39 and one ahead of BD's 44 that came a few months later. In so doing, Rob and RSL raised the bar for hard-core climber-adventurers everywhere. After Rob earned his BASE number, many of his BASE jumping cohorts, who were also climbers and had thought the numbers were silly, suddenly decided they wanted theirs as well.

Rob wasn't quite ready to retire from BASE jumping, though, and his leap off the City Center crane wouldn't be the only time an unidentified maniac would be spotted flying off a skyscraper in the heart of the Mile High City. On a crisp winter weekday, he climbed the stairs of a still-under-construction One United Bank Building, another Denver 700-footer with a distinctive "cash register" top, with fellow BASE jumper and movie stuntman Brian Veatch. Ironically, unbeknownst to Rob, he would work in that same building years later.

The two jumpers arrived at the 50th floor, dressed in work clothes and hard hats to avoid arousing suspicion among the numerous construction crews at the site. Reaching their launch point without detection, they geared up on the building's southeast corner. Rob would jump from a window on the south side and Brian from an adjacent window on the east side. Far below on a bus stop bench, Black Death Heid waited with his camera.

As they climbed into their respective windows, the outside-the-building construction elevator stopped and opened on their floor. When the workers stepped out and saw them poised to jump, one of them blurted out: "Don't jump! It's not worth it!"

Brian laughed and said, "It's okay; we have parachutes!"

Rob grinned his trademark grin and gestured for the workers to join them. "You can watch if you want to!"

Rob and Brian then turned to the business at hand, counted "Three... two... one... see ya!" and out the windows they went.

The jumps were perfect. Both landed without mishap in an adjacent parking lot and, barely a minute after launch, Rob and Brian were whisked away into traffic. The event barely caused a ripple in the ebb and flow of the city's normal business.

BD's photo of the jump appeared soon after in a back cover advertisement in *Skydiving* Magazine, world's most important parachuting journal. In the photo of Brian and Rob under open parachutes, in the windows from which they jumped several hard hats can be seen.

Eventually Rob did retire from BASE jumping, after a career which defied convention, law enforcement and death. To show for it, his name appears in the annals of the sport, he got some great pictures and was even mentioned on TV, albeit as "an unidentified maniac." Vivid memories remained of the purest experiences of exhilaration and freedom. For years afterward, Rob kept a packed parachute at the foot of his bed, just in case the urge struck.

"That's what it all boils down to; committing suicide and living through it," Rob concluded. But what did he really mean by that and why would he say such a thing? Was it just another of his colorful, outrageous statements or did he really feel that way? Did Rob have a death wish or was there something more? Do I have one too? Why did Rob need so much to continually return to that special state and place? To figure out the answers to these questions and the reasoning behind them requires us to go back to the beginning...

Black Death Heid at the Royal Gorge

On the City Center crane

Robbie (left) on casual belay

Chapter II

"Only those are fit to live who do not fear to die; and none are fit to die who have shrunk from the joy of life and the duty of life. Both life and death are parts of the same Great Adventure."

–Theodore Roosevelt

No one is sure who first "discovered" K2, for no written history is kept by the Balti herdsmen who inhabit the Karakoram Range between China and Pakistan. They rely on memory and lore to pass knowledge along to succeeding generations and live today as they always have, in a world detached by time and space from the creature comforts of modern civilization. In fact, debate remains surrounding the issue of what, if any, native name exists for the peak now known as K2. My twin brother always subscribed to the school of thought accepting Chogori, meaning "Great Mountain," though to him it was his Dream Mountain.

It was the first week in August, 1973. Robbie and I were 12. We stood at the base of the cliff, ready to begin our first climb. A series of cracks, broken into pitches by intermittent ledges, ran up the wall of Cascade Canyon flanking the Grand Teton in Jackson, Wyoming, where they met the sky. As Robbie surveyed the route above, his eyes tightened. I could see the picture he had of himself on the rope, high on the wall, higher than we had ever climbed with the clothesline on the rock formations of Vedauwoo outside our Cheyenne home. I had the picture too.

It was clear from the start that some of our fellow students of the Exum climbing school would never come to grips with the height and exposure of clinging to these massive cliffs. They were just tourists and rightfully scared, but Robbie and I were not, for even at our young age, mountain cliffs and rock faces were not new to us. During our many weekends clambering about the Vedauwoo rocks, we had climbed everything we could, in our cowboy boots and often with the aid of a clothesline. We had sat on many ledges peering into space and looked down from the edge of many precipices. We both loved heights. For us, this was a natural progression-the next step.

The instructor led the way, placing a series of small aluminum blocks called "chocks" into the crack. The chocks were attached to a loop of nylon strap onto which a carabiner, an aluminum device which resembled a large safety pin, was clipped. The rope ran easily through the "biners," and if he slipped, the rope would be held taut from below, causing the top chock to catch his fall. This was called protection, or "pro."

At top of the first pitch the instructor anchored himself and set up the belay. The belayer reels in the rope as his climbing partner ascends. If the climber below falls, the rope, which is pulled up around the belayer's back, is immediately drawn across the belayer's waist. Friction prevents the rope from paying out and holds the climber below. There was clearly a special responsibility and mutual trust inherent in the relationship between a climber and his belay. If they're not like brothers they're at least a team.

Robbie's turn came and he started up. He was finally on the rope doing some real climbing. As the instructor offered praise and encouragement, I knew Robbie was just humoring him. It was way too easy. Robbie quickly worked his way up, pausing to remove the chocks and clip the 'biners to the rope around his waist. He moved like a cat, surefooted and in perfect balance on the rock. I followed, also finding it pretty easy, disappointed I didn't get to remove the pro and clip it to my waist. As we sat on the belay ledge waiting for the others, I saw Robbie's eyes dilate staring up at the magnificence of the Grand Teton range, above the massive cliffs to the far-off summits in the sky. A wide, determined grin spread across his face, giving a glimpse of a razor-sharp focus which belied his tender age and which I had never before seen.

The blueness above the peaks boiled, almost imperceptively, like an immense, infinite cauldron forming an overarching canopy above us. I could see his nostrils flare and mouth quiver slightly in an unconscious attempt to smell and taste the icy winds blasting across the highest ridges and hear their distant roar. I sensed in his grin a feeling of total isolation and complete security. I also sensed his recognition of a subtle yet pervasive force. I felt it too. It was the spirit of the wild places. It was a powerful combination of inspiration and reverence. We were in the midst of the mountain gods. It caused a change to come over us both, but it would play itself out differently for each of us in the years to come. Momentarily, our eyes met. Nothing was said, but I knew *he* knew.

K2 was revealed to the outside world as a result of the Great Trigonometric Survey of India in 1856, an ambitious plan to accurately map all British possessions on the Indian subcontinent. From a vantage point 140 miles away, Captain T.G. Montgomery spotted a group of high peaks which he measured and logged in his survey book as K1, K2, K3, and so forth, for Karakoram Range. The other peaks were originally named K1, K3, K4 and K5, but, intent upon using native names, were eventually renamed Masherbrum, Broad Peak, Gasherbrum II and Gasherbrum I, respectively. While the superintendent of the survey, Sir George Everest, had the world's highest peak named after him, no consensus was reached for the second highest and, consequently, no official name was ever approved so it simply retained its designation as K2.

It was not until 31 years later that the great mountain fully revealed itself, at least to Westerners, when Colonel Francis Younghusband crossed the Old Mustagh Pass and the towering pyramid came completely into view.

"It seemed to emerge like a perfect cone, incredibly high,"

the Colonel wrote. "I was astounded."

In many ways, Robbie and I were like any other brothers our age. Whenever one of us tried something new, the other always wanted to follow. Our brother Paul was one year behind us and Tommy, the youngest, two years behind Paul. Inevitably, we ended up trying just about everything. For the usual stuff like football, baseball and basketball, we formed into teams. I was usually with Tommy, because I was oldest and he was youngest. It wasn't enough just to play-we always had to organize it into some kind of tournament, Super Bowl or World Series. We played to win, mostly for short-term bragging rights, but the victory celebrations were never enough to create grudges or prevent a rematch. We also ended up pushing each other into far less traditional-and dangerous-endeavors such as bike jumping ala Evel Knievel and, later, cliff jumping. Sibling rivalry and competition among the Slater boys always led to the envelope being pushed. In many ways this competition was stronger than peer pressure. It meant more to outdo or impress a brother than it did an outsider. It was usually harder, too. This was especially true for Robbie and me.

Like all brothers, we occasionally fought. Sometimes the combat was with fists, but mostly just bickering words. One time when we were preschool age, Robbie and I got into a fight in our backyard sandbox over possession of an old army shovel, the kind used by soldiers to dig fox holes. As we wrestled for the shovel, I accidently smacked my twin brother in the head with it, which required a couple of stitches to close. For years afterwards, when we got into it, I would joke: "I'll kick your ass just like I did in the sandbox." Robbie would always reply, "Yeah, but you had to use a shovel, you pussy." But that day in the Tetons, unspoken, we were together. That day there was no conflict.

We had been to the Tetons before. We were a "normal" family in many respects, but we were also lucky in the sense we not only had each other but parents, Dad in particular, who always made time to do things with his boys. Dad had a medical meeting at the Jackson Lake Lodge each summer and he brought the family. Full family participation in everything eventually gave way to each of us pursuing a more narrow range of activities, but throughout our childhoods there were some things we all liked and continued to do together such as camping, skiing and hiking.

There were many hikes and our own versions of mountaineering expeditions. This summer, Dad had stopped by the famous Teton Climbers' Ranch, home of the Exum climbing school, located at the base of the Grand Teton. Informed the minimum age for participation was 16, Dad simply asked if he could bring his sons anyway. Asked, almost rhetorically, who would be responsible for the boys, Dad replied, "I will, of course." With that, Robbie, Paul and I were allowed to enroll. For Paul and me it was something definitely cool. After all, not many kids got to climb with ropes and real climbing equipment-in the Tetons, no less. Dad hadn't wanted to make a big deal of it; he just thought it would be fun. Dad never dreamed it would lead to a lifelong obsession for one of his sons. From the start, however, it was something more than fun with Robbie.

That morning, there was a slight yet recognizable bite in the air. Looking back, it was a subtle reminder of who is in control any time you go to the mountains. Racing across the Jenny Lake boat dock and beating his brothers to the best seat on the 25-foot launch made Robbie smirk with satisfaction. Being able to attend the famous climbing school, though technically four years too young to enroll, was a kind of unspoken recognition of his yet unproven abilities. But more than anything, I somehow knew the awesome grandeur of where we were made Robbie feel so incredibly alive and, for some reason, indestructible.

After a couple of multiple-pitch climbs, it was time for lunch. The baloney and lettuce sandwiches slathered in mayonnaise fell far short of our expectations. Robbie examined his with a look of incredulous disappointment but said nothing. We agreed something as cool as climbing warranted decent food to go with it.

Following lunch, the focus of the class shifted. "Making the top is one thing, but getting off and making it home is what ultimately counts," began the instructor. There was a previously absent edge to his voice. It was kind of like the change that occurred in Dad's voice when he talked to us about something important – like "values," as he called them. Of course coming back down is important, but it also seemed to be the fun and easy part. I noticed Robbie's eyes immediately focus up the canyon to where we would make the big free rappel. But the edge in the instructor's voice made us both look at Dad, whose slightly squinted eyes and pursed lips demonstrated he knew the importance of these words – and that he wanted to make sure we did too. They would become prophetic.

The afternoon agenda consisted of rappelling, which, in its finest form, allows a climber to literally fly down the face of the rock. Robbie wanted to go straight to the 60-foot free rappel over a large overhang that he'd watched all morning. I'd noticed as he sat on the belay ledges, watching intently as the "advanced" class members, one by one, inched to the edge of the precipice, most with great trepidation, hesitant to lean back and launch themselves into space. Disappointingly, we were led to the top of a rather gentle friction pitch just slightly steeper than something we would feel comfortable down climbing unprotected. It certainly wasn't steep enough to bounce off of the rock in long smooth arcs like we'd seen on television. No harnesses were used – just the rope snaked between the legs, across the chest, over the right shoulder and down to the left hand, which controlled movement down the rock. Given the rope's serpentine path around the body, it was impossible to descend with any speed, much less bounce off the wall and catch some air. But it's a safe and efficient way to descend a tricky section – and a valuable tool when trying to get off a mountain during a late afternoon storm so common in the high country.

Our group gathered on the ledge above the wall. Rigged up, one by one we backed to the edge. "Just lean back, nice and easy," the instructor encouraged, "let the rope slide - let friction do the work."

This was easier said than done as the natural inclination was to keep a death grip on the rope. Nevertheless, it didn't take Robbie long to make it look easy. For all the other students, it was a question of facing and overcoming fear. For Robbie and me, the question was more like "who's going to go for it more?" We obviously felt no need to gingerly approach the edge. Height and exposure caused no concern. We both loved it.

Several summers earlier, when Robbie and I were about eight, we went to West Virginia to visit Grandma and Grandpa Slater. Dad took us to a place called Oglebay Park that had a huge pool with three diving boards. The first two were similar to many we had seen before. The "low board," as we called it, was a standard one-meter board, about three feet above the pool deck. The "high board" was a three-meter board, or about ten feet tall. Towering above was a third board, at least twice the height of the three-meter. The diving board itself was sawed off a couple of feet past the hand railing. It was obviously cut short to keep people from bouncing-which apparently was considered too dangerous from that height. People were jumping off- all older guys. We asked Dad if we could jump off and he said "sure." We went right up-neither one of us was ever afraid of heights. Afterwards, Robbie and I agreed it would have been cool if the whole board was there and we could have bounced even higher.

After our climbing day in the Tetons, Paul and I proudly recounted the accomplishments of the day over pizza, but Robbie payed little mind. He was engaged in the conversation but his focus was elsewhere. I'd been basically satisfied, even though I'd expected a bit more of a challenge. Robbie, on the other hand, was convinced that the climbs were too easy, the rappels not steep enough, and everything was too low. He was fixated on ever greater heights and difficulty. The highlight of the course would be the next day's free rappel off the big overhanging cliff, but I could tell Robbie was looking beyond. Robbie was already talking about summits and putting the skills we had been introduced to into serious application.

As I sat there next to him, it reminded me of something that happened when Robbie and I were in fourth grade. The next door neighbors got a trampoline. My brothers and I lined up to take our turns but, after a couple of times bouncing, Robbie grew bored of waiting and went back to our house. A short time later he returned and declared it would be far more exciting, rather than standing around waiting to jump on the tramp, to jump off the roof. We immediately followed Robbie back to our house, the group's collective interest in the tramp overshadowed, at least temporarily, by the anticipation of perhaps witnessing a leg being broken. From the fence, Robbie climbed to the roof and appeared above us. He inched to the edge, as the crowd below loudly admonished him that holding onto the gutters would somehow constitute "cheating." Robbie jumped, hit the ground with a thump and rolled on the grass as we watched in disbelief. I went up and jumped off as well, though the real admiration rightly belonged to my twin who went first and, in so doing, inspired others to follow. In this case it was just me, but as time went on he inspired many others as well. Robbie was not content with the trampoline and, more specifically, with waiting in line to do something every other kid in the neighborhood could do. I followed, but Robbie led the way.

During that year of fourth grade, we lived in Salt lake City, Utah. Our house was in a new development built at the base of the mountains flanking the western edge of the city. We were on the last street, so our yard literally backed up into the mountains. My brothers and I spent hours, regardless of the weather, hiking, playing and exploring. We had forts, racetracks for our bikes and our own ski runs. Nearby was a large outcropping of granite near the top of steep slope. On it was painted a large "H" for Highland, the local high school. We were warned by the neighborhood kids about exploring it as high school kids patrolled it to keep non-students away. We ended up going anyway, of course. From its base, the huge black vertical sides of the H rose above us. There was so much paint poured on the rocks it looked like it had been covered with smooth black lava. Looking around, we were the only ones there-no patrolling high school kids.

"I'm gonna climb it," Robbie stated, and started up. As usual, I followed.

The next morning at Exum, we again separated into small groups, each with an instructor. As the group left the staging area near the boat dock, Robbie led the hike up the trail to the cliffs. At first I entertained thoughts of passing him, but ended up having to settle for being in front of everyone but him. Over the years, I would spend many miles behind Robbie on the hikes, trying to match him step-for-step along rocky mountain trails. I usually did a pretty good job, though always from *behind*.

Once we arrived at our climbing area, we found that the climbs were more challenging and we got to use more of the equipment. For Paul, it was quite satisfying, though in keeping with his personality, he didn't say much. For me, it was a great, exhilarating experience. I was happy to have had done it and, for that matter, to able to now say I had.

"This is so cool," I said to my twin, who nodded in agreement as his face lit up with his big grin, but at the top of each pitch, it was apparent to me that Robbie's appetite for a steeper, more challenging route remained unsatisfied. In fact, he was hungrier for it now than he had been when we started the class. For him, there just seemed to be no better combination than height, exposure and difficulty. I didn't know the word at the time, but right in front of my eyes Robbie had become insatiable in his desire to climb.

At long last, it was Robbie's turn for the free rappel. As he roped up, I couldn't help but notice the shine on his face, outlined by his thick mop of hair. We all grew it the same way and had it as long and wild as Mom and Dad would let us. In contrast the students who had gone before, Robbie backed towards the ledge with a single-minded purposefulness which demonstrated a total absence of fear. I think everyone watching, including the instructors, was impressed. Grudgingly, perhaps, I was too.

"Be sure and lean back, especially at the edge," the instructor counseled as he has done with all the students.

At the end of the precipice, Robbie felt the knife edge of the ledge under his arches as he bent his knees, pressing on the rock in a challenge of strength. Leaning back, slowly allowing the rope to slide through the 'biner, Robbie knew his next step would be his last before reaching the ground some 60 feet below. Coiling like a rattlesnake, he launched himself backwards and opened his right arm, freeing the rope of friction. For a fleeting instant, the sky's vault opened. Robbie glimpsed the heavens, then only rock. I saw his face, joyfully intense and happy, before he disappeared below. This time I was definitely impressed. Robbie's first arc didn't stop until about 20 feet below the ledge. No one else had flown nearly that far. He felt the give in the rope as he bounced and swung, slowly beginning to spin.

Robbie did not want to stop but, unfortunately for him, he was obligated to land. Opening his arm, Robbie slid down the rope, periodically checking his speed, stopping to enjoy the bouncing, swaying and twirling caused by the interruption of his downward flight. For Robbie, being airborne was clearly an unrivaled sensation. Upon landing, like the others before him, he was greeted with a congratulatory cheer.

"I want to do it again." Robbie was dead serious – especially for a 12-year-old. Part of him may have just wanted to show the group that he really wasn't afraid to do it again. Just about everyone had expressed at least a feigned desire to go back up, but most probably found the experience terrifying and were, in truth, glad it was over. I would have done it again but didn't press the issue, but Robbie truly wanted to go back up. I think it had more to do with him wanting to prove something to himself and push himself further rather than showing off for or trying to impress anyone else. There was a palpable difference between the way Robbie reacted compared to me and the rest of the students. Standing there watching, Salt Lake City flashed through my mind -- when he jumped off the roof in fourth grade, or led the assault on the "H." As he did then, Robbie had again separated himself from the pack.

Rockefeller Memorial Parkway runs parallel to the Teton Range through Moose Flats and skirts the Jackson Lake Dam before turning east to Moran Junction. As our station wagon was loaded, we claimed our seats for the first leg of the journey home. Robbie made sure he got the window seat in the back, behind Dad, which provided him the best and longest-lasting unobstructed view of the Tetons.

It was always awe-inspiring looking at the Tetons; they're not the most photographed mountains in the world for nothing. I saw him wondering how its cliffs compared to those he had just conquered with so little difficulty. In my mind's eye, I could see Robbie on the highest summit, at the edge of the cauldron, dreaming of diving in, or up. I knew he would be back and that, someday, he would stand on the top of every one of the Teton summits and get the chance to fly.

But Robbie was doing more than just enjoying a spectacular natural view. With face close to the glass, he studied the peaks, the Grand Teton in particular. They seemed so far away and he was clearly sad to be leaving. Robbie gazed longingly and knowingly at his newfound love as if he had realized and was now set to develop a relationship he knew would get serious. There was also the component of risk, excitement and adrenaline that came with the courting. He had felt it when he was on a particularly steep or difficult section of a route. He felt it when he had gone to the edge of the ledge on the big free rappel. Robbie discovered an important part of himself those two summer days in 1972. It was an arrival for him but also marked a departure. I wanted to follow, but I was unsure how far...

Robbie, Paul, Richie, age 9

Rob, Paul and Tom, with Sis and Rich in front

With Grandpa Slater and Dad (Robbie on right)

Chapter III

"I'm gonna do it. '
–Rob Slater
"Anything worth doing is worth overdoing."
–Rich Slater

When I was fresh out of law school, trying to build a practice, I used to pass out my business cards in the local biker bars and strip joints. I rationalized it was good marketing because, admittedly, they were the kinds of places I sometimes liked to hang out. Inevitably, I found myself doing a lot of criminal defense cases. Down at the courthouse in Cheyenne, the defense lawyers joked about the old adage that "the nut doesn't fall far from the tree," in reference to some second-or third-generation defendant again showing up in the criminal justice system. While the adage unfortunately held true for those hapless souls, fortunately it was also true for my twin brother Robbie and me. Like everyone, from whence we came shaped our personalities and our destinies.

When Robbie and I were four, Dad took us on our first camping trip. He got both of us a knapsack, and we each put in a bowl, spoon and box of our favorite cereal – Cap'n Crunch. The army surplus canteen with the canvas sheath was filled with milk. Paul, who was only three and Tommy, who was still learning to walk, stayed at home with Mom.

We were living in Salisbury, Maryland, so Dad took us down to the flats along Chesapeake Bay and we crowded into our small canvas Sears and Roebuck pup tent, seeking refuge from the clouds of mosquitoes. There were so many of them, though, that we went home early that night. It was the first and only time we didn't make it through the night.

Many successful camping trips followed and by the time Robbie and I were 10 years old, all of us considered ourselves outdoorsmen. The little knapsack was replaced by aluminum-framed backpacks. Dad always carried the heaviest pack, with the tent, stove, cookware and most of the food. The rest of us vied to see who could carry the second-heaviest pack, lining up at the bathroom scale the night before a trip.

In the evenings, we had campfires. We waited with great anticipation the coming of darkness, when Dad might let us light torches. Sitting around the fire, or in the tent, alone in the wild, amidst the silliness between four boys and a tolerant if not encouraging father, Dad told us stories. We loved hearing about Dad as a kid and the rest of our family history.

As he spoke, Dad would gaze into the campfire. Periodically, he jabbed and rearranged the burning logs with a stick he called a "poker." This was "tending" the fire as he called it. We all learned how to tend the fire and competed to find the best poker.

Grandpaps Hannah, for example, our great-great grandfather on our Dad's side, was a war hero, Civil War, Union side. Leading an escape from a Confederate POW camp, he went back to help a fallen comrade, but got shot in his heel, Grandpaps Hannah still managed to make it to freedom, along with the guy he rescued.

Grandpap's son-in-law, our great grandpa Audrey Vernon Slater, was a farmer in West Virginia near the Pennsylvania line. In 1900, our grandpa, William Alvin "W.A." was born. Four months later, his dad Audrey cut his thumb shucking corn. It became infected and his thumb was amputated, but that didn't catch all the infection, so he had to have his arm was amputated above the elbow. This also failed to stem the tide of infection and his condition worsened and so, at the ripe old age of 36, Audrey Vernon Slater died. Medicine, Dad explained, was quite different back then and many people died from infection. Nevertheless, my brothers and I were sure that Dad could have saved great grandpa Slater. Finishing up this chapter of our family history, Dad told us Audrey's widow Minnie Jane Hannah cared for young W.A. until she died in 1908 at age 40, having outlived her husband by four years.

His Royal Highness Prince Luigi Amedeo di Savoia, Duke of the Abruzzi, was a member of Italian royalty, but he was no soft, pudgy doughboy slacker of the genteel idle rich. He had eyes tightened by weather from peering into the distance and hands roughened by time spent in the wild. The Duke was missing two fingers, lost on an 1899 expedition to the North Pole. He had also led expeditions to tropical Africa to explore the legendary Mountains of the Moon in Ruwenzori and to Mount Logan in Canada.

The Duke carried an array of scientific gear on his expeditions to perform topographical, meteorological and photogrammetrical surveys. On his Alaskan expedition, the Duke brought along a brass bed, perhaps a manifestation of some immutable royal gene or, perhaps, merely for comedic relief. The Duke didn't hang out at the castle, slouching on an embroidered sofa eating cream puffs. He made the most of the good cards life had dealt him and sought adventure for more than just the thrill. According to Robbie, the Duke of the Abruzzi was honed.

"Good work if you can get it," Rob would say.

The Duke set out for K2 in 1909 with 262 waterproofed and meticulously prepackaged porter loads for the final leg of the journey to base camp – minus the brass bed. K2 was serious business and besides, the drafts allowed by a raised bedstead made it impossible to stay warm.

His Royal Highness brought along over 450 pounds of small change, budgeted for hiring and paying local Balti porters the most generous consideration of one rupee per day. The Duke's expedition would become the model for all future ventures into the Karakoram and Himalayan ranges.

The expedition's main camp was established at the base of K2's southern faces at the head of the Godwin-Austen Glacier. After several days on the southeast ridge, the Duke was forced to call off the attempt at 19,685 feet. Although he had set a personal altitude record, he was still nearly two miles below the summit.

The party then directed its efforts around the western base of the peak. Ascending what he dubbed the Savoia Glacier, after his home province, the Duke and his team topped the Savoia Pass at 21,870 feet. Upon reaching the crest of the pass, no acceptable route could be found through the pinnacles, rock towers and massive cornices to the Great Mountain's upper slopes.

"As a reward of his labors, what the duke thus saw utterly annihilated the hopes with which he had begun," Filippo de Filippi, the expedition geographer, would later record. "The excursion to the westward side of K2 had not revealed any feasible way of ascent.

The Duke never made it to top of K2 and, following his 1909 expedition, he never returned to the Karakoram. But in the dreaming and planning of K2 adventures, his spirit has remained.

W.A., or Grandpa Slater to my brothers and me, went to live with his Grandpaps Hannah when he was eight. According to Dad, the young boy and his war hero grandpap lived a rather odd life together, which no doubt contributed to their respective unique personality quirks. Grandpaps was known for smoking Mail Pouch chewing tobacco in his pipe. One of W.A.'s favorite foods was stale popcorn in a bowl covered with tomato juice. "A delicacy," Grandpa Slater would tell us.

Dad's mom, our Grandma Slater, was a quintessential grandmother. There were always large jars of homemade sugar and oatmeal cookies waiting when we arrived for a visit. Surreptitiously, with an irreverent twinkle in her eye, she would let us steal "just one more" before dinner, as long as we didn't tell Mom or Dad.

In 1929, another royal, the Duke of Spoleto, led an expedition of scientific exploration to K2 and the Karakoram area.

In 1937, Brits Eric Shipton, Michael Spender, Harold Tilman and seven Sherpas explored K2's Northern Flank. The next year, an American expedition including Bill House ascended what is now called House's Chimney. House, and Wyoming's most famous climber, Paul Pedzoldt, the founder of NOLS and Rob's first real climbing mentor, reached an altitude of nearly 26,000 feet. In 1939, Fritz Wiessner's American expedition succeeded in establishing nine high altitude camps on the mountain's southeast ridge, now known as the Abruzzi Ridge in honor of the Duke. Wiessner and Sherpa Pasang Dawa Lama reached the height of over 25,000 feet without oxygen. On the way down, Dudley Wolfe and three Sherpas were lost, becoming K2's first four victims.

The summer Robbie and I were 16, Dad took us with him to visit his father, our Grandpa Slater. While we were there, Grandpa, who was 76, decided it was high time to learn to ride a bicycle. A trip to the local department store produced a shiny new 3-speed and, in no time, Grandpa was cruising around the neighborhood. Also in no time, Grandpa was in the emergency room with a broken hip. For the remaining 14 years of his life, Grandpa walked with a limp. Never, though, did he wear a helmet.

"Grandpa Slater is honed," Robbie would say, using his favorite term to pay his highest compliment. I agreed. I liked his unique use of the term "honed" so much that I used it too. Since Robbie was my identical twin, I believed I had license to use it without attribution whenever I wanted. To be called honed by Robbie meant something and it most certainly applied to our Grandpa Slater.

One of our favorite Dad stories was about Bud Ruble. We would all be in the tent, lined up in our sleeping bags. Dad, staring up at the ceiling of the tent and, judging from the look on his face, fondly looking back in time, recalled that he "had a friend who lived a couple blocks over on Alta Vista Street. His name was Bud Ruble and he called himself the "Earl of Alta Vista." My brothers and I would start to snicker. What a great nickname.

"Bud Ruble thought, in his mind at least, he was some kind of local royalty," Dad continued. "One day in sixth grade science class, we were all asked to bring something from home related to the study of biology. Bud Ruble brought a chicken in a bottle."

To this day, Dad isn't sure where Bud got it; he thinks it was some kind of bottled meal. By this point in the story, we were giddy with the excitement of what we knew happened next.

"All the kids and the teacher gathered around and Bud started explaining that it was a real chicken in the bottle. Then the Earl tried to yank the chicken out through the bottle's narrow neck, but it wouldn't come out. The kids started laughing and the teacher was starting to get angry. Bud kept trying to pull it out and started saying 'Come out of there, Bessie.' The teacher's name was Bessie Yater, and she chased the Earl of Alta Vista out of the classroom with ruler in her hand, yelling, "Bud Ruble you come here." It was complete pandemonium," Dad concluded, summarizing the scene with a simple statement.

It would approach pandemonium in the tent at this point as all of us, laughing, would start doing our own Bud Ruble impressions, calling out, "Come out of there Bessie."

"Bud Ruble was a funny guy," Dad always concluded. Years later, after hearing the story for the umpteenth time, Robbie would always add: "You might even say a comedic genius." We all admired the guts displayed by the Earl in this stunt. We also, especially Robbie, admired the honed nickname the Earl of Alta Vista had bestowed upon himself.

Dad grew up in Moundsville, West Virginia, a small town on the Ohio River in the finger-shaped protuberance at the top of the state. The coal industry dominates the region's economy and the mine entrances can be seen amid the thick forests that blanket the surrounding hillsides. Grandpa Slater, at various times, worked as a farmer, school teacher and ran a shop which re-upholstered furniture. He instilled in Dad a basic notion which played an important role in shaping his life: "Remember, the way out of the coal mines is through the university."

During high school, Dad worked at the local pool each summer. It was a place where kids of all ages congregated.

"Someone donated an old rubber World War II raft which, without fanfare, was thrown in the pool for community use," Dad told us. Dad and his fellow lifeguards, who were in charge of pool safety, watched with amusement as the raft quickly became the object of a water-borne version of "king of the hill." Inevitably, "kids started dive-bombing the raft from the high board and there would be bodies flying everywhere," Dad continued. This part always got our attention. "That would be so fun!" my brothers and I agreed, "but didn't they get in trouble for jumping off the board onto kids in the raft?" we wondered.

"Are you kidding?" Dad replied rhetorically, "Back then there weren't any parents coming around interfering or complaining." My brothers and I knew there would never be an old World War II raft at our local pool, but if there was, we also knew our Dad would let us dive-bomb it from the high board, regardless of what the other parents said.

The 1938 K2 Expedition that included Wyoming climber Paul Petzoldt was the first attempt by an American team to summit the world's second-highest but most horrendous mountain. The team was equipped with all the latest in high-tech outdoor gear, including wool mittens, canvas tents and leather-strapped, buckle-up crampons. Climbing without supplemental oxygen, Pedzoldt reached an astounding height of 25,600 feet. It was a world record at the time, but it was still half a mile below the summit.

Petzoldt, who grew up in the mountains of Wyoming, first summited the Grand Teton at the age of 16. Later in life, when asked why he climbed mountains, responded:

"I can't explain this to other people. I love the physical exertion. I love the wind, I love the storms: I love the fresh air. I love the companionship in the outdoors. I love the reality. I love the change. I love the oneness with nature: I'm hungry; I enjoy clear water. I enjoy being warm at night when it's cold outside. All those simple things are extremely enjoyable because, gosh, you're feeling them, you're living them, you're senses are really feeling, I can't explain it."

Many of Dad's classmates followed their fathers into the mines. For those who didn't, it wasn't so much the coal mines were a filthy, dangerous and deadly place to work, but rather an education was the only way to gain true independence. To do something productive, provide for yourself and be your own boss was the means, with independence being the end. To achieve the means, Grandpa told Dad, you had to "get an education."

Football was a big deal in Moundsville and in the many small communities throughout the state. The whole town turned out for the Friday night games. Dad was on the football team and, at six feet, 185 pounds; he played both offense and defense – quarterback and linebacker. My brothers and I already knew Dad was tough because of it; the shoes had real spikes and, although he was required to wear a helmet, it was made of leather and had no face mask. But Dad didn't dwell on that.

"I was pretty good backing up the line," Dad would admit, which was as close as we ever heard him come to bragging. He even downplayed the way his toughness got him that "education" his father had told him was so important. In his senior year at Moundsville High, Dad was selected to play in the all-star game at the end of the season, where he earned the game's Most Valuable Player award and a football scholarship to West Virginia University. When pressed to describe how he had won the scholarship, however – did he score ten touchdowns, make all the tackles, intercept passes – Dad would only say "they had to give it to somebody."

Dad didn't wear his toughness on his sleeve. It was no more necessary than conspicuous consumption. The important thing was that it was there. As kids, Dad taught his boys to box and how to defend themselves. With those skills went a couple of simple rules which were absolutely inviolate to the Slater brothers: "Never start a fight, but always finish one," and, "If one of you boys comes home beat up, you better all come home beat up." The Slater boys never picked fights and they never all came home beat up.

To us, Dad was the manifestation and a living example of the lessons and values he and Mom had always tried to impart upon us and our sister Elizabeth, who we called Sissy. Independence, hard work, doing your best and following your dreams were the unifying principles. Integrity and respect for oneself and others were the foundations of Dad's world view, which he demonstrated by his deeds as much as he taught by his words.

Dad set a high standard. We kids realized we were lucky, being afforded many opportunities and luxuries our father never had when he was growing up. Dad was the kind of man my brothers and I wanted to be. For Sis, it was Mom who she tried to emulate. The fact Dad had pulled himself up out of the coal mines by his football cleats, something we would never have to do, made his success story the more impressive to us.

"Dad's the man!" was a common Robbie proclamation, a notion shared by the rest of the Slater boys.

While we were in high school, Dad drove a white Buick Skylark, complete with a broken-off driver's side door handle. It ran pretty well, so Dad kept it. Dad knew-and so did we-that he could get a Cadillac if he wanted one and that was the point. Dad was sending a subtle message which, over the years, was not lost on us. Perhaps also it was a small act of defiance. It was far better to be able to do something and choose not to rather than do something or try to be somebody you aren't because others expect it.

"Your Mom and I always cared more about our kids going to college than living in some big, fancy house," Dad remarked years later.

Robbie and I were more irreverent and far more edgy than our parents. Dad's irreverent and defiant streaks were there, but kept under restraint. Dad had too much class to be spouting off and acting dumb with the regularity of his boys. On occasion though, even Dad allowed himself to sink into silliness, offering a verbal glimpse of the genesis of this particular family trait. When referring to someone who enjoyed the obvious benefit of second, third or fourth generation wealth, Dad jokingly remarked,

"He got his company the old-fashioned way – from his father!"

"Good work if you can get it," was Robbie's common rejoinder.

Robbie referred to Dad as the "lender of last resort." Dad and Robbie were both neither borrowers nor lenders, but it was a long-running family joke, dating back to a young Robbie going to Mom and Dad with requests for them to "invest" in climbing equipment or parachutes.

Dad also talked about the need to "be in the game." To him, as a student of history and one who loves exploring ideas, life is full of fascination and opportunity. Dad hoped we would recognize this and encouraged us to search for our individual passions and niches. Doing something also entailed the responsibility of doing something productive. To Dad, the ends did not necessarily justify the means.

When we were younger, I believed only Robbie was lucky enough to have discovered a passion for something that approached Dad's love for surgery and medicine. Rock climbing, mountaineering, ice climbing, skydiving and then BASE jumping became Robbie's passion. Robbie was like Dad in a climbing harness instead of scrubs-with the irreverence, defiance and outspokenness traits amplified by several orders of magnitude.

The rest of us Slater boys also liked to see ourselves as some image of our father, but recognized we were merely varying, less refined versions. Dad had the polish of a true gentleman. We each carried the trait, owing to Dad and Mom, but it was something which sometimes bobbed below the surface. Our minds were adequately trained and mostly willing, but the flesh was occasionally weak. Nevertheless, Dad was always the gold standard of honed.

"Those boys just idolize their father," Mom would say. Dad would say to us: "Remember, I'm your biggest fan,' his most common words of encouragement and approval.

The West Virginia high school all-star football game scholarship was Dad's ticket out of the coal mines. Contemplating his own dad's advice, Dad chose medicine, a fascinating field where he could be independent and contribute to society. Following medical school at the University of Maryland, his surgical internship led Dad to Milwaukee, Wisconsin. One day in the operating room, he met a slender blonde nurse named Mary Krizek. After their first date, he said he'd call again. Playing it cool, he waited several weeks and, at the point where Mary had just about given up on him, he called back. Six months later they were husband and wife.

Mary Krizek was a hometown girl, the daughter of a prominent local family. Grandpa Chet Krizek was the long-time mayor of Shorewood, a Milwaukee suburb, a respected attorney and an accomplished sport and gamesman. Oftentimes when we were visiting, sheriff's deputies came by the house for business related to Grandpa being mayor. They were always in uniform, complete with guns, extra ammo, handcuffs and nightsticks. We all thought that was cool.

Three walls of main family room in the Krizek home were covered with built-in bookshelves. Interspersed among the books were many trophies Grandpa won over the years for basketball, billiards and bowling. There were also many photos of a younger Chet, which included basketball team pictures, shots of him playing in billiard tournaments and photos with his bowling buddies.

Grandpa Chet smoked and had slicked back hair which, in my opinion, made him look really cool. My brothers and I agreed that in his day, Grandpa Chet was a bad-ass – or, as Robbie and I said, *honed*.

As he got older, Grandpa Krizek's real interest was taking his grandsons fishing. Although suffering from arthritis, which caused painful swelling in his hands, he was always able to rig up poles, bait hooks and untangle the constant messes caused by four little boys. For us, fishing was a fun new way to experience a different aspect of the wild.

Grandma Betty Krizek had a charm bracelet with a little gold hearts with the names of every child and grandchild in the family. My brothers and I would gather around as she showed each one to us and told a story about that person when they were young. We liked hearing about Mom as a young girl on the swim team

At the age of 92, Grandma was incensed when Mom and her sister Betsy told her it was time to give up her driver's license. Grandma protested vehemently as her friends, themselves well into their eighties, nineties or beyond, would be left without transportation.

"I pick them up so we can play cards and visit. Sometimes we have a couple of bourbons and when we're all ready to go back home, I drop everyone off," Grandma protested. No one ever got hurt and eventually Grandma Betty agreed not to drive. Grandma's defiance and determination were pretty honed, too, Robbie and I thought.

Art Gilkey was a geologist from Iowa, finishing his Ph.D. at Columbia University when he joined the Third American Karakoram Expedition to K2 in 1953. The summer before, he had directed the Juneau Icefield Research Project in Alaska and was well-known for climbing Devil's Tower as a boy and his numerous ascents in the Grand Tetons. During the expedition's descent of the Abruzzi Ridge, despite being secured by two separate ice axes anchored in the slope, Gilkey, in an instant, was blown off the mountain, disappearing in a cloud of white at 25,000 feet. Before his team, badly battered by their ordeal, left on their return to civilization, they erected a 10-foot rock cairn to commemorate their fallen companion. At the base of the cairn they placed a small metal box containing some mountain flowers, the expedition flags intended for the summit, a poem and a statement about their friend. On top, they placed Art Gilkey's ice axe. Since then, the Gilkey Memorial has accrued numerous plaques and mementoes of those lost on the "mountaineer's mountain."

In 1954, an Italian expedition led by Ardito Desio challenged the Abruzzi Ridge. As camps were being established, Mario Puchoz, an Alpine guide of legendary toughness and determination, developed a nagging sore throat. Not one to complain, he was not about to abandon the climb due to a slight cold. The weather then deteriorated, along with Puchoz's condition. In the days that followed, his breathing became irregular and, in the early morning hours of June 21st, Mario Puchoz expired. Rather than call off the expedition, the climbers pressed on and, after an epic struggle for survival and the summit, Achille Compagnoni and Lino Lacedelli reached the top of K2.

Mom and Dad also told us stories about ourselves where we were little. We didn't always remember what we'd done – and even when we did, we didn't remember it from the perspective of our parents. We especially liked hearing stories about our supreme acts of foolishness for which, due to the passage of time, we could no longer be punished. Mom and Dad could no longer be mad and as Dad told them to us in the tent, he also thought they were funny.

One of their favorites – and ours too – happened during our year in Cleveland, when Robbie and I were six, Paul was five and Tommy three. One day, with the efficiency of a veteran fire crew, we dragged the garden hose to Mom's 1962 Chevy convertible, which was parked on the street in front of the house. The hose was placed in the front seat and turned on. Slowly the car filled with water as we gleefully watched. When it filled up we would go swimming. No one was the wiser until the water level reached the dashboard. For mechanical reasons which were never fully explained, the car's horn went off.

Running outside, Mom could do little more than turn off the hose. The horn, however, continued to sound, drawing the attention of the neighborhood, especially the kids. Mom had to call the fire department and then wait, as the horn blared, until they showed up. We were thrilled to see the fire engine pull up, sirens blaring and bells a-clangin', with the firemen, decked out in their big boots, fire coats and hats, hanging off the sides of the truck. The firemen jumped off the truck and eventually got the horn to stop. Exasperated, Mom could only shake her head.

Another one Robbie and I especially liked to hear again and again happened the year prior, in New Haven, Connecticut. A new house was being constructed down the street. We liked watching the workers with their tool belts and interesting equipment. Like garbage men, the workers also had cool gloves. We had tool belts, too. One evening, Robbie and I sneaked out of the backyard and down to the construction site. Believing our assistance would be thoroughly appreciated; we pried open several paint cans and got started. As we worked, we commended ourselves for the job we were doing.

"I wonder how much they're going to pay us!" Robbie proclaimed with a wide-eyed grin. We were not offered payment for a job well done. Instead, Dad had to write the owners a check for the damage.

"We were so mad," Mom recalled, "but what could we do? You guys…"

A few years later a similar situation occurred when, without being asked, we helped out by harvesting all of the vegetables from a neighbor's garden.

Curious minds and fertile imaginations, Mom believed, if lovingly cultivated, could grow to bear the fruit of great adventure and worthwhile accomplishments. This held true for kids as well as adults. Sometimes, though, our curiosity trumped our collective common sense. But Mom always thought that the more we spread our wings, the higher we'd have a chance to fly. In the meantime, Mom didn't sweat the small stuff.

These stories not only filled the tent with laughter, but helped instill in us a sense of family identity. Our favorites always focused on our ancestors' traits of independence, quirkiness and subtle irreverence. It caused us to embrace these attitudes. It gave me – and I know it gave Robbie – a framework which encouraged our own individuality. We may not have been necessarily special, but we were at least different.

When Robbie was older, he seemed to get a kick out of Prince Charles of England, mostly because he was married to Princess Diana, who Robbie found quite attractive. Had the prince's mom the Queen passed or given up her title, Charles would ascend the throne as King. If Charles got his chance, Robbie wouldn't have watched on TV as the new king rode through the streets in his gilded carriage draped in the ermine robe of regality. Robbie didn't fault the prince for being born into a position of privilege – "Good work if you can get it" he would say, but this comment transparently masked an element of jealousy Robbie felt. Charles had been born lucky, through no effort or merit on his part. Robbie and I knew we had been born pretty lucky ourselves, also through no effort or merit on our parts. If Charles got to be king, he should at least try and be a good one. Robbie and I felt we had the same kind of obligation, albeit without a title.

This comment also masked another, though not readily apparent element of Robbie's personality: insecurity. Would he be able to live up to Dad, much less be a great king? Though Robbie never expected anything handed to him he felt, as did I that we had to at least try and live up to the best of our legacy.

Dad always said, "In the end, the only thing you have is your integrity. What counts is the type of person you are and what you stand for. If you want to parachute off buildings or run across Antarctica, that's beside the point."

Or as Mom put it, "It doesn't matter if you're a lawyer or a doctor or a candlestick maker, as long as you're the best one you can be."

Or, as Dad concluded, perhaps less profoundly, "I don't care what you do – just do *something*." Whatever that "something" was, however, we would have to figure out for ourselves.

As part of a lineage of characters with the courage of Grandpaps Hannah, adventurousness of Grandpa Slater, cool confidence of Grandpa Krizek, good-natured defiance of Grandma Krizek, subtle irreverence of Grandma Slater and the determination and self-reliance of Dad, as Robbie got older he felt not only compelled but entirely justified not just in doing something but in carrying that something one step further than anyone else. This was especially true when he was in the mountains, surrounded by the spirits of the wild.

Robbie knew he wouldn't be *a* king, but he also knew he could – and should – seek to become *the* king of whatever something he chose to do.

With Grandpa Chet (Robbie on left)

Robbie at NOLS, age 16

Chapter IV

"I've taken grounders from higher than this.
You guys are pussies."
–Rob Slater

Mom and Dad settled into marriage but they didn't really
settle down. Following his rotation in Milwaukee, Dad still had a lot
of training to undergo before reaching his goal of becoming a plastic
surgeon. A year in Baltimore at the University of Maryland hospital,
where Robbie and I were born in 1960, was followed by a year at

Yale University with the family living in New Haven, Connecticut, where our brother Paul was born.

Growing up, Paul always seemed to be the most reserved of the brothers, which really didn't mean much when considering with whom he was being compared. But Paul for the most part kept his thoughts and words to himself and his nose in his books. After graduating second in his high school class, owing to a lone B from the notorious "Happy Jack" Dabney's "History of the West," Paul graduated from Stanford University and then the University of Utah Medical School.

After med school, Paul took a job at a local HMO in Salt Lake City, but never developed the passion for medicine of Dad. Deciding to give law school a shot, he took the law school admission test and scored at the top of the scale. Hearing this, Robbie thought it may be a wise investment to negotiate having Paul take the graduate school admission exam for him. Robbie called "The Doctor of Love," his name for Paul, and offered him $500 to take the exam as Rob Slater.

"Take it yourself, pussy," was Paul's reply.

Paul went on to finish law school, making him The Doctor of Love, Esq. Rather than practicing medicine, or law, or both, Paul did neither. He ended up marrying a doctor, opting instead to stay home with his twin boys and play golf with the retired physicians at his club. Technically speaking, Paul was a retired doctor himself, having worked as one for a short period before law school.

"He always was the smart one," Rob would muse.

Living in New Haven, Connecticut while Dad was training at Yale, our youngest brother Tommy was born in 1963. Tommy was born with a smile on his face. That smile never left and he has always been known in the family as "Sunny.' Little Sunny insisted on participating in whatever his older brothers were doing and always tagged along cheerfully. But Sunny was no tag-along in the normal sense of the term, becoming an expert skier in grade school and the city diving champ. By age four he was performing flips off the high dive and never shrank from a challenge laid down by his older brothers.

In addition to his own wild streak, Tommy practiced his own brand of independence.

"When I grow up I'm gonna be a kid," he proclaimed at an early age, "Then I'm gonna change my name to 'Bud.'"

When we were a little older, Dad would send us on our bikes to get haircuts, or "smoothed off," as he would say. Tommy, like the rest of us, would implore John Lucas, the official Slater boy barber, to cut only enough off to pass muster with Mom and Dad.

"Tommy would leave the barbershop on his bike, only to return 10 minutes later grumbling that Mom said it didn't even look like anything had been cut off. He looked like a kid who had poked his head through a hedge. I'd cut some more off and eventually he wouldn't come back, having finally satisfied Mom," John remembered years later, earning Sunny Bud the additional nickname of "Hedgehead."

For years, Tommy was intent on attending UCLA in southern California. It didn't take long, though, for Tommy to shear off his hedge once he surmised the UCLA coeds liked it neat and trim. Tommy studied economics, graduated and followed Robbie into the world of banking and high finance.

A trip to Denver, Colorado, for a medical meeting led Mom and Dad to move the family to Cheyenne in 1967. In 1968, daughter Elizabeth, dubbed Sissy early on, arrived. Sis was the apple of her Mom's eye and Daddy's little girl. Sis, however, was no sissy. By the age of five she was on the slopes of Aspen with her big brothers, and although we were always fiercely protective of her, she exhibited a strong vein of independence and determination. By the ripe old age of 14, Sis was sometimes known to sneak out in Mom's red Camaro to take her friends for a late night spin. In fact, she was so successful in her stealth that no one, not even her brothers, found out about it until years later. Not that we would have told on her anyway. It was a honed stunt for a 14-year old girl.

In high school, Sis was a member of the tennis team and the cheerleading squad. Dad would drive her nuts with his requests of "Sis boom bah, give us a cheer!"

Sis also graduated valedictorian, with an A in every single class she took in high school. Sis went on to graduate, also with A's, from Robbie's alma mater, CU in Boulder, with a degree in economics. From there it was off to the London School of Economics for post graduate work, followed by law school at my alma mater, Creighton University, where she left with not only a law degree but an MBA as well.

From the standpoint of her brothers and friends, however, what set Sis apart from the crowd was her tremendous sense of style and incredible sense of humor. There was a somewhat edgy, irreverent component to her personality that made her fun to be around. Guys found her hilariously funny, but in a way that did not compromise her feminine qualities. Sissy was just plain cool.

Mom and Dad, with their four little boys and a baby girl, decided to stay out west, where the air was clean and the climate healthy, to raise their family. About twenty miles west of Cheyenne, the prairie turns into mountains. Nestled on the fringe of the Medicine Bow National Forest, Crystal Reservoir forms the headwaters of not-so-mighty Crow Creek. Although nowhere deep or swift enough to prevent an easy crossing, it enjoys an auspicious start before meandering across the prairie to Cheyenne.

On the dry side, the Crystal dam is nearly 100 feet tall. On the lake side, depending on the year and the season, the top of the dam to the water could be anywhere from five to 30 feet. The lake forms a small finger at the north of the dam, flanked by cliffs which also, depending on the water level, range from 30 to 80 feet in height.

During the summer of 1977, when Robbie and I were 16, my brothers and I were invited to go "cliff jumping" at Crystal. Crossing the dam and climbing the rocks to the cliffs for the first time, we were excited but not really apprehensive. That is, of course, until we reached our destination. All of a sudden, we were standing on a sloping rock which formed a ten-foot launching pad into space. Looking across the lake, we had a great view of the surrounding hills, forests and mountains. It appeared from the top of the cliffs that we were above the horizon, which made the distance to the water below seem that much more daunting.

We examined the ledges below and, as first timers, began to climb down, looking for a better, meaning lower, place to jump. In the meantime, Robbie showed up-and we all immediately scrambled to the top, suddenly embarrassed to have climbed lower.

My twin brother had a way with words. Even back then, he was the master of the pithy comment. His sense of humor was irreverent, ribald and, in many cases, outrageous. He used words like horrendous, hideous, heinous and horrific. My personal favorite was "hellacious," but Robbie's favorite was "honed," and, as I said, it was his ultimate compliment. We liked and regularly used these kinds of terms, partly because no one else did. Over time, people who came in contact with Robbie would adopt portions of his unique vocabulary, which I believe arose out of their desire to be like him. I know that was the case with me.

We thought Robbie would certainly be impressed by the height of these cliffs. Instead, he simply took off his shirt. "I've taken grounders from higher than this. You guys are pussies." With that, he ran off the top. I glimpsed his face as he unhesitatingly began his launch. For a fleeting instant I thought back to the look on his face four years before as he went over the edge on the big free rappel at Exum-the same joyful intensity.

We watched him fly and heard him hit the water far below with a loud splash. Robbie's love of heights and fearlessness were already well known to me and everyone else by this time. I could not help but be impressed. We were identical twins, yes, but he had something extra.

As a group, watching Robbie made us all want to have the courage to follow. We were not offended by his remark. Rather, we were emboldened. Moments like those made me begin to realize how everyone wanted at some level to be like Robbie. This meant to at least try to follow in his footsteps or take things one step further than they otherwise would have on their own. Shortly thereafter, steeled by Robbie's performance, we all jumped too - from the top. Regardless of what phraseology was used, we all thought Robbie was honed.

During those early years, as young men we began to develop our own individual interests. As time went by, it wasn't always the case that, whenever one of us wanted to do something, the rest would automatically follow. The summer before we moved to Cheyenne, when Robbie and I were 11, there was a neighborhood girl, a tall slender blonde two years older who we both liked. This gal played tennis, so I promptly took up the sport. The girl never became interested in either of us, but I played tennis through high school. I liked the individuality of the competition and the way success had nothing to do with a coach's favor. I ended up doing pretty well and collected a number of state championships and a shelf full of trophies, even though my initial motivations for taking up the sport went unfulfilled.

Over the years, there were several girls that Robbie and I both liked. In response, a couple of them liked me, some liked my brother, but many, for reasons that are probably already becoming obvious to the reader, decided to pass on both of us. Nevertheless, there were a few who liked us both. In truth, neither of us was ever much interested in long term, serious-type girlfriend stuff.

My twin brother already had his mistress – climbing – to whom he was true, although periodically there were what RSL and Robbie later fondly referred to as "girlfriend units." To Robbie and RSL, girlfriend units were temporary, fungible and easily replaced, generally soon after their first complaint of "You're going climbing again?" With Rob, climbing was Girlfriend Unit #1.

I wholeheartedly agreed with this approach. To me, the aspect of replacing the girlfriend unit was the main fun of the process. Besides, it would be many years before I thought seriously of collecting potential future ex-wives.

As we progressed through junior high school, Robbie and I still went out for all the sports teams, including football. On the eighth grade team, I was the quarterback and Robbie was a receiver. For one game, the head coach was unable to attend so his assistant took over. Rather than calling the plays like the head coach did, the assistant said I could. I started passing every play, with my twin as my primary target. Even though we were winning, the assistant reclaimed the play – calling authority and returned the offense to a more conservative game plan. We didn't care; we had scored, we were ahead and we'd made some twin-to-twin completions.

On another junior high afternoon, I took Robbie to the tennis courts near our house. By then I was pretty good and could beat the local high school players. I think he respected my tennis and came along as a willing student. After all, if I could do it, maybe he could too. Trying to serve, Robbie tossed the ball, but swung at it and missed. Robbie was left-handed and I am right-handed, but I don't know if that made any difference. From a physical standpoint, we were otherwise very similar, although I was always a little bigger than my twin. Once we were grown, Robbie's hair started thinning before mine, but that was about the extent of our dissimilarities.

A few neighborhood boys from school, who had been standing by the fence watching, began laughing. Rob and I told them to shut up. The biggest of the group kept talking and actually came on to Robbie's side of the court. Sensing trouble, I headed that way also. The guy went straight up to Robbie, running his mouth the whole time. By the time I reached them, however, the "trouble" was already over. The loudmouth was now quiet as he staggered away after being punched in the face a few times by my brother. That turned out to be the only time Robbie and I ever played tennis together, although we both always remembered the incident with a laugh.

When Robbie discovered climbing, however, he steadily gravitated away from other extracurricular endeavors. I think Robbie was simply bored with organized or regimented activities. Basically, he just really wasn't a sports fan. Robbie wanted to *participate* in sports, not watch someone else do them. He was attracted to the excitement, speed and danger of race cars and the Indy 500. Pages taken from *Sports Illustrated* of the race hung on the walls of his bedroom, I think because he felt a common bond with the drivers careening around the track at over 200 miles per hour, seeking a thrill and an experience which few have the courage and daring to actually pursue. Plus, the cars were cool and really loud. But Robbie saw no real point in playing little league baseball, joining the science club or running for office in student government. To him, those were moves in the opposite direction from the freedom and exhilaration he found in the wild.

Throughout our junior high and high school years, Robbie's time revolved more and more around climbing. As we got older, while I was out raising hell with our friends, Rob was usually either climbing-or training for climbing. It wasn't unusual, for example, to see him several miles out of town, pedaling along on Mom's circa 1970 Schwinn ladies' three speed, wearing a large backpack full of water jugs as we passed by on the way to a summer evening prairie kegger.

"Go Rob!" we'd yell out the windows.

"Party" was his usual mock response, though we all knew Robbie had better things to do than "party."

Apart from us, Robbie was developing his own mindset that was beginning to separate himself from the rest of our gang and me as well. I did still climb with him sometimes, and when we did, I saw that changing mindset firsthand. Like Robbie with my tennis, I supported my twin's climbing. Each time we roped up together, usually at Vedauwoo, his progress was quickly and clearly evident. It started at the base of the climb, with his familiarity and ease with the equipment, new pieces of which were continually being added. He talked excitedly about and pointed out a new climb he had recently done, the one we were about to do or the next, invariably harder one he had planned. Looking up that day's route, I often wondered aloud how we would ever make it up.

"Don't worry Junior, it'll be casual," he'd reply. "You can make it."

With that, he took the lead. Although Robbie always made it look easy, I studied his moves, knowing I was soon expected to follow. Since Robbie went first, he placed the protection, though on the climbs he did with me he probably didn't need it. Following, I got to clean, just like back at Exum. While I worked my way up, sometimes straining mightily, there was always a steady stream of encouragement and commentary from above. When I fell, which I sometimes did, I knew the rope would be held taut. As I dangled on the rope, the only thing I ever heard from above was "I got you, man. This time lean out more; don't hug the rock."

Robbie never took me up a climb I didn't complete. Even though the routes we did were easy by his standards, he seemed to always take me up something that was harder than our last climb and at the top limit of my ability level. My twin never failed to bring out my climbing best and, as he progressed, he brought me along at least part of the way.

The entire gang got a glimpse of these changes, and was also brought along at times like that day at the cliffs. While Robbie's independence set him apart, none of us wanted him to be apart. He was way fun to be around. Robbie's individuality, irreverent and defiant personality were quietly-and sometimes not-so-quietly becoming noticed.

One day during high school, Robbie was sitting in the locker room eating a cherry Pop-Tart. A classmate commented they were much better when heated in the toaster. Robbie responded he had been eating them this way for years and only wimps put them in toasters. Robbie laughed quietly, finished tying his shoe and ate the last bite. As he walked past the guy he looked over his shoulder and said, "Mmmmm" and was still chuckling as he left the locker room. This wasn't done to offend, but make the point that he liked to do things his way.

That same summer, Robbie and Sam Gusea, one of our gang who was also interested in climbing, went down to Eldorado Canyon outside Boulder, Colorado. There they were, hundreds of feet above the valley floor, with Sam enjoying the view, watching the raptors circle both overhead and below his belay ledge. Suddenly, it began to rain. On a small, downward sloping flake, they debated continuing up or heading down. The decision was made for them when the rain shower turned into a downpour. They had no choice but to wait it out.

"I was huddled against the rock, just trying to hang on, scared to death we were about to be washed off the rock," Sam later told us, with a gleam in his eyes as he recounted the adventure. "The water was just pouring over us from the sky and in waterfalls from the ledges above. Robbie has this huge grin on his face, and rather than clinging to the wall, he paced back and forth across the tiny ledge, a stream of water flowing up above his ankles."

"Isn't this amazing? When it stops, we'll top out,'" Robbie proclaimed. Seeing this, Sam was still scared to death, but also inspired. Robbie's courage and enthusiasm for the situation had once again proved infectious. Sam easily followed him up the rest of the route after it stopped raining.

By the time Robbie was in high school, his training was paying off. He'd mastered the art of the one-armed fingertip pull-up while hanging from the ledge above a door. This was a skill which paid dividends in areas outside of climbing.

As a member of the swim team, Robbie swam freestyle and butterfly. Even though it was an organized activity, Rob liked the swim team. In a pool full of other competitors, he could swam his laps in a chlorinated cocoon, alone with his adrenaline-fueled thoughts, shielded from any sounds of the commotion in the lanes next to him and the cheering spectators and teammates around the pool. Although it was a team, it was also a totally individual pursuit-just like climbing. It didn't matter what anyone else was doing. Also fun was the camaraderie of the team and the horseplay which inevitably went along with it. Rob ended up being voted one of the team captains, not because he was the fastest swimmer or won all his races, but because he was a guy his teammates looked up to and liked being around. Rob's infectious enthusiasm and independent and outgoing personality rubbed off on his teammates and, as usual, inspired them to be better.

Anyway, at the start of a race when "swimmers take your mark" was called, Rob would bend down and with those super-strong fingers grasp the side of the metal starting platform block. Then, during the short period before the starting gun fired, he leaned forward out over the water to a nearly horizontal position – and then held it. No one else could do this and, seeing him move out over the water in their peripheral vision, other racers invariably false started; or the surprised starter anticipated a false start, disrupting commencement of the race – and the timing of the racers with whom Robbie competed. Everyone agreed his lean was quite honed. Every time Robbie did something like this, my friends and I promised ourselves we'd start training like him, so we could be honed too, but we never did.

One day in high school gym class, the coach demonstrated rudimentary moves on the gymnastic rings, which hung from the ceiling on long straps. Robbie was able to perform the "iron cross," one of the most demanding strength moves in the sport. Afterwards, a guy in the class questioned his masculinity and sexual preference, claiming anyone that good on the rings should be wearing a tight stretchy gymnast's outfit. Shortly afterwards, the same guy was on his knees dripping blood on to the gym floor.

During a camping trip when we were much younger, Dad had told a story about his friends and him "wingin' a few 'maters," or, in non-Moundsville parlance, throwing tomatoes. It turned out to be an expression we never forgot. It sounded like fun, but we didn't have any tomatoes. We did, however, have snowballs.

We extrapolated Dad's expression into countenance, but just throwing snowballs wasn't exciting enough. Robbie suggested we take our bikes down to the local gas station where, with a mere dollar or so, a large can of gas could be easily purchased. A large pool of gasoline was poured out across the street in front of our friend Sam's house, which sat a few blocks from ours on a narrow, tree-lined residential street. When a car approached, the gas was ignited, causing flames and thick black smoke to block traffic. Then, when the car stopped and waited for the flames to dissipate, we let loose with a salvo of rotten apples, snowballs and water balloons from the roof. It was a well-executed ambush, if I do say so myself. Sometimes, in addition to the water balloons, etc., we lit Roman Candles to shoot fireballs arcing over the stunned motorist. The drivers just sat in their cars, their attention on the fire. I don't think any of them ever realized where the barrage was coming from. Even if they did, we figured we had plausible deniability. After all, who would be so stupid to try something like that? Certainly not us, officer!

One day in junior high, we lined up behind the fence of our house and let fly with a barrage of snowballs at a passing vehicle. An angry motorist slammed on his brakes and stormed into our garage and began pounding on the door. Robbie answered the door, meeting the man's angry glare with glazed eyes and a faraway gaze.

"What the hell's the matter with you?" screamed the man. "I don't know what you're talking about, sir," responded Robbie calmly, still with a faraway gaze, "I'm blind." The flabbergasted motorist had no choice but to stomp back to his car and drive away. The nerve and coolness of this stunt, in our eyes, was greatly respected.

"What's he gonna do," Robbie asked rhetorically afterwards, "beat up a blind kid?"

I had no problem throwing the snowballs and when the driver stopped and came after us I ran in the house with Robbie and everyone else. But when the guy banged on the door my inclination was to just wait until he went away. If confronted, I would have been the first to step forward to fight, but Robbie had rendered that scenario moot. It took more balls to do what he had done than it would have for me to open the door and punch the guy in the mouth. Robbie was always the funniest, ballsiest guy I ever knew.

My brothers and I had always agreed Jackson Hole, Wyoming, was the ultimate ski mountain. Unlike other places we skied, Jackson was not comprised of neatly groomed runs carved out of the trees. Rather, it consisted of a huge mountain with massive bowls above tree line, chutes no less steep or narrow than elevator shafts and miles of uncut forest. Also, it was in the Tetons, a place we had been going since we were little and which was always special to us. In the summers when we were little, we looked forward to the day we would return during the winter to ski. It was the biggest and the baddest ski mountain and there was only one way to the top-a tram that climbed high above the towering pines, sheer rock faces and upper snow slopes to the top of Rendezvous Peak. Reaching the four-story steel tower at the top, skiers pile out and descend a long flight of metal steps in single file on either side of the staircase, one arm clinging to the railing, the other to their skis and ski poles. Once off the tower, skiers descend into the swirling whiteness of the Rendezvous Bowl.

Throughout high school, we skied at Jackson every Christmas. One time on the tram, my brothers and I noticed a kid crunched in the jam of skiers heading for the top. What caught our eyes was the kid's fancy ski helmet, just like Olympic downhillers on TV. We exchanged smirks and followed the kid out of the tram and down the metal stairs. Near the bottom, the kid stumbled and fell in a heap in the snow at the stair landing. As Paul went by he commented, "Good thing you're wearing a helmet." The comment wasn't about the kid as much as it was about an attitude shared by all of us but epitomized and driven by Robbie. In his mind, helmets were for pussies-a sign of weakness and self doubt. Without Robbie, it was a concept that probably wouldn't have registered. Without Robbie this comment would never have been made.

In 1965, 27 years after he and Bill House climbed to the upper reaches of K2, Paul Petzoldt founded the National Outdoor Leadership School (NOLS) which he operated out of a small, nondescript office in Lander, Wyoming. In Rob's world, going to Paul Petzoldt camp was akin to a Little Leaguer taking batting practice with Cal Ripken. The two-week course took place in the Cascade Mountains which, owing to their location in the Pacific Northwest, are barraged by wave after wave of moisture-laden weather from the ocean and receive considerably more precipitation than the Tetons in Wyoming. For 15-year-old Robbie, this was like meeting his mistress' just-as-good-looking sister. With her, Robbie got the opportunity to do things he had, to that point, only read and dreamed about.

Above tree line, Robbie ascended snow-covered mountain

slopes and glaciers with crampons, marveling at a world filled only with white and blue. Using an ice axe to cut steps up a massive snowfield, ice climbing on frozen waterfalls and actual high altitude mountaineering all had a profound effect on Robbie. High on the Cascade peaks, the suspicions Robbie harbored up to that time, born in the Tetons three years before, were confirmed. With each step upward, as he climbed into the infinite mountain sky, the exhilaration intensified. It was a feeling of not only conquering what was now below him but being absorbed in and at one with the intense grandeur of the high places of the mountain gods. It was everything-but it still wasn't enough. Each step upward increased his need to go even higher. Robbie had, for the first exciting time, been able to touch his mistress.

I couldn't help but feel somewhat jealous. Hearing him describe his NOLS experience afterward, Robbie had the glow about him of a young man in love-a young man in love with someone who loved him back.

When Robbie returned from the Cascades, he dove into climbing and mountaineering with even more vigor. It was as if he had been validated. His focus now shifted from getting himself actually involved in climbing to concentrating on specific mountaineering goals.

From the beginning, the first big goal was the Grand Teton. During the NOLS course, there was talk among both the students and instructors about Petzoldt famous New Years Day climb of the Grand Teton, which had been held annually the preceding 11 years. Petzoldt himself led the expedition, which was comprised of climbers, selected by Petzoldt and the NOLS staff. Robbie, in keeping with his character, made clear to the instructors his desire to join the assault of the Grand while doing his best during the course to demonstrate his ability and qualifications. Sure enough, upon completion of NOLS, and after clearing it with Mom and Dad, Robbie applied to go on the climb. I asked Dad if he was really going to let Robbie go on the climb. He kind of shrugged his shoulders and replied, "Sure, if they'll take him."

And they did. After spending a fortnight with Robbie high in the Cascades, Petzoldt and the NOLS staff had enough confidence in him and his abilities to give my 16-year-old twin a spot on the 1977 New Year's Day climb team as its youngest-ever member.

I suspected his gung-ho attitude had something to do with their decision. Unfortunately, also for the only time in its history, Paul Petzoldt was unable to participate due to health reasons. The summit of the Grand was no longer a far off, unattainable, unreachable dream for Robbie; it was now on his calendar.

The day after Christmas Robbie headed for Jackson for the first time without his family. It was also his first climbing in the Tetons without me. As he packed his gear, we talked about it.

"Man, it's gonna be way cool," I observed encouragingly, both of us nodding our heads and grinning.

"Yeah, I just hope they don't try to keep me off the summit team because I'm young," Robbie replied.

My brother had acquired a large assortment of new equipment, some from his NOLS trip and some specifically for the Grand. In addition to his ice axe, he had crampons, a headlamp and a full ensemble of cold weather clothing.

"This is the real deal" he said, and I knew what he meant. There was some real danger involved climbing up the Grand Teton in the heart of the winter, but I didn't say anything about it; I had a feeling he'd make the top and I had absolutely no reservations about him trying. I never thought to dissuade him, or even caution him. All I said to my twin as he departed was: "I hope you make the top!"

Robbie set up camp at the lower saddle between the Grand and Middle Tetons with 16 other climbers from the Petzoldt expedition. On our previous trips, we had backpacked up Garnett Canyon and camped at the base of the Middle Teton's east face. Back then, reaching the lower saddle, the low point of the ridge between the two mountains, seemed like quite an accomplishment.

What always stuck in my mind about the lower saddle were the notions of scale and perspective. As we climbed out of the tree line after carrying our backpacks more than four miles up the switch-backing trail through the forested lower Teton slopes, we found ourselves at the base of the hideous scree field leading to the massive Middle Teton. Looking back down into the Snake River Valley, we got a sense of how far we had come and how high we had climbed. But only when we started up the steep, winding trail toward the lower saddle did we begin to get a real taste of their size and the horrendous scale of the realm of the Teton mountain gods. The jumbled, knife-edged slabs of rock which had crumbled from above to form a vast expanse of moss, lichen and mica-splattered granite seemed to go on forever, especially as we fought gravity and gasped for breath in the increasingly rarified air.

We all had, at one time or another, experienced what we called altitude sickness, which is the pathological effect of high altitude on humans. It's caused by acute exposure to low air pressure and oxygen content at high altitude and commonly occurs above 8,000 feet, bringing severe headaches and lethargy. It is cured only by descending. For Robbie to be camped all the way up there was, to us, already an impressive feat.

The weather had been unusually mild that winter and Robbie felt his prospects were good. "This year there isn't as much snow on the peaks as there usually is, which may make the climb a little easier," he told the *Wyoming Tribune-Eagle*, the local Cheyenne newspaper, which ran the story on the front page. Off the record, Robbie was a bit more direct.

"I'm gonna climb it" he said, looking directly at me. I noticed immediately how his eyes widened as he said it, along with the determined grin that spread across his face. "I have to," he continued, pushing his face closer. He had not been so outwardly vehement when he spoke to the newspaper reporter and-at our young age, I wasn't sure if Robbie was engaged in a conscious and premeditated effort to maintain public modesty or simply didn't care about public adulation. As time went by I would realize my twin's quest was intensely personal.

"I know you will," I said, because I knew he would.

In keeping with tradition, the order of the members' attempts for the top was determined by drawing names from a hat. This eliminated the need for or possibility of any drama related to who would go up the mountain when. Robbie was put in the second summit assault team. As the first group went up, he anxiously waited for his chance, hoping the weather would hold.
Back in Cheyenne, we all knew how agonizing his inactivity on the mountain was for him. He hadn't said anything to me specifically, but I deduced from our conversation that he was prepared to wait however long it took for his chance at the summit. On prior trips with the family, Robbie had only been able to get as high as the

upper saddle, about half way from the lower saddle to the top. On some attempts, he had been slowed down by our altitude sickness and on some attempts the weather. But this time, the weather held and there were no sick members holding him back. Robbie became the youngest-ever member of the famous Petzoldt expeditions to reach the Grand Teton summit and matched Petzoldt age for his first ascent. He had trained, learned and waited – and it had all paid off.

Standing on the top, with virtual strangers with whom he had shared a tent and a goal for just a few days, it was almost as if he was alone. Robbie looked down as the brilliant sunlight reflecting off the whiteness of the ice covering Jenny Lake melded into the brilliance of the blue above. As Robbie grew older he became an avid photographer and, although he used to say, "if you don't get pictures, it didn't happen," he did not bring a camera with him to this important first summit. It was a personal, non-public celebration on the summit of the Grand Teton. Reveling in the spirit of the wild in this realm of the mountain gods, Robbie let his thoughts drift down to the lake below, Four years before, when he crossed in the launch on his way to the Exum climbing school, he had gazed up at the far off summit in the sky on which he now stood. But this morning, it was the world below that seemed so far away.

Robbie's climb made the front page of the local Cheyenne newspaper. Part of the story read: "Six members of a traditional New Year's climbing expedition reached the summit of the 13,766-foot Grand Teton Friday. The climbers said the only snow on the mountain was in permanent snow fields. That allowed them to reach the summit earlier than planned."

But for us it wasn't the whole story. It marked a further departure for Robbie. The little kid staring up at mountain summits was gone. In his place was a young man looking down from those same summits. Classmates and the community as a whole began to see Robbie Slater as a mountain climber, though he hadn't done the climb for the accolades or the notoriety of being a local celebrity.

When Robbie got back from Jackson, there was an extra gleam in his eyes.

"What was it like above the saddle and how big is the top?" I asked. "Where did you put your tent at the saddle?"

We all started firing questions at him, eager for the details.

My Dad and other brothers and I had never been higher on the mountain than the spot Robbie camped with the expedition. We never even made it to where they had to rope up for the first time.

"We camped right below the ridge to stay out of the wind," Robbie began. "Then I had to sit it the tent and wait for two days before going for the top."

There was a vein of impatience in his voice. We all knew Robbie didn't like to wait around for anything.

"Some of the other climbers were slow but I just wanted to go," he continued. "We roped up at the top of that last scree field above the saddle and went all the way up. The top's about as big as this room. You can see everything. It's so cool."

What was also cool was the pure, unadulterated excitement on Robbie's face as he recounted the climb – especially the part that brought us back to where it had all started for him.

"On the way down there's a huge free rappel down to the upper saddle – higher than the one we did at Exum."

Other than the stories to his family, I never heard my twin bring up his Grand Teton climb with others. If anyone asked, Robbie would sure retell the tale, but he didn't go around broadcasting it. I never heard him say, "Did you see me in the paper?" or anything like that. I don't believe that was of any importance to him whatsoever.

The Grand Teton summit was tremendously satisfying for Robbie. It was as if he had lived up to a part of the destiny and fulfilled a part of the legacy he had begun to create for himself that first day at the Exum climbing school.

That first Teton summit made him hunger for more. That extra sparkle in Robbie's eyes convinced me that he would keep looking up to the heights. He would continue to seek that special thrill, the self-satisfaction and that deeply personal state of mind which could only be reached in the wild's highest places.

In the Cascades

Rob hanging out at Eldo

Chapter V

"If you're not falling, it's too easy."
                                                    –Rob Slater

"That was pussy. My twin brother Robbie's taken grounders from much higher than that."
                                                    –Rich Slater

Sprawling below the leading edge of the Rocky Mountains northwest of Denver is the University of Colorado, Boulder. Nearby, giant exposed slabs of rock lie against the mountains like huge granite dishes in a drying rack. The Flatirons are a prominent feature in the college's promotional literature, which boasts top-notch academics and a big-time sports program. Many aspiring young people seek entry into CU to pursue dreams of education and, perhaps less realistically, athletic fame and fortune. Others, cut from a slightly different cloth, seek out Boulder for another reason.

Just south of the Flatirons, unnoticeable to motorists on the Foothills Highway and not even listed on many maps, is a tiny town called Eldorado Springs. It consists of a few wood-framed houses and an old hotel and hot springs pool which saw its heyday before World War II. Continuing through town on the rutted dirt road past the dilapidated hotel, you cross a narrow, single lane bridge to the entrance shack of Eldorado State Park. From there, the road winds through the bottom of a canyon flanked on either side by steep cliffs several hundred feet high, crowned by clouds and circling raptors.

Eldo. This is what brought Rob to Colorado.

As Rob and I closed in on high school graduation in the spring of 1979, there was little doubt in my mind Rob would end up attending college in Boulder. There was absolutely no doubt as to the reason why: climbing. By that point we were well aware, due to the steady counsel of Mom and Dad, of the importance of an education, although neither of us had given a great deal of thought to careers. With a doctor dad, the obvious choice would have been medicine, but I wanted to rebel and do something else-anything else-just for the sake of rebelling. I was a rebel without a cause-or a clue.

Rob, on the other hand, had a big-time rebellious streak himself, but was smarter than to let it interfere with his career decision. He just wanted to climb more than study, so it was no big surprise when he chose geology as his major. It made sense that Rob would study rock formations when he wasn't climbing on them, though his interest would wane as his interest in climbing grew. For my part, I chose college in Florida, mostly because it meant going as far away from home as possible without leaving the country. The only thing I was interested in climbing on was coeds.

Unlike my twin and his climbing, I had not yet identified my summit for which to strive, though I knew it was up there in some form. One thing that did keep my attention was Dad's mantra of "get an education-be your own boss." When I met with my student advisor before my first semester, I was asked to declare a major.

"Pre-med, I guess," was my response.

"That will be a lot of work," my advisor advised.

"Whatever," I advised back. I figured pre-med was as good as anything else. Although I had earlier decided against pre-med as a clueless act of rebellion, I guess I was now rebelling against my rebellion. So, for the time being, I figured I would take some classes, grow my hair really long, raise hell and have some fun.

Rob liked coed climbing as well, but leaving every weekend and summer to rock climb inevitably got in the way of any long-term relationship-and most of the short-termers as well. Sooner or later, climbing tugged on his heart more than any current or pending "girlfriend unit" possibly could. True to his mission, in the fall of 1979, Rob moved his impressive rack of climbing gear into Sewell Hall, a freshman dorm at CU and, without delay, immediately took off for Eldo.

Rob soon discovered a kindred spirit in fellow student Jim Bodenhamer, who had also became immersed in and transformed by the climbing as a young man. Jim grew up in Arkansas, which is not a place which immediately springs to mind when the subject of rock climbing arises. The same summer Rob was at the Exum climbing school in Jackson, young Jim attended a summer camp where he was introduced to climbing ropes, equipment and the thrill of rappelling. At 15, Jim got to spend a whole month in the Mount Ranier and Mount Adams region of the Cascades in Washington State. Like Rob, he became hooked and, in a move which surprised none who knew him, Jim also set his sights on CU in Boulder. Jim wanted to be a doctor and avail himself of CU's fine pre-med program but, in all honesty, he went to CU for the climbing.

As the future Dr. Bodenhamer checked into Sewell Hall, he noticed a guy a few rooms down with wild hair, covered in climbing chalk, carrying in a big rack of climbing gear. Jim went to introduce himself.

"Are you a climber too? What kind of climbs do you do?" inquired Rob as he eyed Jim somewhat suspiciously. Jim had a similar brown mop of hair, although he kept it combed sometimes, and a strong, wiry frame like Rob.

"I've been leading some 5.8s" Jim offered. Climbing routes are graded, by degree of difficulty, from 5.4 up to 5.13.

"Oh, so you're doing the easy stuff," observed Rob, noting he had just finished doing the 5.11 Naked Edge. But Rob also liked the Eldo "classic routes," as he called them. "Let's go do the Bastille," Rob suggested.

The next day, the two did the Bastille crack, a 5.7 Eldo classic, thus beginning a lifelong friendship and climbing partnership between Rob and "Hammer," as Rob called his new friend. They formed a bond like brothers, pushing each other and enjoying great adventures and climbing successes, their friendship accentuated by a shared irreverence-laced brand of enthusiasm. Hammer, like Rob, found freedom and exhilaration high on the cliffs where he could escape the pre-med grind and the uncertainty of medical school admission. Climbing in Eldo, especially with Rob, was everything he imagined climbing should be. He also knew, from his first trip to Eldo, that when he climbed with Rob, they would always get to the top, sometimes only on the strength of Rob's infectious drive and enthusiasm.

"If you're not falling, it's too easy," Rob often proclaimed as he urged Hammer onward and upward. Rob had developed a system that measured progress by "flight time." Falling was not only an accepted, but, to Rob, an expected part of climbing. The further you fell, the more flight time you accrued. A short fall with a belay from above might only be worth a tenth of a second in flight time. A plummet from 15 or 20 feet above protection, resulting in a 30-footer, would yield a full second-and-a-half.

"Without Rob, I never would have done the climbs that I did," Hammer acknowledged. Hammer was able, with Rob, to go as far toward the edge as he ever wanted or imagined. For him, that was enough.

The same held true for another young man named John Sherman. Born and raised in Berkley, California, "Verm," short for vermin, couldn't wait to get out on the rock. Shown some photos of Eldo by a high school climbing friend, Verm was terrified by the immensity and steepness of the Eldo cliffs. The friend was going to CU and told Verm he should do the same. Without even a visit to campus, John Verm Sherman enrolled, also choosing geology as a major. But in truth, like Rob and Hammer, he went to CU for the climbing.

Also true to his mission, Verm hung out a lot at Eldo, with its small, tight climbing community. One day at Eldo, he met Rob. It was climbing and "both our vulgar and disgusting senses of humor," according to Verm, which caused the pair to hit it off immediately. Verm had a similar unruly, wavy brown mane, lean frame, sparkling eyes and a devilish grin. Rob introduced him to Hammer, forming the nucleus of "The Team," as Rob called his climbing family.

Jim Whittaker's 1975 American expedition attempted the

North-West Ridge of K2, making it to 21,000 feet before being turned back, but the second ascent of K2 did not occur until 1977, when six Japanese and a Pakistani climber followed the Abruzzi Ridge. In 1978, following the death of Nick Estcourt in an avalanche, Chris Bonnington's South-West Ridge assault was halted. That same summer, four Americans led by Jim Whittaker completed the third successful ascent of K2, following the 1976 Polish route to the upper reaches of the Abruzzi Ridge. In 1979, Rheinhold Messner and Michl Dacher, after abandoning their route up the "Magic Line," reached the summit along the Abruzzi Ridge for K2's fourth ascent. The fifth successful ascent established a new route up the South-West Ridge by Eiho Otani and Pakistani Nazir Sabir in 1981.

Rob always welcomed the chance to climb with someone new, but the number of climbers on The Team remained relatively small. All shared Rob's zest for the sport, enthusiasm for life and, importantly, an appreciation for his individual brand of off-the-wall observation. As his first spring break approached, Rob had his heart set on going to Joshua Tree, a climbing area in the desert east of Los Angeles. Someone had placed a card on the student bulletin board seeking a passenger to "JT." That someone was Chris Archer, a student climber and aspiring lawyer. Rob gave him a call and when classes ended the two headed west for a week of climbing.

Rob liked driving even less than taking his own car, so Mr. Archer was alone behind the wheel for the 15-hour drive. To stave off inattentiveness, Chris chain-smoked and guzzled an endless stream of coffee. Chris also liked to drive really fast. On a lonely stretch of road in the Arizona desert in the dead of night, Chris barreled by a Highway Patrol car. Pulled over, he first had to excuse himself to heed the call of nature. The coffee, it seemed, was going right through him. When the cop inquired about his excessive rate of speed, the future attorney responded, "I thought you were a milkman with his lights on." Not persuaded of the legal sufficiency of this defense, a speeding ticket was issued for 110 miles per hour. Back on the road, Rob seized the opportunity to use his new climbing partner's affinity for nicotine and caffeine to come up with his new name. Henceforth, Chris Archer was known as "Nic Café." Years later, when Mr. Archer, Esq. welcomed his only son into the world, he named him Nick.

In addition to Nic Café, Hammer and Rob's long-time climbing and parachuting partner Robin Black Death Heid, Rob had friends he had affectionately nicknamed Great One, Senator, Awesome Liz and The Party Cub. Rob would also commonly use terms of endearment such as Chief or Junior as a means of encouragement. I never knew anyone offended by the light-hearted monikers Rob used for them. Looking back, I believe the genesis of Rob and his nicknames lies with Bud Ruble, a/k/a The Earl of Alta Vista. Rob didn't try to be friends with everybody, but I know those he did choose felt it was a kind of honor or privilege to be a friend of Rob's. Getting a nickname from him was a sign of affection and demonstration one had been accepted into Rob's "family."

Folsom Field sits like a giant sandstone horseshoe at the center of the CU campus, imbedded in the hillside. Its imposing outer wall looks more like it's been excavated from the underlying bedrock rather than quarried from the nearby Flatirons formation, hauled by mule teams and stacked with symmetrical precision. Its walls loom like a medieval castle designed to keep marauders out, or a penitentiary perimeter designed to keep savages in.

But Rob didn't see it quite like that. "That's an easy 5.9," he opined, offering his own brand of architectural analysis. In the late evenings, he stopped by the stadium after visiting the library. He could scale the 30-foot face in a matter of seconds. Passersby stopped and watched but for the most part paid little attention or simply didn't notice. Occasionally, a good citizen would tell him he couldn't climb on the wall.

"Then come up here and make a citizen's arrest," Rob would reply.

During the summers in the early 1980s, Folsom Field hosted rock concerts, some of which drew 70,000 or more fans. It was before band disintegrations and reformations spawned perennial reunion tours and the music, as Rob and I remembered, was about rock 'n roll and girls, instead of lawlessness and misogyny insipidly passed off as "culture." "That's weak-tit," he would say.

The Who came to town and when the band took the stage, Folsom Field was full. Rob casually strolled along the outer stadium wall, anonymous among the milling crowd. He could hear the music overhead, muffled as it reverberated within the stadium. Arriving at his well-practiced route he stopped, glanced about and then quickly scampered up and over the wall. Emerging over the top, a few looked at him surprised, but soon returned their attention back to the stage. Of the few who noticed, fewer cared. Rob was just another anonymous concert-goer and how he got to his seat was nothing they stopped to ponder.

Rob didn't climb into the concert to avoid buying a ticket, hadn't told anyone he was going to do it, didn't brag about it afterwards, or do it to prove any point about concert security. The Who wasn't his favorite band and their concert was something he could miss. It was just fun climbing the stadium wall and the fact that a major concert was taking place inside just added an extra degree. I know if I could have climbed that wall I would have been with him.

Once Rob got inside, he didn't even sit down but made his way straight to the exit. He saw the band, heard a couple songs – and was back outside in less than 15 minutes.

Meanwhile, I was doing a little bit of architectural analysis and urban mountaineering myself. The student union building at the university in Florida I attended was three stories high, with a brickwork lattice covering the outside windows. At the top, the roof overhung about five feet. Letting go of the bricks, I could lean out and grab the top edge of the roof lip with my right hand, swing out into space and then pull myself up and onto the roof. Once I let go of the bricks I was committed, but once up, I could enjoy the view and even a beverage. As I swung out into space 30 feet above the pavement by one arm, I was never scared. I felt the same way I did when Robbie was above me on belay. I knew I wasn't going to fall. I also knew my twin would think my stunt was honed.

I even encouraged my roommate to join me.

"It's an easy 5.9," I told him.

"No way," he replied, "If you miss or slip off the roof edge you go all the way down." After watching me do it a few times, though, he finally agreed to follow. His initial evaluation, however, proved correct. One night I did get off balance on my lunge out to the edge and ended up, just like he predicted, at the bottom. I landed in a heap near a bush, but stumbled to my feet, shaken but not stirred and in no way deterred. I didn't even break my smokes. My roommate was astonished, but I told him, "That was pussy. My twin brother Robbie's taken grounders from much higher than that."

By the end of 1983 another climber had graduated with a degree in math and physics from CU. Rather than proceeding too hastily into the "real" world, as he called it, Al Torrisi became a ski bum in Steamboat Springs, Colorado. Al knew Rob's friend Hammer from a couple years earlier climbing in Eldo. Al had occasionally seen Rob at the rec center,

"cranking off dozens of chin-ups and bragging, or what I thought was more likely exaggerating, about his latest exploits. But as I found out later, he never exaggerated, in fact to the contrary, I was sandbagged on many a route by his under-exaggeration of the difficulties of a climb or even the climb's approach."

In April of 1984, Hammer called Al and said he was going to Joshua Tree with his friend Rob Slater and suggested he meet them there. As Al had already skied over 100 days in a row, he was itching to climb. Financing the trip, though, was the problem. Luckily, every day when Al came home from his work as a waiter, he threw all his loose change into a jar. By April, it was two-thirds full.

Immediately following Hammer's call, Al emptied the jar onto the floor and counted out a total of around $320. After paying for his airline ticket and big bags of rice, beans and granola for the trip, along with a couple of boxes of wine, Al was left with $60.37 to fund his four week trip.

Al's big day finally arrived and he left Colorado for the warmth of Southern California. As he walked down the stairs from the plane wearing his favorite heavy wool sweater, a down jacket and winter hiking boots, Rob and Hammer were waiting for him in shorts and t-shirts. It was about 84 degrees.

"You can probably take off the down jacket," Rob suggested. Rob also immediately suggested they go climbing.

As they began the approach hike to the climb in increasingly overcast weather, Al remarked it looked like it was going to rain.

"It never rains in Joshua tree in April. Hammer and I haven't seen a drop of rain in the two weeks we've been here," Rob replied.

Rob led some 5.10 or easy 5.11 with Hammer following as Al watched the sky get darker. When Al's turn came to climb, he got about 10 feet up the pitch before the skies let loose. The holds were now covered with slimy wet chalk. Al, who had come from "off the couch in Steamboat," scratched his way up in the pouring rain, cursing Rob and Hammer for pushing him to climb when he should have been taking a nap in his tent.

"They both laughed at me as I struggled up the route. I begged Rob to lower me down, but they both wanted me to clean the pitch. I was miserable and thought I'd be swinging across the face at any moment. I swore that I'd never climb with these guys ever again," Al recalled.

"Somehow I made it to the top without swinging across the face. Minutes after I finished climbing, the skies miraculously cleared and the sun came back out. Joshua Tree was beautiful again. All the misery I experienced on the climb was quickly forgotten."

"So began my climbing apprenticeship with Rob," Al remembered. "Rob made me a better climber. From day one he saw potential in me that I didn't even see in myself. He pushed me to do things I would have never thought of doing."

Ten years later, on December 21, 1994, the shortest day of the year, Rob and Al were on Alexander's Chimney on the Diamond, the huge front face of Long's Peak in Rocky Mountain National Park, about 60 miles northwest of Denver. It was well below zero, snowing and blowing a gale.

Two pitches below the top, Al took a 40-foot leader fall. Rob, on belay, caught him. When Al got back to the belay ledge, both his elbows were swollen the size of cantaloupes, his arms wouldn't bend and he couldn't hold onto his ice axes. He knew there was no way he could have rappelled down from their position.

"What are we going to do Rob?" Al asked as he writhed in pain on the belay ledge.

"Going down is not an option," Rob said, checking out his injured friend, "so we're going to finish this thing."

After about 15 minutes, Al regained some movement in his arms and they commenced to finish the thing.

"Rob brilliantly led the last mixed rock and ice pitches in the twilight," Al said of the much-longer-than-planned climb. "I somehow followed him on what I'm sure was a very tight rope."

As they trudged with headlamps across a frozen Chasm Lake at the base of the Diamond and down towards the tree line, they had to stop several times to warm up their faces and fingers. Later, on the trail below tree line, they both stopped dead in their tracks. It was a pair of eyes looking back at them from about 10 yards down the trail. The eyes belonged to a very large mountain lion who was no doubt wondering if Rob and Al would make a tasty dinner.

Rob took the pair of ice axes off of Al's pack and they each held one up in the air to make themselves look big and threatening, but the mountain lion didn't budge. It stayed in the middle of the trail, staring at them for what seemed like an eternity, before finally sauntering off into the woods. Al took Rob's ice axes off of the back of his pack and they hiked the rest of the way out, both with an ice axe in each hand. Every so often they stopped on the trail to listen. Any little sound spooked them because they both knew that mountain lion was just off of the trail stalking them as they went. Luckily, the mountain lion rightly figured that between the two of them there wasn't enough body fat for even a meager snack. Rob and Al never saw the lion again that night.

When Al got home, he took a few pain killers with a glass or two of wine. He went to the hospital the next morning to get both his arms X-rayed because the swelling and pain was still so bad. Although the doctor and the X-ray technician were both convinced that Al had broken bones in both arms, the X-rays amazingly came back negative.

It had been quite a trip, but even after the fall, the cold and the mountain lion, the thing Al remembered most about that climb was the approach hike in to it.

"Rob was one of the most vicious hikers ever to set foot on the planet," Al told me later-which was something I already knew. "You never passed him no matter how big a load he was carrying. For the climb of Alexander's Chimney on Longs, we left Boulder around midnight the night before the climb and were on the trail around 2:00a.m.

"Because the trail was hard-packed for the first three-plus miles, I had the brilliant idea that we should wear tennis shoes instead of our mountaineering boots to make the early part of the approach hike easier. I remember Rob pulled up his pant legs to his knees as we hiked below tree line because we were so warm. As I watched his legs in the light of my headlamp – from behind, of course – they transformed from human legs to that of an animal, with hoofs and everything. I swear that the lower half of Robbie changed right before my eyes into an antelope or eland or gazelle or something that wasn't human, and I kept asking myself how I could ever expect to keep up with this animal. It was an amazing thing to witness and I will remember it for the rest of my life."

Speaking of impressive, a friend of mine and I came across a nomination form for our college's Homecoming King.

"That might be a good way to meet some more sorority girls," I surmised, especially when I saw the prominent section that required a listing of the nominee's campus activities. Considering the kind of guys who actually applied for stuff like this, it was no big surprise that there were several lines to fill in.

We decided to nominate each other, but figured we should at least provide honest qualifications. So, instead of the mundane "honor roll, student president, helps homeless old ladies across the street," my activities listed were "raising hell, partying, chasing women and smoking. My buddy's "resume'" was similar, although "chewing tobacco" was substituted for "smoking." We didn't win. Perhaps I should have added "falling off buildings" to my list.

Rob, on the other hand, never got involved in the party scene as a student. He never tasted alcohol, smoked or touched any kind of drug, regardless of what even those closest to him might be doing. To him, all that nonsense that was life-dulling, not life-enhancing. If I told him of a particularly heinous example of drunken foolhardiness of a mutual friend, Rob would shake his head slowly, smiling, while repeating "lame" or "weak" or, mockingly, "that's so honed." Like Sissy said, "I don't think Rob wanted to miss a single moment or opportunity the world had to offer him in terms of combining his imagination with testing his physical abilities."

It took a lot to get his heart racing, but he never resorted to cheap enhancements like keg beer.

It was during those years of college that Rob and I began to develop our worldviews. This came about, for both of us, I believe, perhaps unwittingly as much as consciously or intentionally. While in many ways we were still the same, and although these views were based on similar premises, they would manifest themselves quite differently – or would they?

Rob dutifully went to class, wrote his papers and was content to fly below the radar. His academic interests progressed from geology to the oil industry and eventually to business. For one paper in a business class, Rob used a multi-day climb to illustrate how to organize and develop a business plan, and enlisted Black Death Heid to help him with the editing.

The concept of capitalism began to register and gain footholds in his brain. It seemed to me Rob liked the idea of competition and testing himself against the marketplace. He read about Carl Icahn, an original corporate raider who, with facetious self-deprecation, referred to himself as "a simple man of commerce" as he made millions through hostile takeovers.

Rob didn't give up his reading of climbing, mountaineering history or his intense study of maps and topographical charts, but it seemed to me that Rob was also developing the kind of balance in his life that Dad and Mon had long preached. Unlike climbing and swimming, where the competition was primarily against himself, business was all about competing against others.

Around this time, Rob also read of Charles Darwin and his famous *On the Origin of Species* and its concept about natural selection, or "survival of the fittest." I know this concept also found resonance in his psyche, as it applied both to the real world of career and his ideal world of overcoming the challenges of mountains and cliffs. Only the most able and dedicated made it to the top of the capitalist heap, just as only the fittest, most daring and strongest of constitution made it to the summits that pierce highest into the boiling blue sky.

As time went by, this became more and more important to him. Even if he were to fail the test of the marketplace, he would not fail himself in the mountains. There, Rob felt supremely confident. He believed that, in nature, competition was pure and he saw in climbing the purest form of all. There, it was him against the rock, him against nature. Nature wasn't motivated by greed or envy like competitors in the market, which allowed him to more easily put aside any feelings of inadequacy he might have in other areas of his life.

As I viewed it, Rob saw himself entering two arenas which to some would seem vastly different but to him were nearly identical in theory if not in practice. Each demanded that he put aside any fear of failure and all self-doubt. The market threatened utter humiliation and destitution but offered the prize of fabulous wealth and its offspring, total independence. The mountains offered the ultimate thrill of challenging and overcoming the force of nature but threatened death. Rob challenged himself to reach the summit of both. Could he become a king of the market? Could he become a mountain god?

Rob atop Eldo

Rob on the Wyoming Sheep Ranch, El Cap

Chapter VI

"Who wouldn't want to be a mountaineer?"
–John Muir

During the winter of his freshman year in college, Rob saw an article in a climbing magazine about El Capitan and the mighty walls of Yosemite Valley, California. The story described "aid climbing" and how a vast array of hooks, pins and other specialized equipment were used to scale otherwise unclimbable cliffs. In the free climbing Rob knew, equipment was used strictly for protection. Utilizing it otherwise to ascend or even rest was considered to be "poor style."

In contrast, aid climbers rely on their equipment to bear their weight and literally as the means by which they ascend sections of rock where there are no handholds or footholds. Aid climbing routes, depending on their degree of difficulty, are graded on a scale ranging from A1, the easiest, up to A5. Rob was enthralled and promptly proclaimed his intention of becoming an aid climbing "A5 Master."

On his first foray to the A1 Practice Roof in Boulder Canyon, as Verm Sherman would later recount, Rob backed off meekly. This was a new deal altogether. He had to learn to rely on his equipment in addition to his own balance and nerve. The equipment was no longer "just in case." This was tough at first, but in usual Rob fashion, he was not easily deterred and soon became not only comfortable but daringly confident. Rob determined he would spend the upcoming summer climbing on El Capitan, or "El Cap" as it is fondly and reverently referred to by climbers. Good work if you could get it, I thought, without a twinge of jealousy or irony.

A bit more than 125 years earlier, a young man named John Muir departed his family's Wisconsin farm to begin a 1,000-mile walk to the Gulf of Mexico.

"Only by going alone in silence, without baggage, can one truly get into the heart of the wilderness," Muir said. "All other travel is mere dust and hotels and baggage and chatter."

John Muir was a true lover of the wild places. Tales of his wanderings are legendary, and his deep appreciation and respect for nature formed the basis of modern environmentalism and the founding of the Sierra Club.

Muir also became known for a streak of defiance. Although he abhorred the notion of common folk trampling Yosemite, he realized mass awareness of natural beauty was the starting point of preservation. In what may have been seen, except perhaps to Muir himself, as a blatant contradiction, he was more than once fined for overstaying his camping permit as he lived "among the sublimities of Yosemite," where he could "forget that ever a thought of civilization or time-honored proprieties came among my pathless, lawless thoughts and wanderings."
During these subliminal, spiritual treks, Muir slept under pine needles. He ate only what the land offered. He walked for miles and miles each day, every day, for weeks on end. Muir was honed.
During a spring more than a century later, Rob decided to experience for himself those same Yosemite sublimities.

Rob ended up spending every summer of his college career in the Yosemite Valley. Like Muir, the grandeur of Yosemite occupied a special place in his life and consciousness. Unlike Muir, Rob looked condescendingly on the throngs of everyday "sheeple," as Rob called them, who flocked to the park to soak up its natural splendor. Though they had just as much right to be there as he, and came for the same basic purpose of communing with nature, Rob was still for some reason scornful of the "touristies" who had the audacity to show up without the guts or wherewithal to get up on the huge walls – or even venture off the paved road.

To me, Rob's view of the sheeple and touristies demonstrated his personal Darwinian view that being able to climb the hardest routes gave him exclusive first rights to the park over those who could not. It was a corollary of his belief that the strongest gets the prize.

John Muir revered the Yosemite Valley and believed in encouraging mass appreciation of its natural beauty. Nevertheless, he apparently believed the rule limiting length of stays at campgrounds did not apply to him or that he was somehow entitled to disregard it. Could the same case could be made against Rob concerning the Indian desert where, as you will see later, apparently in the face of his professed reverence and respect for the lands containing the sacred sandstone spires, Rob saw fit to ignore the climbing ban and scale every single one of them? Or were Muir and Rob simply worthy exceptions that underscored the importance of the rules?

More than a million years ago, the Sherwin Glaciation, one of the numerous glacial periods of the Sierra Nevada, carved and sculpted out the now-famous cliff formations of Yosemite Valley. Since then, wind, weather and erosion have added the smoothing finishing touches. More recently, the Mariposa Battalion in 1851 gave El Capitan its name, which is believed to be a translation of the Native American name "Totokonnlah," for "rock." As it turned out, the boys in the battalion were right on the mark, for El Cap is the biggest single block of granite on earth. It's even bigger than the Rock of Gibraltar. As Rob liked to say, it's "hideous, horrendous and heinous."

The vast majority of the massive face is made up of pale, coarse-grained El Capitan Granite, with the top sections composed of Taft Granite. Diorite, a dark igneous rock formed by solidification from a molten state, is the final component, which seems to splash across the face forming a rough map of the northern hemisphere on what is aptly called the North American Wall.

For quite some time, eons apparently, El Cap was considered impossible to climb. But in 1958, Warren Harding, Wayne Merry and George Whitmore laid siege to El Cap. After 47 days of shuttling up and down fixed ropes, the team made the summit. Two years later, the first non-siege continuous climb was made by Royal Robbins and his climbing buddies in a mere seven days. In the ensuing 20 years, El Cap became universally regarded as the ultimate in big-wall climbing.

Along the Yosemite Valley approach to El Cap, the giant objective of Rob's summer of 1981, he joined a long procession of RVs and cars packed with a diverse array of visitors heading into the park. The place crawled with touristies but, amid the throngs, a tiny enclave existed, reserved for real climbers and protected from outsiders by an imaginary but impenetrable barrier. This was the legendary Camp 4, the climbers' base camp, the heart of the Yosemite climbing scene and launching pad for Rob's big wall ascents.

Camp 4 was also used by members of the rescue team. All expert climbers, they served on a volunteer basis when a climber was injured or needed to be extracted from the cliffs or, more usually, a touristie stumbled while scrambling around on rocks in street shoes. In consideration for their service, the rangers graciously waived the 14-day maximum rule and allowed the rescue volunteers to stay for free at Camp 4 all summer long. Otherwise, the group would have certainly, and continuously, found themselves on the receiving ends of citations for overstaying the campsite time limitations. They, like John Muir more than a century before, would have stayed anyway.

Yosemite had some of the world's hardest climbs and the climbers of Camp 4 talked about the newest and toughest routes they would soon be conquering. As conqueror of a new route, a climber could avail himself of the simple rule that whoever climbs it first gets to name it. Big-wall aid climbers are, pretty much by definition, an independent, free-spirited lot. This helps explain some of the imaginative names previously bestowed upon routes such as Mescalito, Tangerine Trip, Scorched Earth and Magic Mushroom. The first-up-it-names-it rule rightfully allows the first ascender the privilege of immortalizing himself or herself and, as is often the case, choosing a name indicative of the physical characteristics of the route and/or personality of the climber bestowing the moniker. The main El Cap wall, with its variations in color due to rock composition and the effects of water, weather and time, resembles a map of the North American hemisphere. With this in mind, it is no great leap to visualize the Sea of Dreams, Pacific Ocean Wall or Lost in America.

The Camp 4 climbers were a diverse lot. Cliques inevitably developed, based on country, state, climbing sites, or on partnerships and alliances formed during previous climbs together. There were even cliques from the northern and southern parts of California and a local chapter who were particularly possessive of what they considered their home climbing arena. When not on the walls, the climbers hung around Camp 4, talking about climbing in general and, more specifically, new routes.

Rob, for his part, had his own idea for a new route on El Cap, which would mark his arrival as a true A5 Master and appropriately memorialize and immortalize his skill, daring and comedic talent.

In addition to tents and sleeping bags, the site was dominated by mountains of climbing gear and ropes, to be sorted by order of anticipated use and packed into haul bags for upcoming routes. Given the size of the El Cap walls, it took several days to complete each climb, requiring overnight stays hanging on the cliff face. Food and jugs of water, further amassed in large piles about the camp, had to be included in additional haul bags.

Big walls require climbers to be entirely self-sufficient. Once they get on the rock, there is no turning back to retrieve anything. There are no Arby's on El Cap. Each climber had a "port-a-ledge," a collapsible aluminum-framed platform spanned with nylon webbing on which to spend the night. About two feet wide and seven feet long, Rob and his partners had to remain clipped into the rope, lest the throes of a wild wilderness dream roll them into space.

The rule of self-sufficiency on the wall holds true, in the starkest of ways, for food and drink. Aid climbing is extremely strenuous. Pounding pins, drilling bolts and hauling oneself and several hundred pounds of gear up each pitch, all in the blazing California summer sun, saps the strength even of young climbers who trained all winter for these walls. To fight fatigue, many wall teams were willing to accept the extra weight in their haul bags to provide themselves appropriate sustenance. Rob, however, had no objection to a diet limited in variety. While some climbers even went so far as to bring canned vegetables and fruits and gallons upon gallons of water, Rob was more inclined to keep it simple.

"We weren't the healthiest on the wall," Hammer remembered. He had foolishly trusted Rob with the responsibility of organizing the food and water for one three-day climb – a short ascent by El Cap standards.

Hammer didn't realize until it was too late that, in the early spring of 1978, Rob had set out on an attempt to climb Longs Peak with a high school climbing buddy who had also foolishly allowed Rob to provision the climb. That time he simply purchased 30 Arby's roast beef sandwiches and stuffed them in his pack. Nothing else was brought, not even ArB-Q sauce.

Halfway up the El Cap climb, Hammer and Rob were caught in a torrential rainstorm. They decided to toss several haul bags from 2,000 feet, believing it would allow them to speed their progress and get to the top and off the wall quicker. The bags containing their food and water were retained but, to Hammer's dismay, contained only Nilla Wafers, Sara Lee coffee cakes and Pop Tarts. More disappointing, they had agreed to bring four gallons of water for the two of them for the three-day climb. As they discovered half-way up, one of the jugs had been left in the car – on purpose Hammer suspected – in Rob's effort to conserve weight.

As they neared the top, Hammer got a firsthand look at Rob's well-cultivated capacity to do the big walls without much food or water. After a day-and-a-half without water, Hammer was so parched he couldn't even talk. Rob, on the other hand, talked non-stop, showering Hammer with a continuous commentary on any and every subject. He was in his element, pushing himself and intensifying the challenge of the climb by deliberately limiting the food and drink.

Rob loved spending summers in the Valley and on the walls of El Cap and Half Dome. Night after night on the cramped port-a-ledge didn't give rise to complaints from the guy who normally preferred sleeping on the ground. A limited diet coupled with extended periods of intense physical exertion only made him lean and feeling more committed. The fact he was on an extremely limited budget, which he good-naturedly accepted as the consequence of being unemployed, didn't bother him either. When he returned from a climb, he'd hang out at a park concession stand and finish off meals left on picnic tables by touristies or even grab the last few bites of a pizza slice from a garbage can.

"Better me than the bears," Rob would say. "At least I don't knock the cans over."

On his way to becoming an A5 Master, Rob started with the classic El Cap routes, doing the Zodiac and Tangerine Trip during the first visit in 1981. During the following summers, he completed Zenyatta Mondatta with Randy Leavitt and Sea of Dreams, which he started with Randy "RSL" Leavitt but finished with Mike O'Donnell. In all, Rob did more than a dozen different routes with many different partners – and the first-ever solo of the Pacific Ocean Wall.

On a brilliant clear morning in the summer of 1982, Rob and RSL started up "Sea of Dreams," one of El Cap's toughest routes. On the third day, more than 1,000 feet above the canyon floor, they came to one of the most difficult pitches of the climb, called "Hook and Book." About 30 feet into the lead, RSL lowered himself about 20 feet from a fixed rivet so he could do a prescribed pendulum-like "swinging traverse" to reach the next spot where he could place another hook.

"That went fine," said RSL, "but after I set the hook and put weight on it, it blew and I pendulumed again and as I swung my right foot hit a protrusion."

RSL felt pain but didn't think anything was broken, so he shook it off and led the rest of the pitch – the most dangerous one on the route – on one leg. It was an epic lead.

"I thought it would be all right in the morning," he said, "but when I woke up it hurt more than before and was so swollen we knew it was broken and there was no alternative but to go down."

Rob evacuated his friend down to the Valley as RSL urged him to find another partner to finish the route. Rob quickly hooked up with fellow Boulderite and legendary tough guy Mike O'Donnell. Together, they went back up the ropes and spent ten heinous days climbing pitch after hideous pitch until they finally topped out, triumphant.

Soon after, Rob decided to try the second ascent of Shortest Straw with another Boulder climbing partner, Bruce Hunter. Bruce had a quiet demeanor, more like a young man on his way to Wall Street than a guy who lived on cliffs. Around Rob, however, like so many others, Bruce's usually-hidden irreverence and outlandishness was brought forth.

Rob decided that Verm Sherman should come along too, even though he'd never done a Yosemite climb. In a demonstration of his supreme confidence in his friend, Rob insisted Verm lead the first pitch. Bruce went right along with this as Rob talked Verm up so much that Verm actually began to believe he could do it. It was part of Rob's Team mentality and it was the same way he made me feel whenever I climbed with him.

Up Verm went on the first pitch, putting in a succession of zipper placements, meaning if the highest piece of protection failed the rest would "zipper" out as the climber fell. Verm just hoped they would hold and keep him from "decking it," or crashing on the ground. As it turned out, Verm never found out if his "pro" would've held because he finished the pitch without falling.

This didn't go over well with the full-of-themselves locals, who were miffed that such a beginner could lead what they thought was such a difficult pitch. In lame response, for years afterwards they rated that pitch as A1+, just slightly harder than A1, the easiest rating on the aid climbing scale.

As Rob told me this story, I thought less about the locals' pansy offendedness and more about how it was another example of Rob's ability to push and elevate the people around him to do better than they ever thought they could. To the Team, his approval meant more than that of the locals. While most of his partners did not live constantly for the thrill of pushing the envelope, they got caught up in the excitement, at least in the short term, when they were with Rob.

The summer of 1982 saw the sixth ascent of K2 along the Northern Flank, but Yukihiro Yanagisawa died during the descent. That same summer a climber with the Polish expedition died of a heart attack on the lower part of the mountain. K2 was successfully climbed in 1983 and 1985 by Italian and Swiss teams, respectively. The 1985 French and Japanese teams conquered the Abruzzi Ridge as well, but K2 claimed Frenchman Daniel Lacroix during the descent.

The year 1986 occupies an infamous place in the annals of K2 and alpine mountaineering. That summer, the attraction and deadliness of the Great Mountain were shown in vivid detail. After summiting the Abruzzi Ridge, Franco-Polish expedition leader Maurice Barrards disappeared in bad weather. Americans John Smolich and Alan Pennington, along with Italian July Casarotto, met their deaths as they attempted the South-South-West Ridge. On the same ridge, Polish expedition members August Wojciech Wroz and Dobroslawa Wolf (Mrowka) were killed on the descent. Austrian expedition members Alfred Imitzer and Hannes Wieser met their demise on the Abruzzi Ridge, as did Julie Tullis of the Italian expedition. A new route to the summit on the South Face was established by Poles Jerzy Kukuczka and Tadeusz Piotrowski, but during the descent Piotrowski fell to his death. Alan Rouse of the British expedition reached the summit via the Abruzzi Ridge, but died on the way down. In all, 22 climbers made the summit while 11 were killed; a deadly ratio in anyone's math book.

It didn't take a space shuttle designer or a graduate of an accredited sixth grade to know El Cap was also deadly. By the late 1970s, no less than half a dozen climbers met their demise when their ropes were cut by the sharp rock, their jumars failed or their belay anchor gave way. Jeff Hall fell to his death off the Nose trying to free a jammed rope in 1978. In 1981, David Kays was caught in a storm 250 feet from the top of his solo of the Nose and died of hypothermia. Three years later, two Japanese climbers froze to death in a snowstorm a mere 50 feet from the top of their last pitch. El Cap was indeed horrendous, hideous and heinous.

As the difficulty of Rob's El Cap routes increased, he found himself clinging to the overhanging cliffs by increasingly "thin," or less secure, placements. Compounding the danger were ever-lengthening "run-outs," which is the distance from the climber to the last piece of protection. A climber with a 20-foot run-out, for example, risks a 40-foot fall-the distance of the run-out back to the protection, plus the same distance below. Quite literally, Rob was going further and further out on the edge.

At the same time, Rob realized that the limits against which he was now bumping were not set by his skill, courage or lack of good sense, but by the equipment itself. For Rob, an unemployed college kid who lived in tents and on port-a-ledges all summer, bathed in rivers or restrooms and regularly ate table scraps and leftovers from the trash, it wasn't a lack of cash to buy the most high-tech gear available that limited his plans. Rather, the gear he needed to make the climbs he envisioned simply didn't exist.

So in true Western pioneer spirit, Rob decided to create the necessary hardware himself, in concert with some of his climbing buddies, especially "RSL" Leavitt.

It was a labor of love, as Rob and RSL enjoyed the creativity and engineering involved in thinking up and actually making the kinds of aid climbing equipment they needed to succeed on the extreme aid climbing routes Rob increasingly insisted on undertaking.

Rob and RSL called their vision for revolutionary new aid climbing equipment "Extensive Trickery," or "ET" for short. The crowning glory of their ET endeavor was the "Lovetron," a 15-foot tent pole outfitted with duct tape, a steering cable and a small metal "skyhook" at the end to grab the rock. This allowed them to place pro far beyond the length of their arms, which meant they could now "Lovetron" past previously unfixable sections, and thus climb previously unclimbable routes.

While the Lovetron literally expanded their reach, it also greatly magnified their risk, owing to the inherent instability of placing hardware with a 15-foot pole. It was like trying to feed a baby with a sharp fork attached to the end of a stick from across the room. But with practice back in his Boulder apartment, Rob wielded the Lovetron with amazing precision.

"See that light switch across the room? That's A1," he chuckled one time to me as he hooked it effortlessly – then followed it by hooking the top of a molded switch plate. "And that's A3. Now trying getting on it," he added, his pupils dilating as a big grin spread across his face.

"Try that 3,000 feet above the ground," I would say to anyone listening as I described the Lovetron, trying lamely to associate myself at least somewhat with my brother and his adventures. This was part of my own insecurity, I guess; Rob had certainly found his passion, for which I was glad, but I had not.

Back in Florida, a basic lack of interest in responsibility and academics led me nowhere. Unsatisfied with simply squandering an opportunity for an education, I took the next step down the clueless rebel path to oblivion by dropping out of college after my first year. Before I knew it, I was pounding nails. It didn't take long, however, for even me to figure out that swinging a hammer in the Florida sun was far less desirable than hanging out in any campus library. For one thing, let's just say, the scenery was way better. By the end of the summer, I had had enough. One Friday afternoon as I picked up my subsistence wage check, I told the foreman of my resignation.

"You can't quit without two weeks' notice," I was informed.

"I'm not spending the rest of my life being bossed around by assholes like you. I'm going to school," I informed him right back.

At my ghetto apartment complex that evening, I used the community pay phone to call Dad, collect, and tell him of my desire to return to school.

"Nothing would make me happier," he assured me. I believed him, and, as perhaps a first sign I was finally growing up, realized Mom and Dad had been right all along. Immaturity masked as wild-ass, hell-raising rebellion can only get you so far.

I was isolated in Florida, but it wasn't the kind of isolation I liked, so I went back to Wyoming. While I wasn't consciously aware of it at the time, I was being pulled towards the realm of the mountain gods that had already captured my twin's heart and soul.

The weather had something to do with it also. Florida was just too hot and humid for my taste. When I was in sixth grade, I asked Mom and Dad if I could get a mini bike. At the time, Evel Knievel was one of my heroes.

"I've sewn up too many kids in the E.R. who've been in motorcycle wrecks," Dad responded, "and besides, you'll just want one that's bigger and faster." Even though I took his answer as a "no," I kept on him. Finally, Dad relented, but only if I earned all the money myself. To that end, I got the neighborhood morning paper route, which meant getting up at 5:00 a.m. every morning to deliver 80 papers, regardless of the weather. Dad agreed, but with certain conditions:

"You better not wake up your mother, we better not have a bunch of people calling here complaining they didn't get their paper and, under no condition will we drive you to deliver the papers."

"I promise," I assured my parents.

I carried the *Wyoming Eagle* morning paper until I went to high school. Through the winters, I many times found myself on foot, hauling my load of papers in canvas shoulder bags in blizzard conditions in the predawn darkness. Never once did I even think of asking for a ride in the car. In fact, I grew to really enjoy being out in the bad weather alone. I found some kind of weird security knowing I was doing something productive by myself.

I also got my mini bike, which, as Dad predicted, almost immediately made me want something bigger and faster. I ended up racing motocross in high school on a bike that would reach nearly 80 miles-per-hour. One of my favorite tricks was going as fast as I could while standing on the seat.

In any event, with newfound determination I was soon an engineering major at the University of Wyoming in Laramie, which, I would relate with great pride, routinely boasted the coldest temperatures in the continental U.S. I had decided I wanted to design factories or something equally manly and impressive.

During those college summers in the early 1980s, Rob always stopped in Cheyenne, either on his way to or from Yosemite. I always stayed in Laramie, just 50 miles away, finding a summer job and taking a class or two, but I headed to Cheyenne when Rob came to town in order to catch up with my twin. Sitting around with Mom and Dad, any conversation involving Rob invariably turned to and then remained focused on climbing. As he described the equipment he used, I was always at first brought back to the old days when simply using a rope was considered a milestone. I imagined Rob on El Cap, using all the sophisticated hardware he described, and was amazed at how far he'd come. I also realized that he'd truly found his passion. It made me happy to see him so happy, but made me kind of anxious that I had not.

Rob would then shift the conversation from what he had climbed to what he was going to climb. His plans were always bigger and bolder than the tales he had just told. He had all kinds of ideas for new equipment which would enable him to do even more. It was obvious he spent a considerable amount of time thinking about his passion. Hearing him talk about it always made me think, "No wonder he's so good at it."

And he *was* good – really good. During the summer of 1987, Rob and RSL did the first ascent of El Capitan's Scorched Earth, considered at that time to be one of the toughest, most dangerous routes ever done on El Cap. Many loose, multi-ton rocks and a pitch called The Leavittator, a 5.11/A5 off-width crack that went from knife-edge to 24 inches in width made Scorched Earth weinously horrendous, as Rob would say. The route remains so demanding that, almost a quarter century after Rob and RSL's ascent, it's been climbed less than half a dozen times – and some of those who say they've climbed it actually went off-route to avoid The Leavittator.

Rob and RSL also made one of the first ascents of Zenyatta Mondatta, where they discovered that additional rivets – small anchors drilled into the rock – had been added since it was first climbed in 1981 by Jim Bridwell, Peter Mayfield and Charlie Row. Old-school climbers like Rob, RSL and The Team call such additions "chicken bolts" because the climbers who placed them obviously weren't brave or skilled enough to do the route as originally climbed. RSL carefully led the pitch around the offending bolts, followed by Rob, who chopped them off.

"Aid climbing should be imaginative," Rob always said. "The leader should make every effort to get through a stretch of rock with the least amount of permanent damage, but someone will get scared, put in a bolt and ruin the whole character of the pitch," he lamented, shaking his head with a sneer.

Lounging in Camp 4, Rob studied the rough outline of the United States on El Cap's North American Wall. On previous trips, he had surveyed possible routes. One area in particular had caught his attention. Up through the "western" part of the United States, about where Wyoming would be, ran his proposed new route. This line had never been climbed before, and the reason was obvious; it was the hardest line on the wall. Its vast overhangs, expanding flakes and smooth rock seemed to go on forever. Pinnacles and pillars jutted below the most difficult sections, ready to skewer anyone foolhardy enough to attempt to scale the faces above.

Three members of the local Camp 4 clique had also been scoping out a new line on the North American Wall. Apparently visualizing the route through the heart of the continent, or maybe just because it scared them, they called it "Heart of Darkness." Later, perhaps to be more specific, they began referring to it as the "Iowa

Pig Farm." One of them, Greg Child, had done the first nine pitches before bailing, saying it was too loose, too rotten.

"You can't climb it," he asserted.

One day in Camp 4 Rob showed up and joined in the Heart of Darkness conversation. Rob saw the locals as more talk than action, as no new climbs were being put up. They had a way of saving, or putting their dibs on, a route by fixing a rope or leaving some gear on the first pitch until they maybe got around to climbing it. This state of affairs applied in particular to Heart of Darkness, about which there was plenty of talk, but no action, other that Child's aborted try after nine pitches.

Observing climber courtesy, Rob asked first if anyone else was actively planning to do the route. Then, in a move sure to rile the locals, proclaimed he was also intent on doing it first and, in keeping with the rules, naming it after he topped out. Rob wasn't going to call it Heart of Darkness or Iowa Pig Farm either, as he didn't consider them to be quite appropriate. Instead, Rob started calling the route "Wyoming Sheep Ranch," even before he climbed it.

"I'm gonna climb the Sheep Ranch and all your other routes too," he announced to the group and, as they fumed, he walked away laughing.

With Wyoming Sheep Ranch, Rob wanted to establish a new route that was really hard because, to him, extreme difficulty made it that much more satisfying and fun. He also wanted it to be fun in another sense. Being from Wyoming, he met many people in his travels that had never been there or knew little about it. Inevitably, he heard the tired cliché: "Wyoming, where men are men and sheep are nervous."

This didn't bother Rob, who was secure in his masculinity and not offended by ignorant arrogant urbanites who thought hailing from Wyoming also meant a proclivity for intimate relations with barnyard animals. Instead, he used his new climb and its attendant naming rights to uniquely and irreverently mock his detractors, pay homage to his home state and get the last laugh in a big way.

John Barbella, along with Mike O'Donnell and Randy Leavitt, was part of the Camp 4 scene. It was through this scene John Barbella met Rob. Barbella, who would do five first ascents at

Yosemite, including the Atlantic Ocean Wall, Bermuda Dunes and Lunar Eclipse, had a route of his own half-way put up on Half Dome, but abandoned it when Rob enlisted him for the Wyoming Sheep Ranch. It would be his first and only climb with Rob. In John Barbella's mind, Rob had a good ability to size people up. When you started a climb with him, you knew you'd finish it.

"Rob was straight-laced, but wild as shit," John remembers. "He had a good temperament and was never impatient, but he was also super-motivated and confident. When we started Sheep Ranch he said, 'We're not coming down.'"

So up the Sheep Ranch they went, expecting to take at least seven days before topping out 2,000+ feet above. The route was aid climbing in its purest and finest form. With razor-sharp virgin diorite edges never before touched by climbing equipment, the line followed the contours and textures of the rock. Incredibly thin and subtle, there was just enough relief to allow ascent without resort to drilling an endless succession of bolts. It was the hardest thing ever done in aid climbing. The Wyoming Sheep Ranch was even more demanding in skill and daring than Zenyatta Mondatta and Sea of Dreams, then the current gold standard for the most hideous, horrendous and heinous of the Yosemite climbs.

On the second day, Rob smashed his thumb with the piton hammer while leading a pitch. Immediately it began to swell and throb with pain.

"Lower me down to the belay" he called to John, who was secured at the belay point 40 feet below. When Rob reached the belay, he dug into his pack while Barbella watched, unsure what Rob had in mind.

Rob found his Swiss Army Knife, folded out the corkscrew and, with determined haste and without a word, drilled the corkscrew through his thumb nail to relieve the pressure. He then went back up to finish leading the pitch, saying over his shoulder to Barbella, "we're not going down."

Notwithstanding the lack of amenities on the wall, including a first-aid kit, Rob, unlike some climbers, liked to be neat and was diligent about his personal hygiene. He used a wet rag to wash his face, even shaved sometimes and was fastidious about brushing his teeth. Never, though, did Rob spit out the toothpaste.

"I swallow my toothpaste all the time because my Dad does," he explained.

Rob also liked to have tunes while hanging out on the cliffs and his "wall box," a large ghetto-style boom box complete with radio and cassette tape functions, was an important piece of climbing equipment which was never be left behind, regardless of the extra weight. For protection, it was almost completely covered with duct tape and, for luck, sported a portrait of Mr. T.

Mr. T, who played a menacing tough-guy mercenary on the television series "The A-Team," had a famous Mohawk and wore dozens of outlandish gold chains with large medallions around his neck. In real life, he lived in the ritzy Chicago suburb of Lake Forest on an estate with many huge, beautiful oak trees. Not long after he moved in, Mr. T unceremoniously chopped them down, leaving a vast expanse of stumps where a forest had been. When asked the obvious question of why, Mr. T responded in his characteristic growl, "They give me the sniffles, fool!" Rob would never have cut down any trees, but he appreciated Mr. T's defiant, irreverent exercise of his property rights. Mr. T was honed.

A climbing route is made up of a series of sections called pitches, which are determined in part by the length of a standard climbing rope and also by where the best belay points can be set. The Sheep Ranch, at almost half a mile high, contained many pitches, each with its individual characteristics and each of which was given an appropriate name in keeping with the Wyoming Sheep Ranch theme.

"High Boots on a Full Moon Night" conjured images of romantic interludes on the high plains under moonlit skies. The perils of "Cattle Prod Pillar" were accentuated by a large plastic phallus that Rob affixed to the rock. After a tough day of climbing, Rob and John could call it a day at the "Woolly Box Bivy." Rob thought future climbers might enjoy a "Fuzzy Pile Substitute."

Before the climb, he'd purchased a number of cute, fuzzy sheep dolls. Along the route, he stuffed them into cracks at what he considered to be appropriate spots. Rob referred to them as "Love Ewe-nits" or "sheepalopes," relatives or their better-known Western cousin, the "Jackalope," a cross between a jack rabbit and an antelope. At the belay of the "Welcome to Wyoming" pitch, Rob bolted a Wyoming license plate to the rock.

Another day of extreme aid climbing led to the "Sheepalope Bivy," a place as magical and awe-inspiring as its namesake. Aptly named "Ewephoria" captured the thrill, excitement and overall good feeling of the Wyoming Sheep Ranch. "Liz Is Tight," while not sheep-related, Rob named in honor of a girlfriend. Though he was pissed off at her at the time, he still called by her original nickname, "The Awesome Liz." In my opinion, however, the best name Rob gave to a pitch was the one that represented the high point of all previous attempts on the route: "Gumby's Gallows." Rob was the first to make it past that pitch.

"If you don't like the name, then you should have climbed it first and named it something else," Rob said to anyone offended by the mockery or uneasy about their own suppressed ovine inclinations. "If you're offended by the toys, then I suggest you do a different route."

As far as Rob was concerned, the significance, if any, of the names of or props left on the pitches was for others to debate. There was little debate, however, that the Wyoming Sheep Ranch became the new gold standard of super-honed big wall aid climbing in Yosemite.

To me, the Wyoming Sheep Ranch was a reflection of Rob in several ways. It demonstrated his credo of not taking himself too seriously. To do something so challenging, dangerous and daring, to maintain the intense drive necessary to follow through with completing the Sheep Ranch was extraordinary in and of itself. To be able to do it with such irreverent and independent flair was something that set him apart from everyone else.

I truly admired that about Rob. The names and props, along with the connotations associated with them, were a good-natured snub of convention and, some felt, good taste. Rob saw a comedic quality in the prudish, somewhat sanctimonious responses the Sheep Ranch evoked. That was part of the beauty of it. But that aside, the Wyoming Sheep Ranch was the world's hardest aid route and you had to respect that fact. In this aspect, my twin was much further up towards his summit than I.

Hearing Rob tell about the Sheep Ranch, though, was like encouragement to me to keep climbing toward my own summit, whatever it might be. Rob was his own man and went his own way. I remained determined to do the same. You could say he marched to his own drummer, a drummer who wailed away like John "Bonzo" Bonham of the mighty Led Zeppelin. I always liked to think I did too. Rob's inspiration, along with Mom and Dad's mantra to "get an education and be my own boss" kept me going.

When Rob and John Barbella got to the top, there was no huge celebration, cameras or hoopla. They simply threw their gear off the edge of El Capitan, rather than make several trips ferrying it to the bottom, and hiked down. The route was now officially the Wyoming Sheep Ranch. Rob had become an A5 Master. He had become the King of El Cap. But for him it was not enough. It wasn't even close.

In Camp 4 making sure the diet is balanced

Atop a desert tower

Chapter VII

"Oh, to be in the Desert with Hammer, Al and
a truck full of gear!"
                    –Rob Slater's K2 Journal, May, 1995

The Colorado Plateau encompasses the vast area around what
is known today as the Four Corners region, where the boundaries of
Utah, Arizona, New Mexico and Colorado converge. Some 300
million years ago, a sea flowed into the region, leaving a salt bed
thousands of feet deep in places. Compounded by geologic faults,
the surface became unstable, resulting in huge displacements like the
2,500 foot Moab Fault. Surface erosion stripped off younger rock
layers, exposing the famous balanced formations, delicate arches and
towering spires of Castle Valley, Arches National Park and
Monument Valley which are still visible today.

As Rob drove into the desert for the first time in the spring of
1980 during his first year of college, he knew immediately it was a
special place that became known to him simply as "the desert."

At the end of the last ice age 10,000 years ago, as the ice sheets covering much of North America receded, the ancient peoples arrived. These and the ancestral Ute, Fremont and Puebloan tribes scavenged the arid wastelands in search of stone for tools and weapons and plants and animals upon which they could subsist. Their stay in this hostile environment was unobtrusive, leaving but a few artifacts, pictographs and petroglyph panels. Quietly, they disappeared into the wind and dust of the desert.

Years later, a succession of non-Indians arrived, seeking fortune, fame or perhaps some form of personal redemption. The Spanish conquistadors, with their fancy helmets and shiny armor, searched in vain for fabled lost cities of gold. Imagine the look on their faces as they crested a rise and came upon not a metropolis of solid gold but the Grand Canyon! Sadly, with nothing or no one to plunder in the name of their religion, they were forced to return south to complete the job of exterminating the native Mesoamerican cultures. Mineral speculators and cattlemen followed the route into the desert, only to eventually abandon their quests as well among the endless expanses of rock and sand.

Eventually, much of these desert lands were set aside as Indian reservations, with the most desolate going to the Navajo, Hopi and Ute. Those lands perceived as most scenic and valuable were kept by the government and have become national forests, Arches National Park and the Glenn Canyon National Recreation Area.

A drive through the area is a study in contrast. The national parks, with their gleaming visitors' centers, boast high-definition videos of the park's highlights and history. The well-maintained roads offer the occupants of an endless stream of RVs the chance to see nature's finest without having to leave the comfort of a sofa.

Out on the "Res," as Rob fondly referred to the Indian reservation lands, the situation for the natives was as seemingly bleak as the landscape. Along desolate stretches of highway, wooden half-garages called kiosks, sat in rows, many vacant, where tourists could stop, brave the heat and dusty wind for a bit and peruse the wobbly benches covered with Native American arts and crafts offered for sale by the locals. One had a sign that simply said "Nice Indians." It was hard to not buy something, perhaps because of a twinge of personally assumed national guilt.

From Moab, Utah, the Scenic Byway of Highway 128 snakes its way along the Colorado River to the northeast, comprising the southern boundary of Arches National Park. Past Negro Bill Canyon, Jackass Canyon and around Big Bend, visitors get a close-up look at the river that carved the Grand Canyon and the amazing geology of the area. It's a place to look back in time millions and millions of years. When I was there years after Rob's first trip, looking about made it easy to understand why Rob could be interested in geology. The Colorado's power is accentuated by the quiet of the surrounding desert and the pervading heat. In June, the water level is high as the river carries the melt from the snowfields south of Laramie and Woods Landing, Wyoming, to Lake Powell, through the Grand Canyon and toward the sea. Chances are that most, if any, of the cool, silty liquid will never reach the Pacific. Instead, it will either evaporate into the hot, dry air or end up on a field of crops somewhere east of Los Angeles. For years, Mexico has indignantly complained how the mighty Colorado River, by the time it reaches its territory, is but a trickle.

After about 10 miles, the sheer cliffs melt away into the broad expanse of Castle Valley, dotted with giant red sandstone monoliths and towering spires. Perhaps it is called Castle Valley because, as Verm Sherman has written, the "towers resemble the drip sand castles children make at the beach." Another 10 miles leads to the Colorado's confluence with the Dolores River and the Fisher Towers just to the south.

During Rob's college days, there were relatively few desert spots commonly recognized within the climbing community, but serious climbing aficionados had all heard about and wanted to climb in the desert. Along with Eldo and Yosemite, the desert spires were the dream destinations of American climbing. Like giant magnets, they beckoned adventurous souls like Rob – and when he arrived in 1980, many of the towers had either never been climbed or climbed just once, sometimes decades earlier.

The crown jewel of the Fisher Towers is the Titan, a 900-foot-high red sandstone prong jutting from the end of an ancient rock fin. The approaches consist of steep rock gullies washed out by eons of erosion and dotted with desert sagebrush and yucca. Standing at the base of the Titan looking up, it's hard not to lose your balance as the giant monolith appears to sway imperceptibly below the clear, broiling-blue desert sky.

During Rob's freshman year in college, Boulder climber Bill Feiges enlisted Rob to accompany him on an ascent in the Utah desert. Bill, an acquaintance of Rob's from the Eldo climbing community, had been to the desert before but Rob, at that point, had never even heard of the Titan. On the Titan's first pitch, he learned how to use mechanical ascenders, often called "jumars" after a particular brand. Staple-gun-looking devices that slide over and clamp on the rope, they allowed Rob to climb up the rope itself. A few pitches up, Rob led the crux, the most difficult section of the route. During his lead, while performing a body weight "jump test" on the pitch's only bolt, it pulled out, nearly sending Rob off the tower. Barely maintaining his balance, he recovered and continued the ascent. At the top of the pitch, even with the hardest part now behind them, Rob insisted they back off, or "bail." Inexperienced on the desert towers and out of his climbing element, he was scared. Uncharacteristically, Rob had been spooked.

Silence filled the car during the seven-hour ride back to Boulder. Feiges was less than impressed with Rob's performance on the Titan; anybody who bailed like that would never amount to an aid climber of any stature, much less be able to stomach the big-time, exposed aid routes of El Cap which Rob, during their long drive to the desert, had declared he would do that upcoming summer. "Aid climber indeed," Feiges fumed. "What a pussy."

Meanwhile, Rob brooded. The assertion that he could never be a real aid climber served only to fuel his determination. A few years later, after many return trips to the desert, on the night of New Year's, 1985, Rob went back to the Titan, sans Feiges, and climbed it via a harder route.

I wasn't on this trip, but could easily picture the look on Rob's face as he stewed, silently staring out the car window, his frustration and anger exceeded only by his newfound focus to prove Feiges wrong. In a situation like this, I might have let the anger get the best of me and simply lashed back, turning a negative into even more of a negative. But Rob, in a show of what I would consider to be indicative of his character, used it to his advantage.

Rob not only returned to the Titan, but became a kind of

desert and Res local. In places such as Mexican Hat, Bluff, Bridger Jack and Mexican Water, he was a regular where many tourists would never consider stopping. To the local celebrities he gave nicknames, like #1 Grandpa. In the local diners where he ordered huevos or Navajo tacos, depending on the time of day, he looked forward to seeing his favorite waitresses. These anonymous souls were an integral part of the Rob's desert experience, demonstrated by him bestowing upon them "family" names.

Near the tiny town of Mexican Hat in Monument Valley in the extreme southeast corner of Utah stands a sandstone spire of the same name. Rob and Hammer, along with fellow CU student Al Torrisi, stopped in at gem and gift shop before the climb. Al, with his thick, bushy black mustache, was a close member of Rob's Team. On the wall was a huge, five-foot diameter Mexican sombrero, complete with intricate stitching and rhinestones. Rob, Hammer and Al looked at the hat and then at each other.

"We've got to have that sombrero for Al's first ascent of the Mexican Hat," said Rob, vocalizing what they were all thinking.

Since Rob and Hammer had already climbed the Mexican Hat tower, but this was to be Al's first ascent, they agreed it was appropriate to do something a little bit special to commemorate the occasion. Rob, with his friends' backing, talked the owner of the shop into letting them take the sombrero to the climb.

"We promise we'll be careful and bring it back," they assured him. Believing the lads to be trustworthy, the owner didn't even take a credit card or cash deposit; he just let them take it.

At the base of the climb the wind was howling at 30 knots, with gusts even higher. Someone had chopped off the lower bolts on the route, so they had to break out the "Lovetron," Rob's El Cap invention, to clip a bolt almost 20 feet out and aid climb to the top. Al put on the big rhinestone sombrero and started up the rope. It takes little imagination to picture how a five-foot diameter sombrero behaves in a 30-knot wind. As Al clung to the edge of the tower, swinging in the wind with his five-foot sombrero, the sombrero slipped off his head. With the chin strap cinched tightly around his neck, Al thought he might actually be strangled to death.

At the same time, Rob and Hammer were laughing so much Al didn't think they were actually on belay. The only sound louder than the howling of the wind was the howling of the laughter below.

Of course, Rob and Hammer insisted that Al keep the sombrero on.

As Al struggled high above, Rob looked up at him and then over at Hammer sitting on the ledge next to him. "From now on his name is Poncho," Rob declared. And that was it; when Rob gave someone a name, such as Nick Café' or Great One or Hammer, that was his name. From then on, Al was Poncho. Eventually, they all made it to the top of the Mexican Hat, where Poncho Torrisi posed for a summit photo in his big Mexican hat.

When they returned to the base of the tower after the climb, Poncho put the sombrero on a ledge as the gear was packed. When they turned around, the sombrero was nowhere to be found. Frantically they searched the base of the tower, with no luck. Dejected and frustrated, because the shop owner had trusted them with the sombrero, Rob, Hammer and Poncho hiked back to their truck. There, just off the side of trail, was the sombrero lying in the dirt.

A few weekends later, Hammer and Poncho were ice climbing in Ouray, Colorado with Mike O'Donnell, Rob's partner from the Sea of Dreams on El Cap. As he sat on belay, Mike looked down at Mr. Torrisi and said, "We should call you Poncho." Hammer and Poncho looked at each other and then told Mike Rob had beaten him to it.

Indian reservations are considered separate, sovereign nations within the territorial boundaries of the United States, subject to the control of their inhabitants. Despite their beauty and obvious attraction, climbing is strictly prohibited.

"I have great respect for the Navajo lands," Rob said. "The worst thing that could happen would be to allow climbing there. Where John Q. climbs, destruction follows. The Navajo should patrol the place with machine guns."

Rob was happy the Res was closed to climbing and could relate to the natives' point. He didn't want anyone else out there, but he wanted to climb on the Res regardless and was happy to take his chances.

Increased numbers of visitors, especially those whose presence was obnoxiously advertised in their wakes, rightfully drew a reaction of increased vigilance on the part of the natives. Nevertheless, while Rob and his partners were careful to leave no trace of their visits, they each carried a blank check in their wallets, prepared to remit the $500 fine if apprehended.

"Worrying about getting busted by the Indians, having your windows smashed, getting your gear stolen, that adds something," Rob surmised, perhaps rationalizing the seeming incongruence of his concurrent respect Navajo lands and disregard for their laws. But what, really, was the reason behind this contradiction?

Indian Creek outside of Moab was a popular desert climbing training area, right off the main road. With a 150-foot crack in the rock, it was a great place to practice and a nice rappel back down. On the way into the desert, Rob and his climbing friends drove past Indian Creek many times, but never stopped. It was always crowded with helmet-wearing wannabees and other non-serious climbing types. Rob wanted to "nail the mud curtains" instead, as he referred to the red sandstone layers of the spires. Rob wanted to do real climbs and make it to the coolest summits. For him, the greatest opportunity for adventure lay off the beaten path.

At times in the earlier days during college, Rob and his cohorts used mountain bikes. Arriving to do the Mitten Thumb spire, Rob and Hammer checked into a Moab motel, waited until 2:00 a.m., then biked out to the base of the climb and efficiently made their ascent unnoticed in the moonlight. They then hid all day in the brush with their bikes and gear, waiting for the return of darkness to make their escape back to the motel.

As time went by, more and more mountain bikers started showing up. On another trip, as he and Hammer were biking in for some climbing along the White Rim Trail outside of Moab, they came upon a rather serious group of mountain bikers. One of them told Rob he needed to be wearing a helmet. Rob was clearly offended by the presumptuousness of this remark, but said nothing. Instead, he simply waited at the bottom of a long, steep hill and watched as the group began their ascent up the trail. When they had a good lead, Rob took off up the trail, passing every one of them. As he reached the top, the group was just approaching the half-way point of the climb. In his own way, Rob had eloquently and compellingly made his point without saying a word. Helmets, to him, represented an overreaction and succumbing to fear of the most elemental of risks. Hammer and he never even brought a first–aid kit.

Rob was always a hellacious hiker. I never caught my brother on the way to the cliffs that second day at Exum and figured out quickly trying to best him was an exercise in futility. Poncho Torrisi had a similar experience with Rob's hiking stamina-and stubbornness-on the approach to the Castleton tower along the Colorado River in Utah. Poncho was training for the Houston Marathon at the time and was really fit, especially aerobically. Poncho was honed. At the start of the hike, Poncho told Hammer and Becky Hall, who were along for the climb, "I'm going to do everything in my power to pass Rob on the approach hike up to the climb."

Starting the hike, Poncho was right behind Rob, breathing down his neck. The approach was relentless and slippery as they picked their way up first through the desert sand and scrub brush and then through the mass of sandstone scree under the tower's base. Poncho picked it up a notch and tried to pass Rob, but Rob clicked it up a notch as well and wouldn't let him pass. Poncho picked it up again and again the same result. This occurred at least a dozen times until Rob and Poncho were full-fledged running, or rather sprinting, up the approach trail, each carrying packs loaded with ropes, harnesses, water, shoes, and every camming device known to mankind. Not a word was ever spoken between the two during this exchange.

"You'd think that somewhere in there Rob would have turned around and said, "Poncho, what the fuck are you doing, you're never going to pass me," Poncho recalled. Even after they reached the base of the climb, sweating and gasping for breath, waiting for Becky and Jim, Rob never mentioned it. Neither did Poncho. "It was like we were just out on a casual stroll," Poncho told me afterwards.

The Totem Pole is a sacred site to the Navajo. For this ascent, Rob and Hammer just drove out to the base of the tower and parked. As a ruse, they scattered maps, camera equipment and photography magazines in their vehicle in case anyone came by to investigate. It would be assumed by the Navajo, they reasoned, that it was just some tourists out taking pictures and not illegal climbers on their sacred spire. From the top, they watched nervously as two Indians arrived on horseback and circled their truck. Luckily for the intruders, the residents eventually rode off into the desert. They realized they would have to figure out a better way to climb in the desert without being caught or even noticed.

Their concern was realized in the starkest of fashions following their climb of Jacob's Ladder, another spectacular spire in the heart of the Navajo desert. Upon returning to Hammer's truck, two Navajos showed up. It was immediately evident they were not a welcoming committee. With great haste, Rob and Hammer commenced to vacate the premises. The Indians gave chase and the two vehicles bounced across the rough, rutted road through the sand and scrub for several miles. Eventually the pursuers gave up the chase, not due to any lack of exuberance on their part but only because they were pulling a huge horse trailer.

The Middle Sister, a 700-foot spire, was another awesome desert tower Rob just had to climb, illegal or not. Rob and his climbing buddies simply needed to figure out how.

The Middle Sister soars from a group of spires a short distance off the highway, tantalizingly close for a would-be climbing suitor but yet, given her close proximity to civilization, so far away. It's right out in the open. In fact, at the base of Middle Sister was a compound of Navajo houses, or hogans as they are called. To bag this sister would take some ingenuity, finesse and, perhaps more importantly, some luck.

In the visitor center parking lot near the Middle Sister in Monument Valley stood a number of the kiosks with Navajos selling Native American jewelry and arts and crafts so common on the Res. Rob, Hammer and Poncho Torrisi were drawn to one in particular, largely because the young woman tending the crafts was "super hot." They starting chatting with her and soon a young Navajo man joined in the conversation. As it turned out, this young man, Elroy, was the attractive Navajo gal's brother. Rob and his climbing partners admitted they really didn't need any jewelry and were really just visiting the area to see the sandstone towers. Hearing this, Elroy announced he was "an official Navajo guide" and could take them "off the road where the white man is not allowed." Rob, Hammer and Poncho quickly took Elroy up on his offer. As it turned out, his real name was Elroy, but because he didn't think it sounded "cool to pale-faces," he sometimes used the name Kevin.

The next day, with Elroy as their guide, they spent an incredible day exploring primitive trails in Monument Valley. Their last hike led to the top of a cliff band overlooking the Middle Sister. Eventually, they came to a dead end at a chasm hundreds of feet deep. Without a rope or any form of protection, it seemed they had no choice but to turn back. Instead, Elroy leapt across. At that point they really didn't have a choice, and they jumped across as well. Maybe Elroy was testing them to see if they would actually jump. Maybe Elroy just jumped across the chasm without giving it a second thought as he scrambled through his people's sacred place of sand, cliffs and sky. In any case, Elroy, Rob, Hammer and Poncho had formed a bond.

Across the chasm, enjoying a great view of Middle Sister, Rob and Hammer started talking about how cool it would be to climb the tower in an effort to illicit Elroy's response. Elroy got excited and immediately started in about how he would like to learn to climb. Seizing the opportunity, Rob and his cohorts offered to teach him, which was an offer Elroy quickly accepted.

During that same conversation, they mentioned the group of hogans with fences and livestock at the tower's base. In a stroke of great luck, or perhaps greater irony, it turned out it was Elroy's homestead. Elroy invited his new climber friends to stay with his family that night, which turned out to mean they could throw their sleeping bags down between a couple of old Econoline vans on blocks. But it also included the chance to attend a native celebration Elroy was planning with his family.

As Rob and Hammer went off to the tower to deliver rope and gear for the climb, Poncho sat about 10 yards from Elroy's grandfather, watching him butcher and skin a sheep, put it on a spit and begin roasting it on an open fire. Thinking he had to get a picture, but not knowing if the old Navajo would think it was OK to snap his picture, Poncho nonchalantly took out his camera and pointed it towards the old Navajo sitting peacefully next to the now-roasting sheep, occasionally turning the spit. As soon as the shutter went "click," he looked right at Poncho and started yelling something in Navajo.

Elroy's grandpa then grabbed his rifle and started charging towards Poncho, with his rifle aimed right at him. The old Navajo started shooting. Bullets whizzed past Poncho's head. As Poncho's life passed in front of him, he thought, "If I ever make it through this mess I'm going to kill Rob and Jim for talking me into this misadventure."

But the old Navajo ran right by Poncho, who turned around to see that the real target of the rifle shots was a coyote that had gotten into the family's sheep pen.

That evening, Rob, Hammer and Poncho joined Elroy, his family and nearly three dozen other Navajos for a traditional Navajo ceremony and dance. There was a huge camp fire whose light reflected off the sandstone cliffs, casting eerie shadows of dancers in native ceremonial dress and head dresses in the desert night, all set to a soundtrack of singing, drumming and chanting. For Rob, Hammer and Poncho, the only white folks there, it was a truly magical experience.

The following morning, Rob, Hammer, Poncho and Elroy stood at the base of the Agathla, a 1,000-foot-tall volcanic plug located just outside the park boundaries but still illegal due to its location on the reservation. Notwithstanding his agility and fearlessness on the cliffs, they discovered Elroy had never been schooled with or used modern climbing equipment. Elroy joined them on the climb of the Agathla and, as they ascended, was taught how to jumar and other basic safety techniques.

Climbing a steep 1,000-foot rock was quite an impressive introduction to rock climbing. The route had some 5.9 pitches which Elroy managed with relative ease. Elroy thus became the first Navajo to scale the tower. Rob took a summit photo of Elroy which he developed and framed, with the intention of presenting it to Elroy during their next trip to the desert. Rob, Hammer and Poncho also did Mitchell Mesa and several other desert ascents with Elroy during that trip.

That evening, the plan was to meet Elroy back at his hogan and all climb the Middle Sister at night, due to the route's high visibility from the road. This would certainly alleviate the would-be serious issue of having to sneak by the compound, make the climb, descend and escape unnoticed. When Rob, Hammer and Poncho arrived at Elroy's homestead around 11 p.m., they discovered, in what they considered to be a sad commentary on youth on the Res, that Elroy intoxicated and unable to climb. Rob and his group asked if it was OK with Elroy and his family if they climbed the Middle Sister that night. Elroy replied with a big smile and two big thumbs up. Rob, Hammer and Poncho had a great moonlight climb, which may have been only the third or fourth ascent of the tower.

On their next trip to Monument Valley, they were unable to find Elroy, despite driving all over the Res looking for him. Elroy's family told them Elroy "is here, there, everywhere and nowhere." Rob and his friends never saw Elroy again. Rob gave Elroy's summit picture to a family member.

The bond Rob developed not only with Elroy, but with his entire family, was instructive. Through Elroy, Rob had an opportunity few non-Indians enjoy. It wasn't just jumping across a chasm between cliffs that caused Elroy to open up to Rob. It was something on a more personal, visceral level. It was something that allowed them to cross a chasm between cultures. Elroy saw a person, not just a white person, who was interested in more than finding a cool place to climb. He saw a man who truly understood his people's appreciation and reverence for their sacred places of sand and stone. Elroy and his family believed in and respected Rob's desire to scale their towers; otherwise they certainly would not have been party to it. Rob climbing on their towers was not, in Rob's mind or in theirs, a disregard for their laws or rights.

Over the years following Rob's first tower ascent, he undertook a quest to climb them all, which firmly took hold when he climbed the Citadel in June of 1992. Rob climbed many of the Fisher Towers with Stu Ritchie, a fellow Colorado University student and desert rat. Since no one had climbed all 23 of them, in Stu's mind it was a race to climb them all. As towers were scratched off the list of the unclimbed, Stu needled Rob about who would be first.

"The race will be over when I finish. No sooner," Rob responded, somewhat agitated by Stu's pestering.

Upon his return from one desert trip Rob ran into Stu, who started in again on the Fisher Towers "race." Exasperated, Rob told Stu he had now climbed them all, just to shut him up. But he had not done every one, for he lacked the Pink Pussycat. As soon as the conversation concluded, Rob called Hammer.

"I told Stu I did them all, but I haven't done the Pink Pussycat. You have to go with me next weekend to do it."

Hammer agreed and that next weekend, in November of 1994, they bagged the Pussycat. For the last move to the summit they either had to drill a bolt into the rock or, in crude cowboy fashion, lasso the top notch of the spire to pull themselves up. Rob chose the lasso and, moments later, stood atop the Pink Pussycat as the first climber to do all the Fisher Towers and making good his slightly premature boast to Stu. For the sake of the historical record, it bears mention that Rob, over the course of climbing every one of the towers, never took a single leader fall. This means, simply, that in addition to going up first he never fell while leading a pitch. That, in itself, was an extraordinary accomplishment on the mud curtains.

Sometime later, Rob discovered that someone had bolted the last move on the Pussycat, thereby eliminating the lasso move. He promptly went back and unbolted it. On other "mud routes," as Rob called climbs on the sandstone spires, he did find it sometimes necessary on a first ascent to drill bolts into the rock to provide protection for the lead climber. But the rock wasn't always solid and, in a living example of time and erosion, was in some places so porous and unstable that he had to scrape off or dig down several inches before his bolt could find purchase. Once placed, a bolt is given the jump test to determine if it will hold his weight if he fell. If it held, everything was fine. If it didn't, a decision had to be made whether to go up anyway, without protection. On many of Rob's desert ascents, if he wasn't the first, there had been only a small number of those who had gone before. If he came upon a bolt where the surrounding rock had eroded to the point of instability, he might put in a replacement. Never, though, did he add a new one to a previously climbed route.

Differing schools of thought exist concerning this and other issues of "climbing ethics." Scholars debate the demarcation points along the subjective, sliding scale of what constitutes a "clean ascent" versus the "poor style" of defacing nature by placing too much protective hardware. After all, if an actual step ladder was affixed to even the most difficult of climbing routes, it would be relatively easy and safe to complete the ascent. Rob was of the opinion that if someone else could do it without, so could he.

In the early days of his desert climbing during college, Rob enjoyed what he considered to be true solitude among the spires. But as time went by, the desert was "discovered," leading to all the havoc which invariably follows man. In many places, the Navajo lands took on a new character. Rob was disappointed to come across a set of mountain bike tracks in a spot he believed no one ever visited, even though he himself was leaving tracks. It was downright maddening for him to come upon more blatant examples of John Q's failure to leave the desert in at least the same condition they found it. If Rob came across a piece of litter in the wild, he picked it up and carried it out. This was true for trailhead parking lots as well as the most secluded spots.

Meanwhile, I had drifted from engineering and then careened into economics, history and political science. I was covering all the bases as far as subjects which interested me, but none of which evolved into any form of life-long passion. Nevertheless, I was at least getting a well-rounded education.

It was the Age of Ronald Reagan and without really trying, I found my political conscience as I joined the world of academia. Instead of embracing the idealism of youth and the hope and promise of mankind and governments existing in utopian harmony, I went the other way. Changing my major to political science, I took on my liberal classmates and professors in the Cold War debate. Supporting what I called the "hard line against the communist menace," I submitted letters to the editor signed "Red Blooded American."

"Are you serious?" one of my professors asked, after reading a paper of mine which included the line, "The United States, with the great forearm of capitalism across their throat, will drive the Soviets to their knees..." "I've never had a student with such extreme views," he told me, scratching his head.

"I get it from my Dad," I replied proudly.

"What is he, in the military?" the professor wondered, apparently starting to make to sense of my attitude.

"No, he's a plastic surgeon and history buff," I responded.

My time as a "poly sci" major in the early 1980s also coincided with the disintegration of the old Soviet empire and the call for freedom in Poland. Out front in the Polish independence movement was Lech Walesa and the Solidarity trade union.

My friend Ken "The Chief" Bull and I considered ourselves history and politics aficionados. The Chief, a history major, could draw a map of Eastern Europe on a bar napkin. It didn't necessarily attract the hottest chicks, but I still thought it was pretty cool. We respected the courage shown by Solidarity and the Poles in standing up to the totalitarian Soviet regime that had held them down for so long. As the protests raged in Poland, the Polish national basketball team was touring the United States. They made a stop in Laramie, home of my University of Wyoming.

The school administration made it clear that no political demonstrations would be tolerated. The Chief and I, however, thought the university trying to deny us the right to show support for the Polish freedom fighters was on the same level as the Soviets stamping out free speech. So, in a small act of defiance, we made a Solidarity banner out of a large bed sheet. I snuck it in the arena and, right before half time, The Chief and I unfurled it and paraded around for the entire crowd of 15,000 to see. We were met with a huge ovation and, inevitably, by a group of uniformed police officers.

We didn't resist or even try to get away. The cops escorted us out of the arena amid the now-booing crowd and down to the police station. After holding us for about half an hour, they let us go without so much as a ticket. I think they agreed that what we did was honed. They even let us keep our banner, which we took to our favorite tavern and hung up. For participating in this stunt with me, I thought The Chief was honed.

Eventually, I ended up in international relations, which was a shorter way of saying I had a political science major with minors in history and economics. I had thereby astutely positioned myself for a high-level job with the State Department, such as an ambassador to some peaceful Caribbean island nation with a young, single female population. But even I wasn't dumb enough to put much stock in that happening. In other words, I was basically as unemployable as I was before college, so I had to come up with a back-up plan.

The path of least resistance led to law school. I rationalized that all I had to do was get into law school. Once in, all I would have to do is get out. Once out, all I had to do was pass the bar exam and I would be set. History and science were far more interesting to me, but I hoped the study of law would turn out to be a fascinating pursuit. I figured lawyers did well and it would give me an opportunity to pursue whatever it was I decided I wanted to do. I admired and was somewhat envious that Rob had a passion, like Dad and his surgery, but I felt I would eventually discover mine. After all, I was still young and could do much worse than *only* becoming a lawyer. But that was about as deep as it got.

With no great haste, I finally graduated. Mom, Dad and Rob came to the graduation ceremony, with Rob and me both wearing gray suits, white shirts and black wingtips. The graduation speaker intoned the usual platitudes about going forth to do great things.

"Yeah, whatever," I thought to myself, concerned mostly with going forth to have a great time. In the process, though, I would get myself a law degree.

By the time Rob finished college in 1983 and finished off the Fisher Towers in 1994, he had evolved into a real Darwinist. He felt no guilt over the white man taking the American West from the Indians. The white man would make better use of it, as they were more enterprising and stronger. They deserved it so they took it. It was part of his principal belief that the stronger wins.

In the words of our sister Sissy, "Even though Rob knowingly trespassed on the Indian lands, he clearly acknowledged it was theirs. Climbing on their sacred lands was really a gesture of respect, or at least he didn't view it as disrespectful. Rob revered the land and the towers as much, he believed, or more than the Indians, but for different reasons. The fact the land was sacred to the Indians only heightened his reverence for the towers and added to the allure of climbing them. The fact it was illegal added to the challenge, but he wasn't climbing them to trample on the rights of anyone."

Rob left bottles of whiskey at the bottom of the towers as peace offerings "to placate the Indians," as he would say. Beyond the practical considerations, it was an offering not only to the Indians as owners and stewards of the towers, but also to the mountain gods and spirits of the desert. Rob paid the same homage in the boulder field below Longs Peak. There, he regularly left a Pop Tart not only for the small, furry marmots that lived there and normally subsisted on the moss and lichen growing on the rocks but to the mountain gods of Longs and their spirit guardians. As our brother Paul observed, "to Rob, whiskey for a few hours on the tower was fair trade. He just wanted to climb, not despoil their beautiful spires or disrespect their rights as property owners and believed his token peace offerings would suffice."

Rob felt he had some right to make the best use of the towers and had shown reverence to the Indians, including Elroy and his family, and honored their land by climbing every one of their towers without trashing them. Rob climbed the towers on Indian lands in pursuit of what he believed was his own noble cause, his own destiny. It remained to be seen where this pursuit would ultimately lead.

Looking up at Rob from the desert floor

Al and Hammer in the desert

On the Grand Teton summit (Rob on right)

Chapter VIII

"I'll wear a coat when it gets cold."
–Rob Slater

In 1848, 25 Chicago businessmen founded the Chicago Board of Trade to instill order in the chaotic grain market. By the mid-1980s, the CBOT had grown to become a national financial center and one of the busiest commodities exchanges in the world. Within the 68-story downtown skyscraper where it has been housed since 1930, everything from corn to pork bellies to silver futures to U.S. Treasury bonds is traded in face-to-face markets overflowing with frenzied profit-seeking. Rob took me there in 1988 during one of my breaks during law school. The place reeked of history, power and wealth. It was big-time honed.

Rob called the bond pit at the CBOT the "wild animal pit of capitalism." In a small area about the size of half a tennis court, dozens of traders screamed, jumped, pushed and used their own special hand signal language buying and selling bonds. Fortunes were made and lost in seconds and nerves of steel were a minimum prerequisite. Talk was cheap and those able to survive the Pit were the true kings of the capitalist jungle.

This cutthroat competition was what had originally attracted Rob to business. It fit squarely within his then-emerging Darwinian views. Outside the climbing world, it represented the epitome of the rule that the strongest wins and to the victor go the spoils. Rob realized quickly that the market was smart, totally unforgiving, and had an insatiable appetite for dreams of quick or easy fortune.

As college graduation approached in 1983, Rob, like his student brethren across the country, had started looking for a job that would hopefully launch a successful career. But jobs were rather hard to come by and even getting a little bit of positive feedback during an interview was tough.

"I went to an interview at one of the big brokerage houses and the guy screamed and cussed at me for 45 minutes," Rob told me, almost incredulously. "He even criticized the color of my socks. Who the hell was I to expect a job involving tons of money when I had no experience and just a shitty business degree from Colorado? When he finished, I stood up, shook his hand and said 'thank you for your time.'"

Rob ended up spending a year in San Diego working for a real estate developer, but kept his sights set on Chicago and New York. Eventually, he was able to land an entry level job in Chicago with Goldman Sachs, one of the country's oldest and largest financial houses. Armed with his business degree and a year of work experience, he packed his one grey pin-striped suit, white dress shirt, conservative blue power tie and a pair of wing tips, along with his huge climbing rack and library of climbing and financial books, and headed to the Midwest to seek his fortune and the perfectly honed, slender blonde with a well-defined collar bone.

Each morning, after some Cocoa Puffs or Pop Tarts, Rob rode the bus to the Loop to fight it out in the Pit as a member of the Goldman Sachs trading desk. It didn't take long to realize how hard it was to wrench any money out of the market. Everybody there, along with everyone on the other end of the thousands of ongoing phone calls from the floor, had the same thing in mind, and they had obviously been doing this a lot longer than he. Profit, in the form of good trades, appeared with enticing regularity, but the hyenas of the Pit pounced instantaneously and each, it seemed, had its own angle of attack and method to take a nick off the margin. It also didn't take long for his cohorts at work to discover Rob's no-nonsense view of economics and life in general. Risk was necessary to reap rewards and nothing was free. It was all very simple to him and no good purpose was served by making things more complicated than necessary.

On the streets of downtown Chicago, Rob was periodically confronted by panhandlers who, of course, wanted something for nothing. This offended Rob's basic sense of economic fairness.

"Why should I just give you money when I have to get up every morning and work my ass off for it? I'll tell you what, if you give me five good pushups, I'll give you a dollar."

When every so often someone would get down and give him five – or at least try, Rob always paid up, with a final bit of advice: "That's a good effort. Don't waste it all on liquor."

Politically correct and other self-professed do-gooders were offended, but in Rob's mind handing a bum a dollar really wouldn't do him any good. To him, it wasn't a question of being mean but whether his world view applied to everyone. Rob thought it did, so it was "give me five and I'll give you one" – or nothing.

But in Chicago, when Rob applied it to himself, he believed he came up lacking and began directing his anger and frustration outward. Though he was a loyal and giving friend, with increasing edginess and a decreasing component of compassion, he applied his own Darwinian rules to everyone from bums on the street to strangers he met at parties.

One time, Rob needed some help carrying a bookshelf up to his second-floor apartment. Members of the "Swiss Family Washington," as he called the family that lived upstairs, could not tear themselves away from the Price is Right and declined his offer of payment. He then had to search elsewhere for labor for this five-minute undertaking. On the street he encountered a guy whose hand-held sign professed he would "work for food." When offered $20 to help carry the bookcase up one flight of stairs, he simply refused but did, however, offer to accept a donation.

"Amazing," Rob thought as he dragged the bookshelf into his

apartment by himself.

Rob had a doctor friend, Geoff Tabin, who in addition to being a renowned climber and adventurer, for a time worked emergency room duty at Cook County Hospital in the heart of the city. ER duty at CCH was like working in a MASH unit at the front line of a war zone as the results of gunshots, knife wounds and stomach-churning trauma poured in constantly with a diverse sea of humanity.

Rob wanted to experience what it was like to be a doctor, like Dad, so he badgered Tabin until his friend allowed him to don a white lab coat and join him during his shift, introducing him as a young doctor there to observe. They encountered a woman with a deep laceration on her arm that required several stitches. As he finished numbing the wound before suturing, Tabin was called away to assist with a more pressing emergency. Several minutes later he returned to the exam room, expecting to find Rob and the injured woman waiting. Instead, he heard the woman scream, "Oww, what do you think you're doing? I don't think you're even a doctor. Get away from me."

In Tabin's absence, Rob had tried to suture the woman's arm. Although he got in three stitches, he couldn't get the knots to stay tied. Rob discovered it was tougher than the real Dr. Tabin made it look. Though he may have rationalized he was only trying to help, in truth, he did want to be a doctor like Dad. That frustration overshadowed any real concern he had for the patient. Tabin could only shake his head and "ask" Rob to please not practice medicine in the ER for the duration of their shift.

Following college graduation and a year of graduate studies in history, I headed to the Midwest, just like my twin brother. In the vacation and humidity capital of the tri-state region, Omaha, Nebraska, I rattled into town in my in my old Jeep on a sweltering August day in 1985. I had about three days to find a place to live, get settled and start law school.

Creighton University, where I was enrolling, was an old-time Jesuit school founded 107 years before I got there. The campus was a mixture of really cool old buildings interspersed among ultra-modern structures. There was definitely history there. The Jesuits have cash and, as I learned in later years, they are phenomenal at keeping track of you after graduation to solicit donations. It was a place where people were serious about their religion. I couldn't help myself, but sometimes I referred to it as "Satan" instead of Creighton. Even though I was now a law student, I still had my sense of humor.

It was a place where girls used more names than they did in Wyoming. By hyphenating their maiden and married names into very business-like, lawyerly-sounding monikers such as R. Jessica Weatherly-White Hollingsworth Von der Hosen, they sounded like they were their own law firm. I decided I would get serious about school and, to be on the safe side, only refer to the ladies by their first names, regardless of how many names they had following. To be sure, though, some of them had what I called "the professional thing" goin' on.

In law school, students are taught how to "think like a lawyer," whatever pompousness that connotes. It's done by the Socratic Method, where the professor calls on some poor sap and browbeats them in question-and-answer format. All the while, the rest of the class tries to figure out what the hell the professor is talking about while furiously taking notes. One notorious professor was claimed to be the worst of them all. On the first day of class, according to law school lore, he would call on the male student with the most Irish-sounding name and verbally abuse him mercilessly.

At the pub after the first-year student orientation, my new buddies and I sat around our pitchers of beer eyeing the class list, considering the most likely target. Upon unanimous consent, it was resolved Brian O'Brien was the obvious victim. As it turned out, the dubious honor went to Patrick Doyle.

A few weeks into the semester, my turn came on a Friday morning. No matter how well-reasoned my answer, the professor's response was a thundering "bullshit" or "why?" And so it went. In fact, I was called on each Friday during the succeeding weeks, faring as well as anyone else, I suppose. Since it was torts class, and I had seen an editorial in the Wall Street Journal about a tort issue, I went to professor's office and asked him about the article. We had a nice chat and I quickly recognized his political bent, my political science training coming in handy. As I was leaving I told him matter-of-factly,

"I just want you to know you can call on me every class. I'll always be ready."

"OK" he said dismissing me, unimpressed.

After that he never called on me again. He did, however, give me a "C." In the end, I guess he showed me. Or I showed him. Either way, I was satisfied. I was never very good at backing down. I had stood up to the professor and still passed his class.

For Rob, Chicago was very different from Colorado University and Boulder in terms of outdoor access and interest. In Boulder, the outdoors occupied a prominent place in the collective psyche of the residents and some of the best climbing in the country was a literally a five-mile bike ride away. In the Windy City of steel, cement, traffic and crowds, it was tough to find even a thin slice of wild solitude, much less any good climbing nearby.

So Rob compromised. By taking a part-time evening job at the Aerehwon Mountain Outfitter in downtown Chicago, he was at least able to talk with people of like mind – and drew decent crowds to the slide show seminars he put on about his desert climbs, BASE jumps, and big wall ascents in Yosemite.

In Rob's world view, some people were smart, some were blessed with great athletic talent and some were good looking. These people were just lucky; they were pretty honed without having to do anything. Others were not so smart, didn't have natural gifts bestowed upon them and, frankly, weren't all that attractive by society's skewed celebrity-worship standards. These folks could also be honed, as a result of their own efforts and daring, which Rob greatly respected. One of Rob's biggest pet peeves, however, was with those he considered to be poseurs. A poseur, in Rob's mind, was someone who made a conscious decision to appear to be something he or she was not, rather than put forth real effort. It was a choice to attempt deception at the basest level.

Rob especially hated poseurs when it came to the outdoors. Popular among the young urban "hipsters" as Rob called them, was a new activity called "sport climbing." It entailed "climbing" for "sport" on man-made walls to which molded plastic handholds and footholds were affixed. Conveniently located on the ceiling above was a pulley for holding a belay line. In the event of a fall, the "climber" simply swung out and was lowered down to the padded floor to try again. Rob had a bumper sticker on his car which read

"Sport Climbing is Neither."

Poseurs talked big games, but Rob eventually exposed them in his own subtle fashion. One evening a snooty North Shore woman, dressed in all the latest outdoor gear, came in shopping for a tent for her next big outdoor adventure. Rob listened patiently while the woman explained how she needed the latest technology in a tent that could handle the most extreme conditions. The woman made it clear she was willing to pay anything.

As she painted a picture of an epic journey, he actually became quite curious, thinking maybe this gal was the real deal. Rob inquired as to where she was going which demanded such equipment.

"Wisconsin," the woman proudly answered. After a long, thoughtful pause, Rob replied, "Lady, you don't need a tent, you need a Hefty garbage bag."

Rob saw the lady as a poseur, invading the outdoor world where he was a king, pretending to be something she was not so she could brag to her friends. Rob was offended so he offended her, perhaps not bothering to recall how much Feiges had offended him by taking him to task for being a pussy on the Titan.

Another time, Rob and Tabin were seated at a dinner with another high class, society type lady. On and on she went about some film she'd seen and how profound and meaningful to society was this important director's latest masterpiece of art and culture.

Unimpressed, Rob tried to listen politely, but those kinds of movies really weren't his thing. Clearly offended by Rob's disinterest, "You haven't even seen it, have you?" she accusatorily demanded.

"If a movie doesn't have animal sex in it, I don't go see it," he responded lightly. Rob and Tabin agreed later that seeing the resulting look on her face was worth twice the price of admission to any movie ever made.

Rob, though he now lived as a big-city urbanite, was still a wilderness child at heart. He had a Cheyenne friend, Peter Sherman, who lived in Chicago with his wife Amy as he started an advertising career. One night Peter's wife Amy came home with a huge grin on her face. That morning, she told her husband, she was waiting on the train platform on her way to work. It was brutally cold, complete with a howling wind and chill factor far below zero that cut straight through her heavy winter coat.

As Amy shivered, hoping the train would come before she froze to death, someone tapped her on the shoulder. Amy turned around to see none other than Rob, standing there with his big grin but without a coat. When she asked the obvious question, he replied, "Fuck coats. I just moved here from California, and I'm not going to wear a coat all winter. I'll wear a coat when it gets cold."

Another time, Peter had to switch apartments in a single night to complete the move between two leases, so he enlisted several friends to help. On the appointed night, however, Peter got home late from work and, to make matters worse, it was pouring rain. One by one, each of the friends bowed out. Peter felt totally screwed.

Then, the doorbell rang and, standing on the porch in the deluge was Rob, grinning of course.

"What are you doing here, Rob?" Peter asked, surprised and amazed.

"Getting soaked and getting ready to help you move," Rob replied. He and Peter moved the whole apartment that night.

The nearest place to Chicago to actually climb was 200 miles away at Devil's Lake, Wisconsin. When Rob and Tabin arrived one weekend, they were sorely disappointed to find the puny rock formation swarming with people. Some had gear but many just clambered about the rocks like ants on a discarded plate of Mini Mart Super Nachos. When they finally got their turn on the hardest route, it was an anticlimactic end to a three-hour ride through traffic. From then on, they relegated themselves to searching out man-made cliffs in the urban landscape.

Their favorite was a 15-foot-tall, 200-foot-long limestone-block retaining wall south of Grosse Point in Evanston, Illinois. Dubbed the "Great Wall of Evanston" by Tabin, it better approximated actual rock climbing than anything else available.

"Also," as Geoff told a newspaper reporter doing a story about people climbing the wall, "in the climbers' vernacular, it's way hard."

They spent hours figuring out the exact sequence of moves on the Wall's 60 mapped routes.

"We can do 'em right away," noted Rob to the same reporter,

perhaps reminiscing about the stadium wall at Folsom Field. Rob and Geoff drove each other.

"I'll come out alone and work until I can do something Rob hasn't done," said Geoff. "Then Rob cranks one off I can't do, so it goes back and forth."

Rob also sought out the vertical cracks in the cement among the underpasses along Lake Shore Drive. He named one particularly enjoyable route "Head Thrush" in homage to the honed collarbone of a young lady he admired greatly.

Despite these small victories, there was no denying Rob was out of his element in Chicago. He knew he needed to be in a big financial center like Chicago or New York for the purpose of his career, but his heart and mind remained in the mountains, where the competition with nature was pure.

For Rob, the bond pit at the Chicago Board of Trade represented the best example of competition between raw economic forces. In theory, the forces of the marketplace are immutable, much like the powers of nature encountered high on a mountain peak. In practice, however, and unlike in nature, the purity of market can be sullied.

In an effort to root out lawlessness and dishonest trading practices, in 1987 the Federal Bureau of Investigation sent undercover agents into the CBOT and the Chicago Mercantile Exchange. Posing as traders, they infiltrated the commodity exchanges and trading pits. To avoid arousing suspicion, they made actual trades. Their trades, however, were not entirely on the "up-and-up."

One of these FBI agents was assigned to the CBOT bond pit. Each morning, he arrived and made his way into the pit before the start of the controlled mayhem of trading began. There were no assigned places in the pit, but the traders all stood in the same spots every day. Over time, the agent became acquainted with a young trader with a big grin who occupied a regular spot just to his left.

The trader and the agent always talked before and after the trading sessions. They were about the same age and even went to breakfast together and lunch occasionally. The agent and the traders who occupied the area immediately around him were considered "local traders," who traded their own accounts but would also fill trade orders for the public.

The agent's job was to watch, listen and take note. By posing as a sleazy character, the agent engaged in trades with prearranged terms and prices, thereby skimming thin margins which comprised illegal trading profits. By doing so, the agent was able to identify the nefarious actors within the pits.

The bond pit is a small place and, "although to the outsider it may look really chaotic, everyone knew what was going on and what everyone else was doing," the agent recounted. "When I made trades that were less than legit, the others could tell what I was doing."

The young trader with the big grin who was befriended by the undercover FBI agent in the bond pit was Rob Slater.

"What are you doing? Why are you doing that with those scumbags?" Rob asked the agent. "You don't need to be doing that."

"I could tell he was disappointed and bothered by it," recalled the agent. "Rob wasn't happy about it personally, because it wasn't fair to the honest traders."

"It made me feel bad," the agent told me, "to think Rob thought I was letting him down by being dishonest. Rob didn't do *anything* like that. Rob wasn't about that at all."

Aside from his undercover duties, the agent enjoyed hearing Rob's stories each Monday about his training to trek to the poles or across Antarctica or skydiving over the weekend. In particular, the agent was fascinated by Rob's talk of his ultimate skydiving goal, what he called a "chute-less jump." Rob's plan was to dive out of an airplane without a parachute, track over to a friend, hook together and ride the canopy to the ground in tandem.

"I couldn't believe it, and had to laugh," the agent recalled. "Almost rhetorically, I'd ask him 'a chute-less jump?' But what struck me the most was Rob's reaction to my response. Rob never gave any sort of long-winded explanation, but looked at me like I was the one who 'didn't get it.'" Rob simply didn't understand how someone couldn't see how honed a stunt like that would be.

After nearly two years of investigation, dozens of traders were indicted on federal racketeering charges. The illegal practices involved the defrauding of customers by trading after hours, and destroying evidence of losing trades. There were many long and drawn out trials, followed by long and drawn out prison sentences.

"If I would have done even one thing wrong over those 18

months," Rob remarked to Black Death Heid when he realized he had been standing next to an FBI agent for a year-and-a-half, "I would have been busted."

At the conclusion of the investigation, the agent wanted to talk to Rob and 'apologize' by telling him he wasn't dishonest-just doing his job. In fact, under different circumstances, the agent told me, "Rob was the kind of guy I would be friends with and hang out with. But I couldn't contact him as it would have tainted or compromised the investigation and because it would have been frowned upon by my superiors." They never saw each other again.

During his time in Chicago, Rob not only wasn't becoming a king of the market, but he was growing increasingly frustrated because he felt he had no control over what he was trying to accomplish. As I saw it, his insecurities with his lack of success were manifesting themselves in a deterioration of his overall attitude and affected his interaction with the people and world around him. I thought Rob was unhappy with this recognition and was taking it out on the world.

But I also believe this contradicted Rob's basic good-natured make-up. He was still a guy who would show up in a rainstorm to help a friend move furniture.

"Dad's the man!" Rob always said, a sentiment shared wholeheartedly by my brothers and me. To us, Dad was the ultimate role model. To Rob, he was the one guy who, when measured against his basic premise of the strongest wins, stood the tallest. Dad was a father in every good sense of the term, a man of integrity who practiced what he preached his sons, a beloved surgeon and a self-made success. We all wanted to live up to the standards Dad set. Flailing away in the market, while billions in wealth swirled around him, Rob saw himself falling increasingly short of his own expectations.

While in Chicago, Rob became involved with a young lady. Blonde and petite, she was the picture Rob was always painting of the perfect woman. It looked for awhile that they might have a future, but the more Rob talked of quitting his job and travelling to the ends of the earth to climb, the more she saw the futility of luring Rob from his mistress climbing. From a well-to-do family, she proposed Rob take a job with her father in the family business, perhaps in a last-ditch effort to get Rob to settle down.

Rob not only declined, but I believe he viewed this offer as a subtle vote of no confidence in his ability to make it on his own in the market. It might have fallen into the "good work if you can get it" category, but Rob didn't want it that way. Having it handed to him was the same as failure. Even more offensive to Rob was the notion of doing something dishonest to get ahead. Rob's time in the pit literally rubbing elbows with the FBI agent demonstrated how, despite his self-perceived lack of success in the market, he would never compromise his integrity. That would have turned him into the thing he most disliked in others: a poseur.

I was never really sure why Rob wasn't as honed in the bond pit as he was in climbing. I imagine there are many factors which, in combination, make up a successful trader, such as intelligence, analytical skills, foresight, constitution and confidence. Knowing my twin as I did, these were characteristics that I regularly saw demonstrated in Rob's personality. The only thing I can figure is that Rob wasn't quite able to get to that special state of mind necessary to process the swirling chaos of the pit and make sense of it instantaneously in the form of profitable trades. Maybe it was simply just a question of confidence. In the end, the result was Rob becoming even more driven to set, reach and exceed the mightiest challenges he could dream up in the world of climbing. It was his way of compensating.

By my third and final year of law school in 1989, graduation, the bar exam and the cold reality of having to find a law job loomed on the horizon. In consideration of a 12-pack of beer, my friend Mark "Corporate Raider" Rater allowed me access to his word processor. I sent an introductory letter and resume' to every lawyer in the Cheyenne phone book. I also sent letters to the district attorney in every county in Wyoming, Colorado, Utah, Idaho, Nevada and anywhere else that had mountains. I then sat back and waited for the offers to roll in.

What rolled in were rejection letters, all in the same form, complimenting me on my "impressive resume" but informing me, unfortunately, no positions were available-even for one as obviously qualified as myself. All we students got them, or at least all the guys I hung around with. Some of the locals got the same one from the same firm. One time we had a rejection letter party, taking turns reading aloud our favorites in between toasts to our impending collective success. One guy had his room wallpapered with them.

Of the several dozen letters I sent out, I received a grand total of two expressions of interest. I got one from a solo practitioner in Cheyenne with a general practice and one from the district attorney's office in Boise, Idaho. That Christmas break, I went home to Cheyenne to see the family and talk to my prospect. Spiffed up and shaved, resembling little my status as runner- up in the "worst-dressed" category of my class, second only to my good buddy Richard Perez, I presented for my interview.

"So, what are you looking to do?" I am asked by the distinguished, lawyerly gentleman sitting behind his desk wearing a gold University of Wyoming jacket. Old school honed for sure.

"I grew up here. I want to come back, be my own boss and build up a huge practice." "Huge practice" was my Dad's expression.

"Well, I'm a one-man firm with enough work for about one-and-a-half lawyers. If you want, you can use that empty office over there," he offered.

I went home and called Boise, cancelling my interview, as I had "taken another position." Instead, I went skiing, not having to worry about shaving or getting dressed up for another interview.

The day after law school graduation in May, 1989, I cruised westward on I-80, across the vast corn fields and prairies of Nebraska toward Cheyenne, in my rental truck towing my beat-up black Jeep. I had an empty office waiting for me, ready to be filled up with a huge practice. I was excited to begin a new and hopefully rewarding and fulfilling challenge.

During early August each year, in keeping with family tradition, Dad and any of us who could get away made our annual trek to the Tetons or to the Wind River Range in northwest Wyoming. The route in, chosen by Rob after his usual careful study of maps and topographical charts of the area, was always long and in many sections very steep.

"Don't worry Dad," Rob annually assured, "its downhill both ways." A 10-mile hike into the Bridger National Forest led to areas pretty much devoid of people. The scenery was pristine and the climbing spectacular. We didn't do the kinds of experts-only routes Rob preferred, but it wasn't The Great Wall of Evanston either. Rob didn't have The Team with him and though I was always game, my enthusiasm to climb with him and our shared love of heights was way greater than my technical ability. We both knew that and didn't dwell upon it.

The Shark's Nose was a towering, 12,000-foot over-sized spire. Rob asked me if I wanted to climb it with him and, of course, I did.

"Don't worry; we'll take the casual route" he assured me, though I knew the casual route for him was not so casual by my standards.

Rob led the pitches, making it look easy. Straining, I was able to follow, fearing not being able to do it far more than any fall. With Rob, I literally had no fear of falling, just failing to measure up. When we came to a section or move at the upper end of my ability level, I could always hear Rob, even if I couldn't see him above on the belay ledge, offering a steady stream of brotherly encouragement that always included some version of "Come on Junior, you can do it."

Even though I was technically older than my twin by a few minutes, he sometimes good-naturedly referred to me as "Junior" or "Chief." Junior was used in instances when he was trying to encourage me, like when we were climbing, while Chief was more of a mock title. In neither case was I offended. They were more terms of endearment than anything.

Rob was never critical of my climbing and I always put forth my supreme effort not to let him down. I suppose he tolerated climbing easy stuff with me because it was better than not climbing at all. More importantly, for both of us, climbing as twin brothers was something special, something that kept us connected. Regardless of where we lived and what adult-world issues related to jobs and career we faced, we always had climbing. When it was just the two of us on the rope, alone on a massive rock face miles from anywhere, it was, even if only for a short time, a respite from the world.

From the top, Rob suggested we rappel off the front face. The slab sloped steeply down about 25 feet before ending abruptly at a knife edge. Rob suggested I go first.

"Go down to the edge and then jump out as far as you can-but you can't look down-you'll love it I'm sure."

I then realized why Rob had insisted on bringing an extra rope; one for the belay and one for the upcoming "huge free rappel." I backed down to the knife edge and looked up at Rob, grinning on belay.

"Go for it, Chief," he laughed. "Just jump."

I did as Rob suggested, trusting my twin brother completely, as I had in previous years when followed him off the high board at Oglebay Park, the roof in Salt Lake City and the cliffs at Crystal Lake. Here, on the Shark's Nose, he was letting me do the honors. I had supreme confidence in his climbing judgment so I launched over the edge – without looking – and met nothing but rarified air. After gliding down the rope about 40 feet, I involuntarily stopped my descent. Bouncing on the give in the single strand of rope, twisting slowly, I marveled at the sensation of being suspended so high up and so far out in space. It seemed like a thousand feet to the bottom of the cliff face, though the ledge where I would land was only about 100 feet below. Very few ever got a chance for such a thrill. I felt lucky and proud my brother had given me such an opportunity, and trusted me not to screw it up. With Rob on belay, I had no problem leaping without looking if he said so. It was also satisfying to be part of one of Rob's climbing stories back at the campfire.

During the car ride up to the Tetons on another summer trip in 1984, Rob started talking about what he called the "Grand Traverse" – climbing all the major Teton peaks in a single day. He offered no history of why it was called that or how many people had actually done it, but whether there was real history beneath the Grand Traverse or it was something Rob came up with himself, I didn't care; it sounded honed.

The Tetons are perhaps the most photographed mountains in the world. Looking from the Snake River Valley flanking them to the east, it's easy to see why. The main group forms a ring around the jewel of the range, the 13,766-foot Grand Teton, the Teton Glacier and Garnet Canyon, which opens into the valley floor. The range's spectacular relief is accentuated by the lack of foothills. In front sits 12,325-foot Teewinot Mountain, with a tiny pointed summit no larger than a fist. Circling counterclockwise, the East Prong and Mount Owen form the northern arc to the Grand. To the south of the Grand sit the Middle and South Tetons, Cloudveil Dome and Spaulding Peak. Opposite Teewinot and Mount Owen, across the space of Garnett Canyon, the Matterhorn-like Nez Perce completes the circle.

"We'll be on the top of Teewinot at sunrise," Rob explained. "Then we'll do the East Prong and Mount Owen. We'll climb the North Ridge of the Grand and go down the Exum Route to the Upper Saddle between the Grand and the Middle Teton. Then we'll do the Middle and South Tetons and just follow the ridge across to Cloudveil and Nez Perce. The whole thing will take us 14 hours and we'll be back down in time to go to Happy Joe's Pizza for dinner," Rob concluded with his usual casual enthusiasm and confidence.

With two packs, one containing the climbing rope and gear and the other cold weather clothing, Pop Tarts, cookies, water and lemonade, we started up in the moonlight before dawn at 4:00 a.m. On the trail we encountered a black bear sitting just off the path enjoying an early breakfast of berries, undistinguishable from the dark shadows until we were right next to him. Startled, there was no time to do anything but continue past, trying to be as nonchalant as possible. The bear paid us no mind and, as soon as we realized he wasn't interested in adding human flesh to his meal, we relaxed but quickened our pace. The meeting clearly meant more to us than the bear.

As the rising sun painted the dawn sky in brilliant purple, pink and orange above the Wind River Range to the east, we took turns posing, unroped, for photos on the summit of Teewinot, which is too small to accommodate two at a time. Surveying the jagged ridge forming the northern arc of peaks from the East Prong to the Grand Teton, we felt confident we would be able to complete the Grand Traverse as planned.

Next was the East Prong, deceptively close across the span of space from the top of Teewinot. Reluctantly, we had to give up altitude and quickly descended the tower to cross a steep scree field. We headed for the day's second summit up a tight, snow-filled gully that appeared to lead straight to the bare granite tower sparkling in the first rays of the new day.

At first the going was easy; the crusted snow held our weight as we zigzagged upward. As we climbed into the sunshine, the snow softened and we found ourselves swimming in chest -deep snow. We soon realized we were losing valuable time at an increasing rate.

We came upon an overhanging serac that was impossible to scale without ice axes and gear, none of which we had. Rob then realized we'd taken the wrong chute and hit a dead end. The next chute over, we now saw, was clearly the proper route.

We looked at each other, knowing just as clearly that our quest was over, at least for that day. We both kind of shook our heads and almost laughed, and then Rob said something very – very – rare for him.

"Let's just go down, have lunch and play golf with Dad this afternoon,"

I was well acquainted with Rob's overwhelmingly intense drive to finish something – anything, everything – once he started. I knew he'd drilled a hole in his thumb on El Cap so he could keep climbing. I knew how many times he had faced down storms and bad luck to finish a climb – or help a friend move. I knew Rob was no quitter.

I also knew, without doubt, that Rob and I would be back to the Tetons many more times, and that we'd finish the Grand traverse some other time. I knew it in my soul and I saw it in my twin's eyes. At that point, why bother stumbling along on an unnecessary epic? We looked at each other again as we wallowed in the chute. We'd bagged Teewinot, we now knew which chute to climb on the East Prong – and besides, we knew how important it was for Dad to be with us this week each year. We should hang out with him. After all, Dad was The Man, so down we went.

We were a bit more successful on other forays to the Tetons. Since our days at Exum, we'd planned to summit all the Tetons together, though in our tent during these family outings, conversation inevitably ended up being dominated by Rob's next big climbing adventure.

When we were younger, it had been the Grand Teton. As we grew older, it became El Cap and the Wyoming Sheep Ranch, then the desert towers. Eventually, the conversational path to which all things led was K2. There was never any question if Rob would do these climbs, including K2. We also knew from Rob's stories that K2 was the baddest mountain in the world by a mile, even if only the second tallest by a little. There were never any objections or reservations to Rob doing them, either.

We climbed the Grand Teton together during college, doing the 60-foot free rappel off the West Face on the way down. It wasn't as cool as the free rappel off the Shark's Nose, but it was a great way to end a successful assault of the Grand.

Another time, Rob and I set out to do the southern part of the Grand Traverse, starting with the Middle Teton. We made the summit in good order, came down and climbed within 100 feet of the summit of the South Teton before sunrise. Then the weather changed, with clouds moving in to obscure the stars and moonlight that had lit our way to that point. A bolt of lightning struck the summit just above us, sending sparks flying.

"That was so cool – let's get the hell off of here!" Rob said to me with wild eyes. I concurred on both counts and down we went, images of the lightning strike still dancing in our heads, waiting to be recounted that night at the campfire.

The next summer, we again attempted to summit the southern peaks in a single day. This time, we backpacked up Garnet Canyon the afternoon before and camped as high up the canyon as allowed by the Park Service, thus getting the approach over with beforehand.

We spent the night in the tent retelling Dad's stories about The Earl of Alta Vista, kids being kids again. Early the next morning, we set off with Pop Tarts and a single rope. As the sun rose in a crystal clear sky, Rob and I watched from the summit of South Teton. This day looked like it would bring no lightning or weather to foil our grand scheme.

All proceeded according to plan as we followed the main ridge to the summits of Spaulding Peak and Cloudveil Dome. The weather was holding and it was still early. Far below, the Snake River crossed through the valley floor roughly parallel to the stream of traffic building on the Rockefeller Parkway. We were in another world, on top looking down like tiny fish in a giant aquarium looking out. We were at the edge of the cauldron. Rob, of course, was wearing his huge grin.

All that remained was Nez Perce. Roping up, we started up the West Ridge, now fully bathed in sunlight. Ironically, the gorgeous weather was melting the intermittent patches of permanent snow above us, deluging our route with streams and cascading waterfalls. It was quite the picturesque scene but made for extremely dicey climbing conditions. Reluctantly, Rob admitted it was too unsafe to continue - a decision I knew he'd arrived at because it was too much for me, not him. He was more cautious because of me.

We returned to camp fairly dejected, but packed up and were back at the parking lot well before noon. The day wasn't a total failure, as we had together bagged three more of the Tetons together. No big deal, we told ourselves. We knew we'd be back many more times in the future. Eventually, we'd get them all.

Following his week with us, Rob always took off for Eldo or the desert to meet up with The Team to do some real climbing. I didn't know it at the time, but Mom and Dad once had to tell him to go with us first. In his excitement to get out of the city, Rob had apparently been focusing on going straight to hard stuff, which would have bothered me more in terms of how disappointed Dad would have been than in terms of my own disappointment.

Rob realized this too, and quickly relented, though it showed how climbing overshadowed everything in his world. It was a troubling omen on the one hand, but my parents also recognized that Rob being stuck in Chicago 11 months out of the year was made bearable for him only by the opportunity to periodically get away. Ironically, it provided some balance in his life. Or was it a catalyst for supreme imbalance?

In the dichotomy of Rob's world, while he had ever-growing confidence he could meet his expectations in the climbing realm, he was growing less confident about his prospects in the world of career and business. On the flatlands, Rob was forced to do more reading, talking and thinking about climbing than actually climbing. In Chicago, Rob's only climbing choices were driving three hours to a veritable anthill or climbing concrete retaining walls. Inside, the turmoil mounted.

During the summer climbing season of 1990, via the difficult North Ridge, Greg Child made the top of Rob's Great Mountain, K2. Not reaching the summit until just after 8:00 p.m., Child enjoyed the top until 9:00 p.m. before starting down. Stumbling through the bitter cold darkness, his descent became "an all-out epic." Hallucinating, Child imagined himself thawing his hands over a warm campfire. A mere 100 yards from the safety and warmth of his tent, he collapsed. He crawled the final distance.

Had Greg stayed too long on the mountain before heading

down? Why would he spend so much time on the summit at such a late hour?

"In China all time zones are set to Beijing time, so even though K2 is far from Beijing, we ran on that clock. Thus, 9 p.m. means little. We were there late, regardless," Child told me later. "Could it all have gone wrong for us...? Sure."

"In the end, climbing such mountains is an exercise in personal choices, personal selfishness, and personal assumption of risk. One should always assume that the worst is possible. Those who are unwilling to take a great risk will never climb K2. But those who turn around in the name of self-preservation are entirely normal and reasonable," Greg added.

Was Child, a big-time accomplished and respected alpine mountaineer, foolish, crazy, both or just plain honed? Rob and I would say honed.

However those questions are answered, Greg Child was lucky to get off K2 alive.

Rather than refocusing and redoubling his energies on his career, instead Rob began to fixate on an ultimate climbing challenge. It would be something over which he felt he had some measure of control and something which, if successful, would completely overshadow any perceived shortcomings elsewhere.

It was during this time that thoughts of climbing K2 – the supreme mountaineering challenge – began to coalesce. It was also during this time, early in 1992, that fate intervened, in the form of a chance to climb the 20,433-foot Nameless Tower in the Karakoram Range in Pakistan, which looms over the Baltoro Glacier along the approach to K2. Notwithstanding the career opportunities available at Goldman Sachs, it was now decision time. But there was really no decision to make. Rob had already made up his mind.

Rob called April 20, 1992, his "last day of work at Goldman Sachs and his first day away from Chicago forever." His co-workers threw him a going-away party, complete with a cake and presented him a large picture of the Chicago skyline with something written on it by everyone. The comments reflected how Rob's unique-if-twisted sense of humor and outlook on life had grown on those who had been subjected to his unsolicited editorializing on a daily basis:

"Keep your playschool mentality."

"Have a great time defying gravity."

"Good Luck – Girl Scout Troop #1212."

As he packed his car to leave, Rob figured the landlord was going to be pissed that the freezer wasn't defrosted, but he was already late so, in what he called the true spirit of Chicago, but was really in the true spirit of Rob doing as he pleased, he just bolted.

"I could stay in the tropical vacationland of Chicago, slogging to my job downtown every day," Rob said to me, rationalizing out loud, "or I could go climbing in the Karakoram and actually see K2. I'm paying my own way, so who can tell me no?" I had to agree. "How to spend $30,000 and have nothing to show for it except 2,000 pictures?" he concluded only half-jokingly.

As Rob spoke, I couldn't help but detect a slight note of resignation in his tone, even though he was almost giddy with anticipation and determination. It wasn't sad resignation, but more like a sense that he'd heard his destiny calling – and was answering the call.

As Rob set off for his first trip to the Karakoram, I wondered if his trip to the Nameless Tower would be enough to satisfy the demands and expectations he had imposed upon himself. In the back of my mind, I wondered if anything would ever be enough.

Dad and Rob on the Middle Teton summit

On the Middle Teton summit

Chapter IX

"K2 is the ultimate mountain. I have to climb it."
                                    –Rob Slater

  A vast canopy of peaks forms the roof of the world between Asia and India. Most prominent are the Himalaya Range between Nepal and Tibet and the Karakoram, which comprises the border between southern China and Pakistan. As most people know, Mount Everest is Earth's highest mountain, rising 29,028 feet from the Himalaya on the Nepal-Tibet border. In 1923, the great British explorer George Mallory was asked, in the true spirit of sycophantic sports journalism, why he wanted to climb the highest mountain. His response became one of the most famous and oft-repeated quotes in history, "Because it's there."
  In 1953, Sir Edmund Hillary and Nepalese Sherpa Tenzing Norgay became the first to step foot on Everest's summit. Since then, hundreds upon hundreds have followed their famous footsteps. Women, children, double amputees and blind folks have made their way to the summit. Nowadays, each summer season the line of climbers on the West Ridge resembles a conga line of adventure

tourists slogging their way up to the ultimate photo op, dragged along by high-priced guides. During the 2007 summer climbing season alone, more than 500 climbers summited Everest. There was a "reality" TV show chronicling the exploits of various would-be stars and celebrity wannabe climbers. One guy even carried a golf club to the top and drove three balls off the summit. Everest became the ultimate touristie trap.

"Everest is covered with tourists from New Jersey and their garbage," Rob would sneer.

To the west of Everest lies the Khyber Pass, where 23 centuries ago Alexander the Great led his armies in conquest of Asia and the known world. The Hindu Kush, the impenetrable mountain barrier between Afghanistan and Pakistan, flanks the Khyber to the north. Crossing the Khyber to the east, over the route taken by countless explorers, traders, marauders and conquerors since Alexander, leads to the Indus River valley. Following the Indus toward its headwaters leads to the province of Kashmir. There, in one of the most desolate, treacherous and awe-inspiring places on the planet, raises the Karakoram. At its heart, between the Sinkiang Region of China and Kashmir, in what has aptly been christened "The Throne Room of the Mountain Gods," stands the chief god: K2.

Randy "RSL" Leavitt, of the Accelerated Free Fall School which bears his name, had remained a close friend and climbing partner of Rob's for more than a decade. RSL was also friends with and had climbed with Greg Child, a Yosemite big wall climber and accomplished mountaineer. Child had made the top of numerous high altitude peaks in Pakistan, Nepal and Tibet, in addition to his harrowing descent from the summit of K2.

Child and his friend Mark Walford, who had extensive high altitude experience in the Canadian Rockies, had their sights set on a 20,433-foot granite spire in the Karakoram called the Nameless Tower. The two had been to the Nameless Tower in 1989 and were intent on returning to climb it.

Rob got wind of the planned expedition, contacted Greg and, as Greg told me, "inserted himself into the climb." Greg and Mark knew of Rob's reputation and abilities as a climber and figured what he lacked in high altitude mountaineering experience he made up for in enthusiasm, determination and one simple, overriding fact: Rob was honed. Greg and Mark accepted Rob on their team.

The nuts and bolts of putting the trip together had already been taken care of by the time Rob joined the expedition. Greg had done the organizational work, secured the permit for the Nameless Tower from the Pakistani Ministry of Tourism and arranged some sponsorship for the expedition. Coming in near the end of the preparations, Rob's role was limited to that of a climber.

At the beginning of the summer of 1992, the three made their way to Pakistan, travelling by plane to Skardu, the last real outpost of civilization near the entrance to the Karakoram. The path to the Throne Room of the Mountain Gods is the Braldu Valley and the Baltoro Glacier. About halfway in stands the Trango Group, a spectacular collection of knife-edged granite spires surrounded on three sides by glaciers. The Trango towers are one of nature's finest examples of vertical. Reaching more than 20,000 feet into the sky is the Nameless Tower, a spire which dwarfs by orders of magnitude the sandstone monoliths of the desert.

At the trailhead into the Braldu, Rob had his first encounter with the native Balti porters, who were hired to carry the mass of expedition gear to the base of the peak. For Rob, it was just like the pictures he had seen as a kid in *National Geographic*, which sometimes covered Himalayan mountaineering expeditions, complete with glossy photos. Rob enjoyed his interactions with the more outgoing of the natives and soon recognized and grew to respect their toughness and work ethic.

As Rob, Greg and Mark and their antlike procession of porters wound their way along the narrow path into the Braldu Gorge, Rob marveled at the scale. He was in another world, growing increasingly excited with anticipation, even if he didn't outwardly show it, as he considered the grand peaks around him and what waited at the end of the long trail ahead.

Base camp was established near the foot of the Trango Group. Armed with the experience of their previous visit, Greg and Mark had devised a well-thought-out plan of attack and route to pursue up the tower.

Rob, naturally, had his own ideas for the line of ascent and climbing strategies which, at least initially, led to inevitable conflicts and disagreements. Without a doubt, Rob's rather assertive personality played a role in creating a high tension situation, though to be fair, pretty much all climbers at that level share the common trait of intense drive and focus, usually fueled by a bit of ego. It was no surprise then, when Rob, Greg and Mark periodically rubbed each other the wrong way. In the end, Rob acquiesced to Greg and Mark's experience and plan. It was an uncharacteristic show of deference on Rob's part, or perhaps he just had something more important on his mind.

Greg and Mark both noticed how Rob could run hot and cold about things and seemingly switch his focus on and off. At night in the tent, Rob took out his books about the bond market and studied. Greg, who knew Rob from the summers in Yosemite, was struck how Rob had converted himself from a "climbing bum" who lived in a tent and ate out of garbage cans to a guy who knew about and worked in the bond market. As time went by, however, it became apparent to Greg that Rob was losing interest in climbing the Nameless Tower – not necessarily because of the disagreements or conflict between them but because his focus had shifted to a much more imposing challenge a little further up the Baltoro Glacier. Rob simply had to see K2.

The approach to the main tower was a long, steep chasm, chocked with ice and loose rocks. The climbers had to go up very early in the morning before the sun began to loosen the snow and ice that acted as cement to hold the rocks in place. As the three ascended the gully during what was to have been their last trip up before the final summit push, they encountered a barrage of rocks, ranging in size from watermelons to cars, clattering down like deadly rain from above. For all of them, being in the gully with rocks tumbling down around them was quite unnerving.

That evening, the group discussed their situation and plans. They were ready for their summit attempt. The weather was good and they were poised for success. The next morning Rob declared he didn't care about climbing the Nameless Tower and he wasn't going up the mountain again. He summed up his feelings by saying, "Frankly, I don't want to be buried in a shallow grave," referring to the gully and rock fall.

It was dangerous just to get to the route and, moreover, Rob announced it had been his intention all along to see K2 rather than climb the Nameless Tower. This was news to Greg and Mark, who had come to climb the Nameless Tower. For them, K2 had nothing to do with it, and they'd had no idea K2 had been part of Rob's agenda all along.

"You guys finish," Rob concluded, "I'm going to K2 instead."

Greg and Mark simply said "OK" and prepared to go for the Nameless Tower summit without Rob, who had decided to hike the extra four days up the Baltoro to Concordia, where the Upper Baltoro and Godwin-Austen Glaciers converge, to get a look at K2 from a distance of less than 10 miles. He hired a porter to help carry his provisions and set off alone.

When Rob reached Concordia and first saw K2 with his own eyes, he, like the Colonel, was astounded. To Rob, K2 was a special place he'd seen only in pictures and read about in the annals of climbing history. Now, as it stood before him like a living thing, its scale and power and grandeur was unbelievable, even to him, a guy who had spent most of his life hiking around in, climbing and gazing from the summits of grand mountain peaks. Then and there he vowed to himself he would climb K2.

Meanwhile, Greg and Mark summited the Nameless Tower, though they almost died in the process. Near the top, a huge chunk of the mountain the size of a building broke free, disintegrating right next to them, obliterating their route and forcing them to descend on a different line. The mass of rock thundered down the spire to the valley floor, creating a cloud of dust that blotted out the sun. Those who witnessed the spectacle from below were amazed that Greg and Mark had lived through it.

Not long after Greg and Mark returned to their base camp, Rob arrived from his trip up the glacier to K2. Rob may have experienced some kind of personal epiphany in the shadow of K2, but Greg and Mark were so preoccupied that they didn't notice.

"At that point," Greg recalled, "we were in our own worlds."

Greg and Mark were overwhelmed, not only with the exhaustion of their grueling summit ascent, but with the emotional aftermath of their near-death ordeal. They were simply too tired and spent to worry about, fight with or engage Rob. On the other hand, Rob was preoccupied as well. But for him it was not about looking back to recent events which distracted him – it was about looking ahead. The only thing on Rob's mind was K2.

For some reason, I naively figured once I graduated law school I would automatically find myself a polished, financially successful attorney. In reality, I had a fancy diploma but no clue about the workings of the real world of law or business. Rather, I had to focus on the mundane matters of supporting myself and preparing for and passing the bar exam. Having brilliantly negotiated the princely wage of $10 an hour, I was shown to an empty office and basically told to practice law. I worked 10 hours a day and then drove an hour to Laramie each night for a three-hour bar review course. Upon my return home, I had to study. Even though I had done respectably well grade-wise in law school, it seemed the only thing the review was teaching me was how little I knew. At the end of July, I took the two-day exam-and passed. I was now a lawyer, but by title only.

After a few months, I was told I worked too many hours to be paid hourly. After all, even at ten bucks an hour, 50 hours a week is $2,000 a month. That was too much for someone not generating nearly that much revenue. Instead, I was made a partner, responsible for half the overhead and entitled to half the profit, if any. I made $900 my first month.

Hanging out in the less-than-lawyerly-respectable local taverns and establishments of ill repute, I passed out my business cards and ended up developing a criminal defense practice. Representing drunk drivers, drug dealers, child molesters, thieves and murderers, however, lost its luster. Eventually, I grew tired of this, though I liked helping my clients and the problem-solving aspect of practicing law.

Slowly, I tried to work my way up the food chain, undertaking the study of limited liability companies, business structuring and asset protection. After all, hardworking, legitimate businessmen and their families deserved to enjoy the fruits of their labors. Here was an area of law and an endeavor I could appreciate and one that coincided with the political philosophy I had cultivated, or stumbled upon, during college.

Back home, Rob talked about his Nameless Tower trip not in terms of the Nameless Tower but in terms of getting to see K2. I had to ask him specifically about the climb to get him off the subject of

K2, to which he would quickly and inevitably return.

"I don't care how many times I have to go back, I'm gonna climb it," Rob declared of the object of his now-all-encompassing dream. While Everest, by Rob's observation, was covered with tourists and their garbage, "K2 is covered with the dead bodies of guys who tried to climb it. K2 is the ultimate mountain. I have to climb it," he said with a combination of determination and reverence.

Following Rob's trip to the Nameless Tower, the more I thought about it the more I realized how what transpired helped provide a clearer view of what was going on in Rob's mind and soul. The fact he brought books about the bond market demonstrated that, whether he liked it or not, Rob had to keep his eye on the ball career-wise. Rob knew he was coming back to the real world and, regardless of his grand K2 scheme; he would for some time have to rejoin and remain in the regular-folk workforce.

The notion of Rob pressing on his climbing companions his ideas of the best line of ascent on the tower, despite the fact they had actually climbed on the tower before, in and of itself wasn't too far out of character. Rob having strong opinions and trying to advance them vehemently was not breaking news, but Greg Child and Mark Walford were the kind of true, big-time high-altitude alpinists Rob himself aspired to be. Having to acquiesce may have made Rob start to stew, just like he had done years before on the long ride home from the Titan with Bill Feiges. Back then, Rob vowed to become a desert tower climber and surpass anything Feiges – or anyone else – would do, such as becoming the first person to climb all the Fisher Towers.

For Greg Child, his 1990 ascent of K2 marked the culmination of an extensive high altitude alpinist career. Rob decided he would do first what most alpinists save for later in their big-mountain careers, and what they consider to be the zenith of climbs – K2. Rob would thumb his nose at convention, just as he had when he learned to skydive by shunning traditional training for the Leavitt Accelerated Free Fall School and the Black Death Heid BASE Jumping School.

Was Rob too afraid of the rock fall in the gully to continue? I doubt it. As far as the Nameless Tower was concerned, Rob simply felt the risks, for him, outweighed the benefits on that particular climb, especially in light of his overarching focus on, and the close proximity of, K2. It was another of several factors that led Rob off on his own up the Baltoro Glacier to see K2. The summit of K2 became Rob's promise to himself, the fulfillment of which would surpass anything he had done in climbing and, perhaps just as important, compensate for the frustration of what he thought of as his failures in life outside of climbing.

When he returned from the Karakoram late in the summer of 1992, Rob moved back to Boulder and secured a job as an investment banker in Denver. His official position was vice president, a title reserved for pretty much everyone below the CEO and above the bank tellers. It was the cut-throat world of big city banking at one of the country's largest banks, but where employees were regularly required to undergo sensitivity and diversity training. Rob put it in proper perspective:

"It's pussy compared to The Pit in Chicago, but I'm right by Eldo."

For me, it was great to have Rob back in the area, so I could see him more often. Mom and Dad were glad not only that he was nearby but that he had a job and once again lived in the West where he could pursue his career and climbing with some reasonable balance.

Each weekday morning, Rob got up early and headed for the Park 'n Ride lot, where he filed onto the bus for the 45-minute commute to downtown Denver. Each weekend, he got up even earlier to go climbing. Sometimes he just went to Eldo, riding his bike the seven miles to the canyon walls. Sometimes he went to Longs Peak, where he would do several routes up the Diamond before running or skiing back down. On special occasions, he got up at 2:00 a.m. and drove five hours to the southern Utah desert to climb the sandstone spires.

There was always a weekend adventure to plan, a new route to put up. All were discussed at length with the family, The Team or anyone else who would listen. But there was always the greatest trip of all, the subject to which all conversations ultimately led.

Anyone who knew Rob even casually during the preceding decade knew the American 1995 K2 Expedition came to represent his obsession with – and quest to summit – the Savage Mountain.

Just as all kids want to go to Disneyland and all surfers dream of being in the Bonzai Pipeline off Hawaii's North Shore, all climbers have probably wondered what it would be like to conquer the world's most demanding and dangerous mountain. But not all kids' parents are able or willing to take them to Disneyland. Hawaii is a long, expensive plane ride away and the Karakoram is even farther away-and far more deadly. So, for most, idle chat of great, death-defying adventure is just that: idle chat. And just as daydreams are rudely ended by a new assignment from the boss, and pleasant night dreams are inconveniently interrupted by the alarm clock, reality always seems to rear its ugly head when it comes to lifelong dreams and plans.

Rob's K2 dream, however, was not about to be ended, interrupted or sidetracked by reality, at least not before he had summited. Upon his return from his first trip to Karakoram, he began talking to Thor Kieser, who had organized and led an earlier expedition to K2 that included Charley Mace, a climber from Boulder. After meeting Charley, who had summited K2, Rob called his new friend "the baddest motherfucker in Boulder."

Since Thor had been through the process before, Rob wanted Thor to help him get another successful K2 expedition together. The first thing they did was submit the paperwork to obtain a permit from the Pakistani Ministry of Tourism to lead a party up the Abruzzi Ridge. Then, while they waited for their permit, they recruited climbers, gathered gear, and organized a an almost military movement of dozens of people – from climbers to trekkers to native porters – along with tons of food and gear to one of the remotest spots on the globe. When their permit was finally granted for the summer of 1995, they were ready: Rob would get the chance to seize his ultimate mountaineering prize.

"Richie, you have to go to K2 with me," Rob started insisting soon after, whenever we were alone.

"There's no way I could climb that thing," I responded, stating the obvious. We'd talked in the past about me going on various trips with Rob, but for the most part, when it came to the serious stuff I reluctantly considered myself an outsider. To be honest, I hadn't really given the idea of actually going to K2 much thought.

"I know, but you could go to the base camp," Rob cajoled,

pressing his argument with the vehemence that always surrounded anything associated with K2. "It'll be so cool. You *have* to see it."

I'd always wanted to do El Cap or a desert tower with Rob, and he always said he could drag me up an easy route, but that remained something we talked about but had yet to follow through with. Trekking to the K2 base camp, when I did start thinking about it, was something I could do-and the thought of going all the way to the Karakoram in Pakistan with my twin, on his expedition, got my gears grinding. Here was an opportunity to really be a part of one of Rob's adventures-his greatest adventure of all, no less.

Subconsciously, I knew it was a chance on another level for me as well. I had the same insecurities of underachievement as my brother. I had made it into and through law school and was my own boss with my own law practice, but still felt I had fallen far short of Rob and my mutual expectations. Here was a chance to do something special, if only as a peripheral participant but, at least initially, I pussied out.

"I would love to go but there are two small problems," I sniveled. "One, it's too expensive; and two, I can't take two months off from my law practice. Moreover, it was a logical, well-reasoned, rationalized response to get me off the hook for participating in my twin's obsession.

"Fuck that," Rob said. "You have to go, Richie. We need to talk Dad into going too.

Money wasn't the real issue; it wouldn't make any difference in the grand scheme of things. I could also leave work for a bit, because I was my own boss. I knew I needed to go with Rob to K2. I had to be there with him and for him. My mind was made up. Rob and I were going to K2 together.

"We have to talk Dad into going too," was always part of Rob's mantra every time he brought up the subject of me going with him to K2 – and I always agreed. It would be great to have Dad along because, for one thing, it would be the ultimate Slater Boys mountain trip, far surpassing the Tetons or Winds. When Rob discussed it with Dad, however, he got an unequivocal answer.

"There's no way I'm going to K2," he said. "That's not a trip for me. I'll only slow you down. Besides," he reminded Rob, "one of us has to work."

Dad knew "of the high percentage of guys who didn't make it down from K2," as he characterized it after reading a book given to him by a doctor friend that detailed some of K2's deadly, hideous history. With respect to the danger of K2, Dad told me Rob "was very much aware of what was going on, but he's committed to going."

In fact, Rob had once said to Dad, "Even if you and Mom tell me not to go, I'm still going to go."

So they didn't. Dad in particular didn't want to turn it into a family fight – or in any way prevent Rob from trying to fulfill his climbing dreams and ambitions.

"He was going," Dad concluded, "and if he didn't he would be forever sulking around about it."

Most importantly, however, Mom and Dad never told Rob he shouldn't go to K2 because they both believed he'd make the top and come home safely, just as he always had.

While I didn't have to ask permission at work, Rob did. He went to his boss and, in all earnestness and sincerity and with a straight face asked for a six-month leave of absence.

"I would like to take six months or so off to go climb K2 in Pakistan," Rob stated matter-of-factly. "Depending on the weather and how things go, it might take longer. When I get back sometime next fall, I'd like to have my job back. I have to climb it."

"Six months off to go mountain climbing?" his boss screamed. "I'd love to take six months off to go on a vacation. Are you serious? No fuckin' way!"

The guy just didn't get Rob, or K2, or Rob and the whole K2 thing, and Rob wasn't going to try to explain it to him. Instead, he rephrased his request in terms the guy might better understand.

"If I was going to alcohol rehab, you'd give me the time off and save my job. Maybe when I come back after summiting K2, I'll have my brother the lawyer sue your ass."
Startled, this was indeed a language the bank understood. Immediately, the guy rethought his position, perhaps deciding that the better part of valor was in fact discretion.

"When you get back, give us a call and we'll see if we can find a spot for you."

Rob had no intention of ever suing the bank or anyone else for that matter and neither did I. Neither did he have any qualms about his employer not holding his job for the better part of a year while he went off on his personal quest. It was just his politically incorrect way of pointing out what he considered to be the idiocy of the bank pretending to be so "sensitive" to "diversity" while doling out preferential treatment to some, but not others. In fact, his idle threat was a joke made simply because his boss had so rudely dismissed his request. I thought his stunt was honed. In truth, Rob didn't care whether he had a job waiting for him upon his return or not. There would be plenty of time to worry about that later. Rob and I were going to K2 and that was all that mattered.

Dad and Rob

Breakfast, lunch and dinner of champions

Chapter X

> "And so it is turning
>   The Great sun is coming up
>   The sun of a great day
>   In the five colors
>   May nothing change
>   May Luck Remain
>   May Everything Bloom…"
>   –First entry, Rob Slater's K2
>   Journal, May, 1995

Rob kept a journal of his journey to K2, which began with the phrase "Last day of Work." Rob believed quitting his job heightened his commitment to climb K2 and helped him focus. Maybe this was just another rationalization that mundane conventions such as being expected to have a job didn't apply to him. So on Saturday, May 6, 1995, as he began his new life as an unemployed soon-to-be summitter of K2, he felt ready.

The preceding February, Rob was in the Canadian Rockies

climbing Slipstream, a 3,000-foot-high ice route he had tried but failed to scale several time before. Pressing on as the day waned, he finally emerged through the narrow couloir at the top. Victory was short-lived as, in a seeming instant, darkness closed upon Rob and his climbing partner. During one of the longest nights of his life, Rob paced around the summit, pounding his and his partner's chest in a vain attempt to stay warm. Marveling at the Northern Lights as they blinked, shimmered and danced in the black sky above, Rob, wearing only a light jacket, ran in place and huddled with his partner as the cold slowly invaded his toes. When dawn arrived, the result was a case of severe frostbite of several of Rob's toes.

In the ensuing weeks, barely able to walk as successive layers of dead, blackened skin sloughed off in excruciatingly painful fashion, it became apparent that Rob's upcoming quest for K2 was in jeopardy. If he couldn't walk, how could he even get to K2, much less climb it? As Rob convalesced, he pondered the stark reality that he might not even be able to go to K2.

"For the first time in all the years I had known Rob, I detected a note of mortality in his voice and demeanor," his old buddy Hammer recalled. What Hammer didn't realize was that it was actually only the second time Rob had demonstrated even the slightest feeling of mortality in the climbing realm. Eight summers prior, Rob was on Scorched Earth with RSL Leavitt. On an early part of the climb, Rob was leading a pitch. In a completely uncharacteristic show of self-doubt, Rob backed off.

"I don't have it any more," he lamented to his stunned friend.

RSL ended up leading most of the rest of the pitches, with Rob following. Scorched Earth was a two-man undertaking, and one of the most heinous and demanding routes ever put up on El Capitan. Rob's bout with self-doubt while completing Scorched Earth showed that, even at what he perceived to be his worst, he was still more honed than the vast majority of climbers at their best.

As RSL said later, "whatever he thought he lost he apparently found again," as his Fisher Tower achievements and most of his accomplishments "on the res" came long after he "didn't have it any more."

Rob's doubt about missing out on K2 was short-lived and, in usual Rob fashion, his determination prevailed. Soon, Rob was not only back on his feet but again immersed in his training regimen for K2. By the time departure day for the Karakoram arrived, the Slipstream frostbite ordeal was just another climbing story, overshadowed completely by thoughts and talk of K2.

Following the tragedies of 1986 through the summer climbing season of 1994, no less than 49 expeditions made their attempt for one of mountaineering's premier prizes. Groups of Americans, Poles, Japanese, Austrians, Basques, Swiss, Italians, Germans, Spaniards, Brits, New Zealanders and several international teams all lined up along the moraine under the shadow of the Gilkey Memorial. They attacked the summit from all angles, as well as the classic Abruzzi Ridge route. Some were repelled by bad weather. Some just couldn't make it. Fewer claimed the prize. As the summer of 1995 began, after nearly a century of attempts, a mere 111 climbers had made the summit. Through falls, avalanches, cerebral edema and hideous weather, K2 had claimed 39 lives. It was a less-than-encouraging statistic to consider when planning a summer vacation. The mountain of dreams was also a mountain of death.

"K2 – I have totally obsessed about it like I have nothing else. I feel totally sure I will make the summit and return. I also hope this climb will change his life for the better," Rob wrote in the first entry of his K2 journal on May 6, 1995. Rob understood Mom and Dad, along with many of his friends, were concerned about him trying something so obviously dangerous, but he felt since he didn't have kids, or, as he saw it, anything for that matter, it was hard for them to understand.

The approval of the initial permit application led to requests for numerous kinds of follow-up forms. There were forms detailing who would be climbing and on what route up the mountain. There was a form for identifying the trekkers and specifying their destination, which for Rob's expedition was the base camp. An American agent for the expedition, who would be Rob, as well as a Pakistani liaison officer, had to be identified and properly appointed. The route and itinerary of the party into, through and then out of the country had to be proposed and approved. The mountain of paperwork, it seemed, would grow as large as K2 itself.

Rob, like any other citizen, had occasional run-ins with the bureaucracy back home in the states and entered the K2 permitting process with an attitude of healthy skepticism. He did, however, hold out the hope that along the way he would encounter some Pakistani government officials who might somehow relate to the importance of the expedition from Rob's perspective and view the undertaking as something more than an exercise in shuffling paperwork. Though he liked to gripe about bureaucrats and government in general, Rob accepted and respected the Pakistanis' point of view concerning their need to protect and responsibly manage their great national treasure K2. But like the Navajos and their sacred desert towers, Rob had no intention of ever letting anyone or anything stand in his way. He couldn't just sneak up to K2 in the dead of night, climb it and steal away without anyone even knowing he had been there, so if he had to fill out forms in quadruplicate, he would comply. Rob also believed that once he got on the mountain, it would be up to him and him alone.

As much as he viewed climbing K2 as a personal challenge, Rob understood he needed a team of climbers with him to have a realistic summit chance. Though he harbored dreams of great alpine solo ascents of the 8,000-meter giants, he went into the K2 expedition undertaking intent, if not entirely content, upon climbing it as part of a team.

Rob and Thor knew many climbers and, as they began their preparations, word got out through the climbing grapevine about their plans for K2. They would need a doctor for the expedition and Rob knew Mike Toubbeh from his Chicago days. Toubbeh was then living in the Pacific Northwest and, through him, word made it to Bend, Oregon and Scott Johnston, who promptly signed on. Scott was a mountaineer who had also been an Olympic-caliber swimmer and cross-country skier. Jack Roberts and Kevin Cooney, experienced climbers from Boulder, heard the word and expressed interest in going. Thor knew Richard Celsi, a southern California college professor who had been up the Baltoro to the Gasherbrum group with him in 1993. While there, Celsi had a good look at K2 and wanted to go back. Rob and Celsi became friends over the phone as they talked regularly about the planning and progress of the trip.

The original plan was for Thor to spearhead the organizing and leading of the expedition, with Rob helping. Thor, however, for personal reasons not having to do with the expedition and without drama, decided to withdraw in the early part of 1994. By then, climbers such as Toubbeh and Jack Roberts were committed, so Rob decided he would take over leadership of the expedition himself. Though it was not his original intent to end up as the logistical leader, it was task Rob willingly accepted rather than scrap the whole trip.

During the fall of 1994, Celsi was in the Himalaya to climb Cho Oyo, the world's fifth highest peak. During his acclimatization process, hiking in towards the Mount Everest base camp, Celsi met a British woman named Alison Hargreaves. Alison was intent on being the first woman to climb the three tallest mountains without oxygen. Celsi, with Rob's assent, invited Alison to join the K2 expedition. Another Brit, Alan Hinkes, was in the Himalaya that fall with Alison. He also wanted to go to K2 and contacted Rob, who readily agreed.

Once the climbing team and the route were confirmed, Rob began to focus on the nuts and bolts of organizing and outfitting the expedition. Before then, he had travelled to the base of K2 and began his ascent on the never-ending snow slopes, gullies, chimneys, chutes and faces of the Abruzzi Ridge countless times in his mind. He had even been there in person, albeit only briefly, during his trip to the Nameless Tower. Now, armed with that experience and with official permission for an expedition, Rob began to visualize in minute detail every aspect of the trip from start to finish.

On the walls were tacked numerous articles from climbing magazines about K2. Glossy photos from the base camp, along with views from the Abruzzi looking up the route and down to rivers of ice and sea of peaks below adorned every room. They served as a constant reminder, lest one was necessary, of Rob's destination. Books and maps of K2 and the Karakoram could also be found in each room, with dog-eared pages testifying to his dedication to his studies.

When the intrepid Duke of the Abruzzi visited the Throne Room of the Mountain Gods in 1909, he surveyed the great pyramid of K2 in search of the most accessible route up, finally settling on the southeast ridge. Today, known as the Abruzzi Ridge, it forms the border between China to the north and Pakistan to the south and is the preferred route for many K2 expeditions.

An assault on a high altitude peak by is done in a series of stages. From a base camp at a strategic spot on the final approach or lower part of the mountain, a series of camps are established at progressively higher altitudes. Climbers ferry up supplies and gear, acclimatizing themselves as they spend more time on the upper portions of the mountain. As this occurs, nature has a way of separating the weaker members of the group, as climbers carry loads to increasing altitudes. From the highest camp, the final push for the summit is launched by those whose stamina and determination have allowed them to remain.

From the northwest, the Godwin-Austen Glacier sweeps south along the base of K2. The glacial moraine known as the Strip, at 16,000 feet, or 5,000 meters, is the traditional site for climbing expedition base camps – 2,000 meters higher than the maximum effective operating altitude for a rescue helicopter.

A couple of miles above the Strip, the moraine joins the ice field leading to the upper reaches of the Godwin-Austen Glacier. Another mile up, a rib of the Southeast Ridge rises from the ice. This marks the beginning of the Abruzzi Ridge and the site of Rob and his expedition's advanced base camp, at an elevation of 6,000 meters, just under 17,000 feet.

By 6,000 meters, fit, unacclimatized humans are unable to concentrate and become confused. Above advanced base rises the mountain proper. From here, the actual climbing begins.

Although Rob's thoughts invariably focused on thrill and anticipated exhilaration of being high on the Abruzzi Ridge, he had to begin with the more mundane components of his responsibilities. Rob began with a notebook. On the first page was the heading "Barrels." Underneath, in numbered succession, the contents and weight of each was listed. On El Cap, the longest routes were 3,000 feet. The Abruzzi Ridge was more than 10,000 feet – two miles in length. It would take a mountain of camping, climbing and high altitude gear to climb the mountain. It would take a mass of gear and effort just to get to K2. The more he worked through the details, the more Rob realized how much there was to do.

The Abruzzi's lower snow slopes rise steeply like smooth white sandstone canyon walls above frozen roiling and foaming river rapids of the Godwin-Austen glacier. Not until a climber has stepped foot on these slopes does he truly begin to comprehend the immensity of K2. In the early morning, before the sun softens the snow, climbers can enjoy relatively easy going along a trail broken by those who have gone before. Later in the day, the top layer of snow turns to slush, making every step a chore as climbers wade up the steep incline feeling like they are wearing lead boots. During these times, avalanches become more frequent, as sections of the upper snow layers give way to gravity and sweep down the slope towards the glacier below. A half mile up, where, for the first time, snow and ice give way to hard, dark rock, a spot is selected for Camp I. Here, at an altitude above 19,000 feet, a small platform is cleared upon which to lash tents, where climbers can spend their first nights on the mountain and begin the acclimatization process.

How Rob started packing showed something about his mindset. The first two barrels contained only ropes, including a dozen 50- and 100-meter lengths. In the next several, he put tents, extra tent poles, sleeping bags and insulated pads for warmth as well as comfort. There were portable stoves and the fuel to power them for cooking meals and melting snow for drinking water. The climbers needed parkas, thermal underwear, or base layers, along with hats, gloves, sunglasses, goggles, socks, boots, over-boots and gaiters to ward off the bitter mountain weather. There were even down suits, which resembled tailored sleeping bags, for the extreme cold Rob knew they would encounter. They had to bring a variety of backpacks, not only for the long hike to base camp but for specialized purposes on the ridge. The big ones would be used for hauling loads while the smaller, less cumbersome packs would be worn during difficult technical climbing and on the greatly anticipated summit day.

Above Camp I the route steepens, ascending through gullies between the rocks filled with ice and snow. Ropes are fixed along the way to allow safer and more efficient movement as the climbers carry equipment and food to stock the higher camps. When the weather cooperates, the ropes remain exposed alongside way, providing protection as the climbers carry equipment and food to stock the higher camps and allowing them to move up and down the mountain with greater safety and efficiency. Just above 21,000 feet, climbers encounter the Doll House Chimney just below the icy, 100-foot vertical chute known as House's Chimney, first negotiated by Bill House of the 1938 American K2 Expedition. With the aid of fixed ropes and ladders, climbers emerge from House's Chimney to find the route slightly less steep. Here, at 6,700 meters, nearly 22,000 feet, another platform is cut from the snow to establish Camp II. By 7,000 meters, fit, unacclimatized humans begin to lose consciousness.

For Rob, the most enjoyable task was determining and procuring all the climbing gear. In addition to the ropes, tents and clothing, he and the climbers would need ice axes, hammers, crampons, jumar sets and a wide range of ice screws and tools used for protection instead of conventional pitons. Pickets to mark the route, head lamps, ski poles and countless carabiners were also added to the lists. With the certainty of encountering falling ice and rock, helmets were a must, as they had been when Rob climbed the desert towers to protect himself from the dried mud and rock which regularly rained down upon him as he belayed his partner from below. The days of snide comments about helmets were long past – unless, of course, they were strapped to the heads of gumbies and touristies.

From Camp II, the route again steepens as climbers toil towards the Black Pyramid, a distinctive pyramid-shaped buttress 1,200 feet high. Its near-vertical cliffs are often covered with giant slabs of unstable snow which combined with the rarified air at 24,000 feet, makes the Black Pyramid the most technically demanding climbing on the route. Overall, the Abruzzi Ridge rises at an average pitch angle of 45 degrees, interspersed with vertical sections of extremely difficult rock and ice climbing. At the top of the Black Pyramid, the route joins the southeast ridge proper, where Camp III is placed a mile and a half above advance base camp.

Far below, the Godwin-Austen Glacier flows southward toward Concordia like a giant muddy river of ice to become the Baltoro. Far above, the summit looms somewhere above the clouds at 8,611 meters, just below the normal cruising altitude of commercial jetliners, obscured from view by yet more snow slopes, ice, serac and cliffs.

There were also a host of miscellaneous items which had to be anticipated but which didn't necessarily come to mind until the details of living high in the mountains for several months were played out in Rob's mind over and over. These included chairs, shovels, cooking utensils, water pumps and filters, batteries, various bags and even several rolls of duct tape. Rob used a seemingly endless number of lists that he revised constantly. He also recognized that no matter what he did and what he brought, something would inevitably be omitted.

A huge aspect of provisioning the expedition was figuring out how to feed everybody. While he knew from his previous trip that perishable items such as vegetables and chapatis, a tortilla-like dietary staple of the area, could be purchased in-country on the way to the trailhead, many items wouldn't be available and had to be procured stateside. One barrel contained 70 pounds of "Gu," a protein gel that came in small individual packets. Two barrels contained nothing but protein bars. In another were 20 cans of chicken, 50 cans of tuna, 10 bags of hard candy and 20 bags of instant gravy. The next barrel contained 80 packets of soup, 20 jars of salsa, 60 packets of hot chocolate and Pop Tarts. There were barrels filled with peanut butter and jelly, dried fruit and beans, more Pop Tarts, Ramen noodles, tomato sauce, coffee and candy bars. One whole barrel had 47 pounds of spuds. But it would be up to Rasul, the expedition cook who accompanied Rob to the Nameless Tower, to make sense-and meals-of it all. The family and I joked to Rob that instead of going to so much trouble securing all the different food, he should hit the local Arby's and pick up about 5,000 roast beef sandwiches.

Human bodies function best at sea level, because the atmospheric pressure allows oxygen to saturate the blood at nearly 100 percent. The higher the altitude above sea level, the lower the atmospheric pressure – and the amount of available oxygen. At 5,000 meters, the height of the K2 base camp, there is only half the amount of available oxygen as at sea level. At 7,500 meters, the body cannot digest food and sleeping becomes extremely difficult.

Amazingly, the human body can adapt to these conditions over the course of several days or weeks, compensating for the reduced oxygen and air pressure. Once in The Death Zone, however, the air pressure and amount of available oxygen drop to about one-third of sea level, and human bodies simply cannot acclimatize, so remaining at this altitude results in a shut-down of bodily functions, cognitive abilities and, ultimately, death. In the rarified air, every step is a chore and even simple decision making and problem solving is a challenge.

Camp IV is dug into the side of the mountain on the Abruzzi Spur right at the start of The Death Zone, and seems closer to outer space than the earth below. It is from here that the final 2,000-2,500-foot push for the summit is launched.

So by design, partial default and owing to the vast distances separating the expedition members prior to meeting at the airport for the flight to Pakistan, Rob undertook the monumental task of organizing and outfitting the expedition. For the most part, this was accomplished from his Boulder apartment. Everything was stockpiled in his spare bedroom and a rented storage garage and included a small mountain of Mint Milanos packages stowed along with the rest of the gear.

Once the gear and food were secured, Rob had to marshal all of it, along with the people going, and get everything and everybody to the K2 base camp on the other side of the world. He also had to figure out how much it would cost and, importantly, how to pay for it. A budget was prepared, which itemized everything from airline tickets, porter wages and those little flags. Then, ala the Duke of the Abruzzi himself, funds were set aside for making "necessary donations" to various officials and bureaucrats along the way. Rob used all the connections he had made over the years to solicit sponsors to contribute funds or at least some equipment or clothing. Little by little, things came together.

In addition to organizing and packing all the expedition's gear in the dozens of blue plastic barrels to be hauled by Balti porters up the length of the Baltoro Glacier, Rob had to be in shape for the ardors of the Abbruzi Ridge. Climbing his way into shape was the preferred method, but wasn't possible with so much to do, even though his days weren't burdened by work and commuting. Rob developed a number of simple activities to get and stay in shape. If he didn't have time to climb, he might just go for a quick run, wearing a pack filled with gallon-sized water jugs. If he couldn't even do that, he might just do 1,000 finger-tip push-ups and pull-ups, and 1,000 sit-ups too. It was cool to watch him do one-armed, two-finger pull-ups on the trim piece above a door. In Mom and Dad's house in California, there was a spot on the exposed roof trusses in the garage covered with climbing chalk where Rob did full crunches, by the thousands.

With the indulgence of the weather and the mountain gods, climbers make their way through the upper reaches of the mountain. Just below the 27,000-foot level, they encounter another seemingly insurmountable obstacle in the form of a giant, overhanging serac of snow and ice. This is the crux of the summit day's climb, through a steep, narrow chute known as the Bottleneck, perhaps the most technical Death Zone climbing in the world. Climbers emerge from the Bottleneck to face a traverse left across yet another snowfield to avoid the serac's giant overhangs until, at long last, they reach the final 500-foot-long snow slope below the summit.

"I think of the summit constantly. What was it going to take? How deep will I have to dig?" Rob wrote as he went about his preparations. While he believed he was going to summit, at that point the crux seemed to be just getting there. "Oh well," he added, "I'll reach the top so the tribulations along the way are really insignificant."

There were many goodbyes to say. Al "Poncho" Torrisi cooked an Italian feast with Hammer, now married with two daughters, and much of the rest of the Team. They were already planning the victory party at Hammers' upon his return. Hammer's wife Melissa cried when she said good bye. Rob was very touched she was so concerned. He had to make sure to come back. The summit was important but was it worth his life?

"NO WAY," he wrote in his journal later that night. "I have a lot to live for. Seems strange to confront these concerns, but K2 is a dangerous mountain."

There was a dinner with Charley Mace, who had summited K2 three summers prior. Rob envied Charley in the sense that he had "already done K2. He doesn't seem to place as much significance on the event as I do, however," Rob noted.

Rob had a last dinner with Mike O'Donnell, his El Cap partner and another talk with Hammer's wife, Melissa.

"I really need to come home safely but I don't seem so worried," he wrote. "I guess I just am going on my instincts- it feels good so confidence is there. Great things are in store for me this summer. I'm actually looking forward to having done K2 and getting on with the rest of my life. I feel as though things will somehow work better when I get home after I have climbed K2."

But in the back of my mind, and likely in Rob's as well, the question remained if K2 would truly prove to be Rob's ultimate conquest, or just another challenge along the road to some greater thrill.

There was also a send-off party from work. In truth, it was a very good group of people with whom Rob had enjoyed working. They had a big cake with a picture of K2 on it along with a Pakistani flag and photo of K2. He explained the process of climbing K2 at least 10 times, feeling it psyched him up to talk about it and increased his conviction to make the top.

Rob believed that the next time he was in Boulder, it would be as someone who'd climbed K2. His excitement grew as the start of his trip approached, but he also knew he couldn't get worked up about anything.

"I have to focus on K2," he said repeatedly. "I have to concentrate on the summit. Climbing is all in the head and K2 will be the same. I know I can do it."

At last, on May 22, Rob had the expedition gear packed into a rented truck and was ready to head for Los Angeles to meet up with the rest of the expedition and leave for K2. He took off in good spirits, feeling like he would be back all too soon. In keeping with tradition, he ate at Taco Johns in Glenwood Springs, Colorado, then drove until midnight before stopping to sleep in his rig on the roadside.

"I awoke at 6:00 a.m. in the Desert! Oh to have Hammer and Al and a truck full of gear!" he wrote in his journal. But there would be lots of time for that when he returned after the summit of K2. He enjoyed seeing the Monument Valley Towers and especially Eagle Rock. "I'll never be there enough even though I'll see it a thousand more times. I had breakfast at the Amigo-Huevos, which were good but not as good as the Navajo Taco's. #1 Grandpa wasn't there, nor was our favorite waitress. I was at first going to skip it and hit the K-Store, but what's the hurry? Better to enjoy myself along the way because this is a once-in-a-lifetime trip that leads to the summit of K2," Rob concluded.

Three days later, Rob said goodbye to Mom and Dad at their house in San Diego.

"I hope they don't worry too much – but I'm sure I'll be back safely soon enough," he wrote.

In this respect, it was like so many other trips he had taken. Rob recognized the danger inherent in these trips and acknowledged K2 was more dangerous than the rest, but it wasn't a solo of El Cap or a parachute jump into a narrow canyon. I believe my parents took solace in this fact-or at least they tried to.

For me, things were much simpler. I perceived no real danger to myself. I was just hiking to the base camp at the foot of the mountain. As I saw it, the most dangerous aspect of the trip involved leaving the security of the United States and going to a Third World country on the other side of the globe. Being miles into the mountains with Rob involved no danger whatsoever in my mind. As to the impending danger Rob faced on K2, I cannot honestly say it caused me to worry. If my parents took solace in the fact that it was just another dangerous Rob adventure, I didn't need to. To me it was a given that Rob would make it. He always did.

As Rob hustled to complete last-minute preparations, I got my passport in order, my duffel bag packed and I was ready to go. I offered to help Rob do whatever I could, but being nearly 100 miles away I was limited from a practical perspective. "I got it, Chief," was all he'd say. "I'll see you at LAX. It's gonna be so fucking cool!" I believed Rob and that was all there was to it.

Everything would be alright. When I came back I would have great stories to tell about travelling to the ends of the globe with my twin. Rob would make the summit and, when he came back at the end of the summer, he would have his own fabulous tale of standing on the top of the world's most hideous, hellacious, heinous, weinous, bad-ass mountain. Neither of us thought for a second that when Rob left Mom and Dad's house in San Diego it was his last goodbye. Neither did Mom and Dad.

Rich, Tommy, son John Paul and Rob at LAX on way to K2

The Islamabad, Pakistan bazaar

Chapter XI

"Welcome to the Fifth World."
– Rob Slater

Rob headed for the Los Angeles airport in his rented rig where, for the first time, the 1995 American K2 Expedition would assemble, with the exception of Alison, Alan Hinkes and Kevin Cooney, who would join us at the mountain. On the way, Rob stopped to see our brother Tommy in Redondo Beach, where he also met up with expedition member and climber Richard Celsi. The tall, slim college professor from the University of California, Long Beach, had an engaging personality and a beard which, if he had been wearing a sport coat with patches on the elbows, would have made him look just like a college professor. Richard also had a quick wit with a seemingly restrained-at-first but recognizable streak of irreverence. More importantly, he seemed to be the kind of person who would not only do anything for a friend, but also put his utmost into everything he did. In this way, he reminded me of my twin. From their many prior phone conversations, Rob felt he already knew Richard. When they met face to face, Rob liked him immediately. When I met him the next day at the airport, so did I.

In Tommy's backyard the afternoon before he departed for K2, Rob and he talked about climbers who had both died and survived storms near the summit of giant peaks like K2 or Everest. Rob described a conversation he had with one of his climbing friends trying to figure out what were the most vital things to have with you and how to handle such a desperate situation.

"We thought a shovel and tent would seem the most vital," Rob recounted, "but those are problematic to lug to the summit, so the conclusion was elusive to both of us."

During that same conversation, Rob told the story of a climber who was unbelievably close to the summit of either K2 or Everest – within 100 feet, when his predetermined time to stop climbing arrived. Showing horrendous discipline, the guy turned around, only to encounter a storm on the way down. He managed to survive, but presumably wouldn't have if he had not turned back when he did. Tommy looked Rob right in his eyes.

"Could you make that same decision?" he asked. Rob stared into his little brother's eyes and pondered for a moment, then answered as seriously, honestly, and thoughtfully as he could.

"I don't know," was all he said.

The next morning, as Rob and Celsi brought the truck full of gear to LAX; I flew in from Denver along with Jack and Pam Roberts, who were from Boulder. Rob referred to Jack as a "pro climber." I didn't know there was such a job; if there was, I figured it would certainly fall into the "good work if you can get it" category. I also figured if such a job existed it would have already been offered to Rob. Since Rob had never mentioned him before, and he didn't even have a cool Rob-bestowed nickname like "Nic Café," "Great One" or "Black Death," I was somewhat skeptical. But to be fair, I viewed everyone somewhat skeptically in the shadow of my twin. Jack was rather quiet and somewhat aloof towards me, but I attributed it to him being a climber while I was just Rob's trekker brother. I had always viewed climbers in terms of Rob and his Team, all of whom I thought were honed, engaging and had what I considered to be an admirable trait: a prominent streak of irreverent defiance and outrageousness. I hoped Jack would prove to be the same once I got to know him.

Jack's wife Pam, who was along as a trekker, was a school teacher. Pam wore a smile on her face and seemed friendly, down-to-earth and unpretentious. Being a teacher, and having the entire summer off, I thought that definitely fell into the "good work if you can get it" category. Considering it was so early in the trip, I still had the office in the back of my mind. As I watched Pam, I wondered what it would be like to be in such a position and I wondered if she ever gave it much thought. I also thought of a joke Dad had told me about "the three best things about being a teacher: June, July and August!"

We hooked up with Rob and Celsi at the airport to begin what would prove to be our first in a long series of layovers and waiting on our way to Islamabad. I remember Rob mentioning to me that he needed to be patient because he'd undoubtedly be waiting for something all summer.

Scott Johnston, another climber member of the expedition, eventually showed up, his flight having been cancelled. Scott, who was in the antique car business, was big and strong with All-American good looks and a boyish quality which softened a toughness the group all recognized was there. I understood Scott had either been on the Olympic cross-country ski team, or swim team, maybe both. He was the kind of guy who inspired confidence. Scott, according to Rob, was "The Man," which was another way of saying he was honed.

Mike Toubbeh, a tall, lanky doctor from Seattle also arrived. To me, Mike seemed reserved and somewhat serious. He also seemed to have all the latest mountain wear, which matched his array of expensive-looking photographic equipment. Not knowing him or anything about him, I tried not to be judgmental but, in all honesty, I couldn't imagine him going to the top of the world's most dangerously heinous mountain alongside my brother. On the other hand, the expedition had to list a physician on the forms for the Pakistani Ministry of Tourism. Rob decided to take a wait-and-see attitude and suggested I do the same. "The mountain will sort us out," he reasoned. Fair enough I thought – and good leadership thinking by my twin.

There were other trekkers besides me accompanying the expedition. We were just along for the ride and would only be hiking to the base camp. Despite any delusions of grandeur we may have harbored in the back of our minds, we would not even step foot on the mountain.

One of them was Ruth, who was apparently Toubbeh's

girlfriend and appeared to me, at least at first glance, to be a similar reserved, serious type. I guessed Ruth to be the sort to also have the latest mountain gear to go with her own collection of fancy camera equipment, which both she and Mike seemed to fiddle with continually as they went about documenting the trip, apparently start to finish. I would take a wait-and-see attitude with her as well, though I wondered if maybe she just had a calm, cool way about her. After all, she would have to be cool just to be going on the trip.

Maureen Stivers was also a trekker. A petite physical therapist from Seattle, she arrived with the Toubbeh and Ruth contingent from the Pacific Northwest. Maureen proved to be outgoing and funny, with an independent streak which became more evident over the course of the trip. I gave no thought to any mountaineering experience she, or the other trekkers for that matter, may have had as all we would be doing was walking. Maureen laughed freely and seemed to be genuinely excited about what she viewed as a grand adventure. It looked like Maureen might have some game.

The next three days became one long blur. As we waited around LAX, Rob introduced us to the 1995 American K2 Expedition mascot, Tony Rigatoni. Tony was a Ken doll bedecked in disco pants and a gold lame midriff-bearing half-shirt. He was a true LA hipster. Thereafter, Tony Rigatoni was always afforded a prime seat on the luggage pile or around the campsite, befitting his pedigree and lofty stature.

Once we were somewhat organized, we checked in and ended up with 50 excess bags. Rob haggled with the airline for a while and settled on 10 excess bags at $100 per bag. Not too bad, he concluded, but not as good a start as he had hoped. The bags were now gone until Karachi, Pakistan, where we all hoped we would see them again. We boarded the jam-packed 747 and took off on our 10 ½ hour flight to London. The highlight of the ride was flying over Cape Farewell on Greenland. We saw the mountains, glaciers and pack ice, which made Rob and me start talking about wanting to go to Antarctica. It really made me excited, as I realized if I could actually go to K2 with Rob, why couldn't we go to Antarctica? Once again, we vowed to go there together some day.

We touched down in London in time for lunch; cold food,

warm beer and very expensive. We then ended up barely making our flight to Dubai in the United Arab Emirates, where we arrived at 2:00 a.m. to wait out the rest of the night in the airport.

Boarding a commercial airliner in the Middle East is a scene that warrants recounting. Having travelled nonstop for well over 24 hours, we were in no hurry to rush onto another plane. With reserved seats, we would get on in plenty of time to wait some more before take-off, so we hung back, not expecting the spectacle which was about to unfold. When the flight was called the Arab men, all dressed in lightweight, pastel leisure suit-type outfits, rushed to the gate. They roughly jostled for position at the front of the line, many with cigarettes dangling from their mouths. Once they had crowded through the ticket turnstile, the women, carrying the baggage and carting the kids, followed in comparatively orderly fashion. Rob, Celsi and I opined that the women of America could learn something from these gals. Predictably, our female travelling companions didn't think this funny, although, to her credit, Maureen may have smiled. We then followed, greeted at the bulkhead by stewardesses who looked like they came right out of Tony Nelson's magic bottle on "I Dream of Jeanie." They handed us menus and we ordered ice cream bars, a real treat in the midst of our seemingly endless travel ordeal.

The flight to Karachi was full of Pakistanis and we finally felt we were getting closer to our final destination. We landed in Karachi in the daylight, again with 2 ½ hours to get through customs, check all of our baggage and catch our next flight. We made it through customs in about half an hour, and we were relieved to discover all our bags had made it. After a crazy period of running around getting to the next terminal, however, we were informed we had to pay a $3,900 excess baggage fee. Rob and Celsi negotiated with the airlines while the rest of us watched the gear. In the end, it was agreed to check it all through and take a chance with how much it cost. Another mad scramble got us through the X-ray machines near where the bags were weighed. After more negotiating, we had everything through for only $627.

Unbelievably, we landed only 10 minutes late in Islamabad. As we taxied to the gate the voice over the intercom said "Welcome to Islamabad, where the local time is 5:30 a.m. and the temperature is 114 degrees."

"Welcome to the Fifth World," Rob announced.

We were met at the gate by Bhaig, the expedition's Pakistani liaison officer, or LO. Rob knew him from his trip to the Nameless Tower and it was nice to see a familiar face. In the process of gathering everything to load into two buses for the trip to the hotel, we rushed wildly up and down the escalators leading to the street level with our dozens of bags and barrels, soaked with sweat in the heat. A large crowd of Pakistanis stood around smoking in their pastel leisure suits, clearly amused but only one offering any assistance. Actually, it wasn't really assistance as he only reached out a hand to keep a barrel from rolling off the escalator towards him as he and his fellow citizens crowded about.

The public restroom at the airport also warrants mention. There were no toilets, at least in the sense of what Americans consider toilets. There were holes in the floor, with large stains resulting from poor aim and infrequent janitorial attention. There was also no toilet paper; it was shake with one hand and wipe with the other, giving rise to Rob's phrase "the Pakistani wipe." It's apparently a social faux pas to offer the wrong hand to shake during an introduction.

We made it to the Shalamar, an upscale hotel in Rawalpindi on the outskirts of Islamabad. It seemed nice by Pakistani standards but hardly the Four Seasons. In the process of adding a high-rise addition, the workers had about four stories of cement structure in place. On the top were many crooked wooden poles sticking up, presumably some sort of construction exoskeleton or maybe Fifth World rebar. During our stay we never saw anyone up there working. The rooms were furnished like the American equivalent of a Motel 4.

When it came time for room assignments, the husband/wife and boyfriend/girlfriend teams paired up first. Then it went climber/climber and lastly, Maureen and I, who were the only ones left. Neither of us cared, because by that point, the only real concern was not having to sleep in an airline seat or waiting room chair.

One of the rooms was a suite so the extra room was converted to storage. While the rest of the group rested or looked around, Celsi and Rob worked all day sorting the gear and getting police registration. Later that afternoon, Celsi, Scott and Rob went to the Ministry of Tourism to obtain permission for Celsi and Rasul, the expedition cook, to go to Skardu one day early to line up the jeeps and porters.

Rasul had been the expedition cook from Rob's Nameless Tower trip, who arrived at the hotel later that evening. He appeared to be around 50, with a thick head of Ronald Reagan-like hair and a weather-beaten face with a wide, ever-present grin that made him seem like an old friend. Rasul was gregarious and seemed eager to please. Everyone liked him right away.

The next day, Rob posted the necessary bonds and paid a guy named Abdul Quddas $18,000 for the permit, trek fee, hotels and other sundry charges. They weren't going to let us even close to the mountain until we paid the bill. The weather, according to Rob, wasn't as bad as July, 1992, during his last visit, but a swim nevertheless did a world of good. I could tell Rob was getting severely run down, having had only about six hours of sleep since leaving LA. Just about everyone was is some way or another starting to feel sick, due to a combination of travel, the heat and general Pakistani system upset.

That afternoon we all went to the bazaar. Nothing can prepare you for the Islamabad bazaar, because it's impossible to account for the two most memorable characteristics; the heat and the smell. The sprawling Islamabad-Rawalpindi metropolitan area was similar in many ways to a large city anywhere in the world. The streets were paved, with traffic signals at the larger intersections. Pepsi and Coca-Cola billboards seemed to be everywhere.

The streets were clogged with large buses, smaller airport-type shuttles and passenger cars, three-wheeled cabs powered by gasoline or leg strength and bicycles. Many were brightly painted in intricate detail and festooned with thousands of little dangling baubles, decorated to catch the eyes of man and Allah. The choking smell of carbon monoxide pervaded the air, mixed with the scents of throngs of people, animals and just about everything else imaginable.

Moving off the main thoroughfares deeper into the bazaar, the traffic became tighter, bumper to bumper in all directions with no signals or lanes. Amazingly, the mass kept moving, albeit slowly. Every driver continually tapped his horn, but tempers were not evident.

The streets narrowed until they become more like alleys and then mere passageways, winding through a never-ending maze of garage-sized shops. At first, it seemed the selection of goods was as vast as the market place itself, but we realized the wares included only a relatively small array of circa 1950s products. There were hundreds, if not thousands, of clothing shops, but all the men wore the same pastel leisure suit. The women were covered in long dresses and veils of similar material. Upon closer inspection, the clothing shops sold only these same few items.

Interspersed along the streets and passageways were a wide variety of food stands. Some resembled a children's lemonade stand with a few stools placed about. All seemed to be doing a brisk business. Others were made up of makeshift benches displaying produce, dry goods, some canned goods and even meat. The produce looked rather wilted in the 110+ degree heat. One memorable merchant had a collection of wooden cable spools, the kind college kids use for tables, upon which were arranged various kinds of meat. Chicken was recognizable, but nothing else looked familiar from the Albertson's meat department. Everything was swarming with a zillion flies.

"I think those might be human hearts," I ventured. Only Rob and Celsi thought my joke was funny.

Adding to the sights and scents of the Pakistani bazaar was the garbage, which seemed to be everywhere. Numerous construction sites, fenced off with chain link, stood in various stages of completion, many of them vacant or apparently abandoned. Cattle, horses, sheep, mules and goats were herded and milled about among the thousands of people. Chickens and mangy dogs pecked, sniffed and rooted around in search of a meal. We saw a few overflowing trash receptacles, but signs of littering were clearly evident.

Overall, the smell of thousands of people and their animals, along with their waste, the choking vehicle fumes and aforementioned garbage, all broiling in the summer sun, produced a veritable cornucopia of olfactory offensiveness. Without question, it affected everyone in our group. The conversation didn't dwell on it after the initial comments of recognition, but, after all, there was little that could be said other than "eeww." Exchanged looks were more than sufficient as we took it all in. Even I, who prides himself in in having an iron-cast constitution hardened by years of poor habits, felt a little queasy under the onslaught. The gals showed some constitution as well.

In the midst of this bizarre bazaar scene were people of all shapes, sizes and ages. Most gave us no notice, while some simply stared expressionlessly. We were quite obviously outsiders, with the guys dressed in shorts and t-shirts instead of pastel leisure suits. The women of our group, out of respect for and uneasiness with local custom, covered their heads with scarves. To accentuate our tourist status, there were the ever-present cameras. Some of the natives, however, were openly friendly and gregarious, while others viewed us with overt disdain.

The native women, covered head-to-toe in long, flowing dresses and veils, seemed clearly a part of a societal subclass. I understood, under the practices of Pakistan's dominant Islamic religion, something about unmarried women not being allowed to be seen in public without a male family member. Considering it was the middle of a work day, I think we collectively assumed this explained the relatively few native females we saw. Some of the women, however, whose faces weren't completely veiled, would make fleeting eye contact before quickly averting their eyes. It struck me that throughout, their ages seemed only to range from under-14 to over 60. It was as if young adulthood and middle age did not exist, with girls passing immediately from very young to very old. Looking around at the conditions, I figured this phenomenon was indicative of being a girl having to live a tough life in the Fifth World.

That afternoon at the hotel, the bus arrived that would take us to Skardu. It was, frankly, a little disappointing. The tires looked terrible and it wasn't as decorated as some of the other vehicles we'd seen, but we quickly christened it the "Magic Bus." After the bazaar we had our last dinner at the hotel. The buffet had rice, boiled and steamed vegetables and various mystery meats, so most of us stuck to rice and veggies along with bottled water. The ice looked good but we were afraid to try it for fear of dysentery, though I must say the food was pretty good. Considering the selection compared to America, i.e. no fast food or Mini Marts to instantly provide for any craving, it's actually pretty healthy to subsist on rice, vegetables and bottled water. Nevertheless, it didn't stop Celsi and me from waxing nostalgically for a Mini Mart chili dog. Celsi was a man next to my own heart.

We planned to get to bed early in preparation for what we had half-jokingly began referring to, once we had seen our transport, as the "The Ride from Hell." We had about 90 separate porter loads at that point, although Rob suspected that number would grow by quite some amount. Rob was still not feeling well so he started taking antibiotics to cure the GI tract disorder that seemed to be affecting most of the group. I felt fine, but we all hoped the group's overall condition would improve once we got out of Rawalpindi and closer to the mountains.

Early the next morning, our last in Islamabad, we started moving our gear down to the Magic Bus. At 10:00 a.m. Bhaig the LO arrived and Rob and he rounded up the trekkers to take us to our briefing. We began with a long ride into a sprawling governmental complex of modern buildings. We passed through several checkpoints, all staffed by uniformed military guys with submachine guns. It was rather unnerving to consider just exactly where we were. If they decided to lock us up, for whatever reason or no reason, we were at their mercy. I made a comment to that effect, but it didn't seem to register with the other trekkers, other than its possible political incorrectness.

We found our way to a nondescript building and went in. After much ado and conversation among our Pakistani hosts and a wait in a small, dingy waiting room, we were ushered into a tiny office for our briefing with an official of the Pakistani Ministry of Tourism. The office was piled high with papers and folders. After a couple of minutes of small talk the officer, a lower-mid-level bureaucrat, informed our liaison officer Bhaig, in Pakistani, he was ready to approve us, for a "fee," of course. Rob paid him, was offered no receipt and left. We never were able to conclude with any certainty whether he was trying to be hospitable or just shaking us down for payment for permission which we had already received. Rob and I suspected it was a little of both and the guy, who was actually pretty friendly, was just doing his job, Pakistani Ministry of Tourism style.

Back at the Shalamar, Rob assembled the climbers and

returned to the Ministry for their briefing. All seemed to be going well until he realized he had forgotten the folder with all the vital info. Rob said afterward the minister Taleh Mohammed was a little pissed but the briefing proceeded and soon they were done as well. Once back at the hotel, we checked out and left at about 2:00 p.m. for the Ride from Hell.

The luggage rack on the roof of the Magic Bus was filled with the bright blue barrels containing the expedition gear. The rows of seats inside were crammed with everything else. We all found places to sit or lie on top, as no seats were vacant. It was crowded but everyone was in good spirits and glad to be underway. The paved road out of the Islamabad-Rawalpindi metro area rolled through gradually more rural areas with many shops along the way. We were amazed by the number of Coke and Pepsi ads. We concluded there's just no escaping American consumerism. After a while it was dark and a bit cool, but we were glad the road was still paved.

We made pretty good time until we suddenly stopped. The bus looked OK, but our driver, who we named the "Marshmallow Sheik," said one of the tires was flat. The Sheik appeared to be in his twenties and showed no interest in his passengers or their grand plans for K2. He had some honed gold lame' sandals with the toes upturned to accent his tan Pakistani leisure suit and a nice beer belly, although there was no indication he was a drinker. Above the driver's seat, the Sheik had rigged up an old 8-track stereo which continuously blared out a horrendously hideous song that sounded like the Pakistani version of the Macarena.

We eventually got on under way again and drove for an hour before we stopped for gas. When this was completed, the lights wouldn't work. We were all a little ticked off with the un-roadworthiness of The Magic Bus, but about 45 minutes later we were on the road again for half an hour, but by now the Sheik needed a rest and he stopped for some tea.

Rob was getting quite impatient at this point and got out to find the Sheik, who he located lying down in the little rest house. Rob got on his case, and the LO's as well and we finally got going. Celsi and Rob had arranged some pads and were able to sleep on the baggage for maybe an hour. I joined them and we tried to laugh off the situation with Rob as part of the trials and tribulations of being an expedition leader. We made another bathroom stop at 2:30 a.m. and upon reloading we took spots by the windows.

It got light really early, about 4:30 a.m. We were on what's called the Karakoram Highway. As the day dawned, we found ourselves in an enormous gorge of the River Indus with massive cliffs on all sides. The road was still paved and in pretty good shape but resembled a mule trail winding up the cliffs of the Grand Canyon. Some of the turns were so tight that we were collectively astonished the Sheik was able to negotiate them without plunging us into the abyss. We seemed to forget the misery of the previous night as we wound up the gorge through low lying clouds, fog and intermittent rain. The scale of the surrounding cliffs was tremendous and somehow soothing after the clamor and congestion and stink of Pakistani cities.

Rob seemed, at least temporarily, to relax a bit, after being harried by the inadequacies of the Marshmellow Sheik and the Magic Bus over the preceding 14 hours. As he tried to situate himself in a good viewing spot amid the piles of gear in the Magic Bus, his attention now shifted above. I could tell my twin was feeling better as he pointed out, harkening back to his BASE jumping days, particularly heinous cliffs, each accompanied by a comment to its "jumpability."

"Black Death and I could do that one," or "RSL would love to fly off that one…"

At 8:30 a.m., we stopped for tea and chapattis, the Pakistani version of a tortilla and a dietary staple. At about 11:30 a.m., we stopped a passing bus and got another spare tire. Soon we came to a town to again change a tire that had blown about 15 miles back. This, of course, took another hour. As the Sheik and his crew casually went about their work, a small crowd of locals gathered, mostly children. They were all dressed in the same leisure suit outfit, some with colorful vests, and were playful and curious like children anywhere.

During the wait, we had lunch in a nearby hotel. Toubbeh and Ruth, the most cosmopolitan of the group, attempted to converse with the wait staff, intent on choosing the best selection from the menu. While friendly, they of course spoke no English and everyone got what they got when the food arrived, regardless of their order.

Once again, we were off with "new" tires. We were now in the Nanga Parbat/Rakaposhi area, but it was cloudy and the 8,000-meter giants were hidden. Celsi, Scott, Rob and I rode on the roof for the next several hours, enjoying the view and taking pictures. I was struck by how much they all seemed to know about the geology, geography and, most impressively, all of the named, major peaks. Moreover, they all knew the climbing histories of each, complete with names, dates and routes.

But what people who never get the chance to travel the Karakoram Highway or trek to K2 don't realize is that seemingly everywhere are spectacular mountains, the majority of which are "unnamed, unclimbed and over 20,000 feet," as Rob liked to say. Since there were just so many of them and the surrounding lands were wild and undeveloped, they were relegated to "dogshit" status, not getting the recognition I figured they deserved. When I mentioned to Rob that, mountain-wise, even the dogshit was way honed, he kind of laughed in acknowledgement, and then grinned at me.

"Just wait 'till you see K2, Junior."

By 3:00 p.m., we were in another town and the Sheik decided to once again change tires. That was the end for the Marshmallow Sheik. Amazingly, and inexplicably, the bus that had picked us up at the airport was there. We transferred a few personal bags and got ready to ride the rest of the way to Skardu in air-conditioned comfort. We left Bhaig with the rest of our gear and finally got going. The rest of the ride was very pleasant and we rolled into Skardu at 9:00 p.m.

The confluence of the mighty River Indus and the Shigar River forms the gateway to the Karakoram. The Indus, arriving from the Khyber Pass region and the Shigar, emptying the glacial waters of Karakoram, join in a sweeping bend. From there it leaves the Hindu Kush and turns south along the fringe of the Thar Desert toward the Arabian Sea south of Karachi. Midway through the desert it passes Mohenjo Daro near present day Sukkar, one of the Indus Valley's first cities, which thrived around 2,500 B.C.

Skardu marked the end of another stage of the journey to K2, and the very welcome end of the Ride from Hell chauffeured by the Marshmallow Sheik. As we approached the city, we passed through many small villages surrounded by apricot groves and ringed with increasingly impressive mountain peaks. Along the stone walls, men crouched in a seemingly uncomfortable position akin to a baseball catcher, but they all did it and it apparently wasn't uncomfortable to them. Smoking and sipping the local tea, a strong, semi-sweet concoction, they eyed us curiously. Many were outright friendly as they responded to our waves and smiles. In the fields, women could be seen toiling away, some carrying enormous stacks of firewood secured to their backs by only a piece of twine or rope. It was the type of division of labor that would certainly never be tolerated by suburban housewives back home. Rob, Celsi and I kept our jokes to ourselves.

Skardu itself looks like the prototype for Lake Tahoe, with the several-mile-wide riverbed and bend surrounded by towering peaks, their snow-capped summits standing out in stark but beautiful contrast to the vivid blue of the sky. Missing, though, was the indelible stamp of modern civilization, including acres of pavement, steel, glass, shopping and neon.

The K2 Hotel sat on the edge of a bench flanking the Indus just below its confluence with the Shigar. A mile or so to the south, atop a high rocky outcrop overlooking the river, sits the remains of a stone fortress, the site of a famous battle between locals and Muslim marauders 800 years ago. It stood in silent reminder of the deep, violent and fascinating history of a place that probably 99 percent of Americans have never heard of.

I went for a hike by myself along the river bank and climbed to the top. There was no parking lot, no gift shop, no restrooms and no sign commemorating the event or the lives lost ages ago. It was awesome and eerie standing on its walls watching the Indus flow slowly by, hearing only the sound of the wind and the ancient spirits of Kashmir. Even though I was close to civilization, it was a very pleasant feeling of aloneness.

At the K2 Hotel, Rob recognized the entire group working there, and they greeted him like an old friend. We quickly unloaded and got five rooms, feeling good to have completed another stage. The Great Mountain was getting nearer.

Our itinerary called for us to be at the K2 Hotel two nights before our jeep ride to the trailhead at Askole. During the interim, final preparatory and organization chores had to be completed to transfer the entire expedition and its gear to a half dozen jeeps and a couple of trucks. We went to sleep to the sound of a rather steady rain but we awoke to a clear sky.

The next morning, Scott and Jack went with Rasul to the local bazaar. It was the last chance to buy food and while they shopped Celsi and Rob organized and separated everything into individual 55-pound loads that would be carried by the porters to base camp. Rob went to bed exhausted and feeling a bit ill, but he said he hoped to recover once he got into the mountains. The group shared the sentiment that, as soon as we got hiking, things should calm down.

"Boy will I be glad to get to Base Camp – got to keep pushing to the mountain. I need to relax and be healthy for the summit," Rob wrote in his journal.

As wild and desolate as the country had steadily become since leaving Islamabad, it really didn't seem like being "in the mountains" while limping along in The Magic Bus or the shuttle that brought us the final miles into Skardu. All that changed as we loaded into open-air jeeps for the ride from Skardu, the last outpost of civilization in a region basically unaffected by the modern world, to Askole and the K2 trailhead.

Leaving Skardu, the pavement disappeared as our caravan of seven jeeps and 125 porter loads wound its way along the banks of the Shigar River toward the heart of the Karakorum. Each jeep had a local driver and carried two or three expedition members along with a portion of the gear. Rob quickly picked out the driver he figured would be the best, meaning the antitheses of the Marshmallow Sheik. Rob, Maureen and I jumped in and, at Rob's urging, sped off at the front of the pack. Our driver, a young man in his late teens or early 20s, had a wry smile and an impressive head of thick black hair. In keeping with his personal quirk of giving nicknames to locals who might bear faint resemblance to famous people, Rob was soon calling the young driver "John-John, the Balti JFK Jr."

We made good time on the rough, dusty road until being stopped at a bridge over the Shigar. Its ancient-looking stone buttresses appeared only slightly older than the cables and wooden planking of the bridge itself and was staffed on each side with a contingent of machinegun-wielding soldiers. Before we approached, Rob warned the group to put the cameras away when around the military, as we might be considered spies. Nevertheless, Mike Toubbeh was spotted by one of the army men trying to video the bridge and the caravan was halted.

"What in the fuck does Toubbeh think he's doing?" Rob demanded. "Doesn't he realize these guys are serious?"

"People think they have American rights because they're Americans. When you cross the border, those rights are gone. We're totally at their mercy," I added, repeating my comment made back at the Ministry of Tourism.

Although Rob was the expedition leader, this was a situation far more serious than negotiating an excess baggage charge with an airline counter attendant. It was left to Bhaig and the liaison officer, the soldiers' countrymen, to smooth things over. They congregated over by the guardhouse at the bridge's entrance with three or so of who appeared to be the soldiers in charge. Based on the soldiers' expressions, it was impossible to know what was going on. We knew they could detain us for minutes, hours, days or maybe even months. Countries used to wars for many centuries took military matters seriously. Rob and I understood our group's vulnerability.

As we waited for what seemed like forever, I couldn't help but think back to my days as a criminal defense lawyer. Each Friday morning, pending criminal cases were set before the district court, for what was referred to as "the Zoo." Defendants, their lawyers and prosecutors all converged in the third-floor hallway of the "old courthouse." While the defendants waited, the lawyers retired to the waiting area outside of the judges' chambers. As we waited for the judge to appear behind the counter, we talked, sometimes jovially, among ourselves. I liked the other lawyers, the judges and always enjoyed the Zoo.

Sometimes we had to wait a pretty good while for the judge. During this time, the defendants who weren't being held in jail were out in the hall, sweating it out. Many likely thought that the more time it took, the more unpleasant for them things would turn out. They didn't know we were just standing around waiting for the judge. I hoped the same was going on over by the guard house, but I was not overly confident.

Finally, Bhaig and the LO returned and told us the soldiers were pissed off, but they would let us proceed. Toubbeh's little stunt did nothing to inspire confidence in him by Rob or me. The silence among the group as we pulled away from the bridge made me think others felt the same.

After crossing the bridge under the watchful and clearly perturbed gaze of bridge guards, the caravan began its ascent into the Shigar gorge between the Haramosh and Gasherbrum Ranges, the road slowly rising above the river bed. It would have been quite a sight to see it at its highest flow during the early spring, but it had since subsided, exposing huge boulders strewn about along the canyon floor. As we travelled deeper into the gorge, the "road" started looking more and more like a widened hiking trail. At times, John-John was forced to crawl through a tight section, but hit the gas anytime the road straightened for even a short stretch. Standing and holding on to the roll bar while peering into the chasm above the river added much to the trip. It reminded me when I was little, riding a chair lift at the Snowmass ski area in Aspen, Colorado, over a particularly high section where the chairs went across a deep chasm. Rather than being afraid, I always wondered what it would be like to simply jump. Eventually most of the group ended up sitting, except for Rob and me. A few times, during a particularly weinous section, we were implored to sit down for the mollification of the others, though we respectfully declined.

"It won't make any difference if we're standing or sitting when we go over the edge," we reasoned.

"It would be kinda cool...," I muttered to Rob under my breath. He looked at me with a knowing half-grin.

The road ended at the Askole campsite, set in a large grove of leafy trees along the banks of a small stream. Rob remarked again how low the water level was compared to his previous visit. We speculated it was a good omen for the long-term weather forecast.

Our jeep was the first to arrive in the camping field and we quickly claimed what we thought was the best, cleanest spot. Rasul and Bhaig began the task of organizing the individual porter loads, for which Rob was thankful, because he still felt terrible. Scott was sick, too, so the two of them ended up spending most of his afternoon lying in Scott's tent.

I know it was a great relief for Rob to finally arrive at the trailhead because it marked the end of the non-climbing, stress- and commotion-filled journey from his Boulder apartment to the doorway of K2. It would have been nice to savor the moment, but it just didn't turn out that way. Rob figured he was merely dehydrated, so he drank about a liter-and-a-half of water, which instead made him bloated and caused a horrible stomachache. That night, our tent was filled not with the raucous laughter of tales of youth and the Earl of Alta Vista, but with silence. Nevertheless, I drifted into sleep hopeful, more for Rob than me, that better days and triumph awaited many miles away in the silent darkness of the Karakoram.

Changing another tire on the Magic Bus

The River Indus at Skardu from the K2 Hotel

At 14,000 feet on the Baltoro Glacier (Rob on left)

Chapter XII

"K2! The perfect mountain."
–Rob Slater

June 5, 1995

We got up at 4:30 a.m. for an early breakfast. As the sun rose, our campsite was slowly illuminated, revealing dozens of Balti porters who had made their way to the trailhead over the previous days. Some crouched around small fires built from nothing more than a few twigs; some stood around in small groups talking. They appeared at first glance to be a motley crew indeed, ranging in age from late teens to early 50s, mostly small in stature. Individually, they hardly appeared ready or able to a 55-pound bright blue barrel 75 miles up the Baltoro Glacier to the K2 base camp. Some didn't look like they weighed much more than the loads they would be carrying.

As we prepared to depart, the LO called a name off the roster and that man stepped forward to claim his load. Each carried a length of twine or rope, which he deftly wound once or twice around the barrel and secured it to a makeshift wooden frame. Then he hefted it on his back and walked away without a word. Some had an extra shirt, or a few sticks to be used as firewood on the glacier, that they placed on top of the barrel and secured with a quick loop of the twine. For the most part, though, they simply had the clothes on their backs and flip-flop shower shoes or open sandals on their feet. No Gore-Tex, no hiking boots, no sunglasses, sunscreen, hats or the latest outdoor gear.

"Man, those guys are tough," I said to Rob.

"They're honed," he replied.

On June 5th, we were "on the trail finally," Rob recorded. It was quite a congregation that first day, but the porters, climbers and trekkers were all on the trail at 6:15 a.m. Rob remembered it well – an easy mile from the camping field across green fields of native grasses criss-crossed by hand-dug irrigation ditches to the entrance of the Braldu valley. The outlines of stone walls and structures came into view, nestled at the foot of the increasingly steep canyon walls on a glacial moraine terrace.

Entering the village of Askole was like time travelling back to the Stone Age. Narrow pathways led through a maze of walls and tiny dwelling huts, all constructed of stacked rocks cemented together with mud. The un-quarried rocks matched the canyon walls from which they had crumbled, giving the village a natural form of camouflage. Along the walls, men crouched in the now-familiar baseball-catcher fashion that seemed so uncomfortable to Westerners.

Through the open doorways of the stone huts, we could catch a glimpse of the women and young children huddled inside on the dirt floors. There was no electricity, plumbing, glass, telephones, television or signs of modern civilization. There was no traffic, except for an occasional flock of small goats being herded through the village to the surrounding pastures.

"Baaaah, baaaah, that little blonde fluffy one's kinda cute," Rob snickered. I picked up instantly on the Wyoming Sheep Ranch connotation.

"I'm partial to that brunette over there," I offered.

We were intruders, gawking at such a simple, basic form of existence in a place the march of time and technology had missed.

Some of the group tried to be friendly, smiling and offering greetings. We saw Toubbeh and his trekker girlfriend Ruth, with their big cameras, taking pictures. It reminded me one of one of those National Geographic specials on TV where Westerners dressed in safari outfits enter a tribal village while the natives stand mutely by, unsure what to think. I felt, and I think Rob did too, an unsettling sense of embarrassment over the intrusion. We looked at each other. Rob pursed his lips and looked down as we simply made haste to be gone.

The trail out of Askole snaked along the sheer walls of the canyon and down along the benches flanking the river. At several spots, glacial tributaries had to be crossed, which we accomplished by wading, as there were no bridges. Immediately upon stepping foot into the fast -moving current, our feet and lower legs went numb in the icy water. As we picked our way through the knee-deep water, we silently prayed we would not lose our footing and fall in. A few of the porters dropped their loads and assisted, walking back and forth in the icy current, obviously unaffected by the cold. Others watched with bemusement as our group, some of who first took off their hiking shoes and replaced them with sandals for the crossing, squealed in the cold water. I saw Rob watching, shaking his head with a half-sneer, half-smile. Once again, the porters demonstrated their toughness in casual and totally unassuming fashion.

Several miles up, the icy river is fed by the leading edge of the Biafo Glacier, which cuts a 42-mile path deeper than the Grand Canyon as it descends from the Hindu Kush from the northwest. It's the third longest glacier in the world outside of the Polar Regions, and, along with the Baltoro, forms the Braldu Gorge through which we hiked. We would cross the Biafo on our way to the Baltoro Glacier, which is just slightly shorter, which we would follow towards K2. Stepping onto the Biafo marked another leg of the journey. We still couldn't see K2, but being on an actual glacier made the Great Mountain seem closer.

Rob and I headed out together onto the glacier, which resembled a huge riverbed of small rocks strewn with larger boulders, but there was no visible ice or snow. We went up to a ridge overlooking the glacier, where we took a break and enjoyed the view of the Latok peaks. It was hard coming to grips with the scale of the surrounding terrain.

"Isn't this amazing?" Rob exclaimed regularly as he looked about, repeating his "unnamed, unclimbed and over 20,000 feet high" observation.

It was indeed amazing, and it was clear that getting on the trail and into the mountains had raised Rob's spirits dramatically. As usual, I found his enthusiasm infectious, and I was happy to come to this amazing place with my twin.

We walked out across the sandy flats flanking the glacier and waded across two separate tributary streams, the first of which was very cold and swift, to the opposite bank where we would spend our first night. Since we were the first ones there, we relaxed and soaked up the view while waiting for the others to arrive.

That morning, everyone had more or less left the campsite and staging area as a group. Obviously, it had something to do with it being the first day on the trail. Over the course of the day, however, owing to hiking speed and time spent sightseeing and picture-taking in the village of Askole and along the trail, the group ended up widely separated.

Each member of our group carried a pack with personal effects and water, but the porters carried everything else. It was ultimate backpacking without any of the heavy lifting. As Rob and I started out, he made a comment that didn't surprise me in the slightest.

"We need to get ahead of the porter train or we'll be slogging behind and having to pass someone all day."

"No doubt," I agreed.

Needless to say, we weren't behind the porters, or anyone else for that matter. Even as I travelled to the ends of the earth, I had yet to come across anyone who could out-hike my twin brother.

The campsite sat on sandy soil near the high water mark of the Braldu River. Among the boulders strewn about by the river in times of torrent, spots were selected to pitch the tents, each housing two members of our expedition. Through the site ran a muddy stream fed by the snow-capped peaks above. The porters, numbering more than 100, congregated downstream nearby in small groups. Each group constructed, or used a previously built small rock wall, a foot or so in height, to form their own campsites about the size of a small bedroom. There they gathered around meager campfires fed by the small bundles of sticks tied to the tops of their barrels, talking and sipping tea. None of them had tents or sleeping bags, though some had rough and tattered army issue-type green blankets. As a group, they were quiet, their conversation and laughter melding seamlessly into the sounds of the river, the wind and the Karakoram. Before daybreak they stirred and were always ready to begin the next leg of the journey. Not once were they heard to complain of their accommodations, menu, the weather or the weight or unwieldiness of their loads.

Everyone in our group seemed to be getting along and moving pretty well, but I could tell there was some tension building. Some in the group felt the others weren't making an effort to "help out and communicate." Others, it seemed, wanted to crawl in to the base camp and take a rest day three times per week. At one point, Jack lodged a complaint about the "protein deficiency" of our diet.

"Don't they know this is a climb of a serious mountain and not some pansy trek?" Rob asked me rhetorically. This surprised me a little because, given the situation, I more expected him to use "pussy" or "gumby" – or another favorite, "weak tit." Being used to Rob and his usual over-the-top, gung-ho attitude about all things K2, and his usually-irresistible infectious enthusiasm, I was frankly surprised by the seeming lack of fervor on the part of some of these guys. Rob, anxious to get to the mountain, pressed to keep the group moving, all the while trying to balance the diverse collection of needs, wants and egos.

In my view of things, the expedition seemed to be divided, or dividing into two groups. Maybe, in truth, there was no such division and I was only projecting my normal if-you're-not-with-my-brother-and-me-you're-against-us attitude. If this indeed was the case, in one camp there was Rob and, by association, me. In the other there would be Toubbeh and Jack and, also by association, Toubbeh's girlfriend Ruth and Jack's wife Pam, who both seemed to be truly nice people. Maureen, while I thought initially would be with the other gals, had an outgoing and independent streak that would, I guessed, over time, push her towards "us." Celsi, possibly due to the relationship he developed with Rob during the organizational phase of the expedition, but also due to somewhat similar personalities, gravitated towards Rob. Scott, on the other hand, seemed too smart to declare a side so early in the campaign. Eventually, though, due to his own drive for the summit, I figured he would side with Rob. Otherwise, in light of what we had all been through together, from the long plane ride to the Ride from Hell with the Marshmallow Sheik, we were all in this together, notwithstanding minor differences that were bound to periodically arise. Either way, I'd just have to wait and see.

Even though it was oppressively hot at times during the day, then downright chilly when the sun disappeared behind the surrounding peaks at day's end by 9:00 p.m. I originally thought that the many small tributaries feeding the Biaho would be crystal clear, like many American mountain streams, but they were all extremely muddy and cloudy. With no vegetation to act as a filter or prevent erosion, everything but the larger rocks was flushed into the water, to be carried eventually to the sandy banks and bars of the Indus.

At first, we treated all water drawn from these streams with iodine, creating a silty tea which served only to stave off dehydration.

We slept well during that first night on the trail at our 10,100-foot-high campsite. Rob felt better and his pulse had declined.

"It finally feels like my body and stomach are settling down a bit," he told me before we both drifted off to sleep.

The next morning, everyone was up at 4:30 a.m. for a 5:00 a.m. breakfast. Rasul, our cook, was always the first one up. He got the coffee and the day's first meal going, before positioning himself centrally, in the darkness, among the groups' still-quiet tents. Then, in a way that was most certainly fun for him, he blasted out several ear-splitting salvos from his coach's whistle. No one ever slept through Rasul's whistle and no one ever held it against him that it was such a horrendously obnoxious way to get people moving.

Notwithstanding the manner by which he so crudely but effectively announced the new day, an encounter with Rasul was always enjoyable. Whenever someone spoke to him, he listened intently while maintaining eye contact. As the conversation progressed, Rasul's eyes always sparkled as he nodded his head in agreement, smiling all the while. I wasn't quite sure if he completely understood everything that was said to him, but it didn't make any difference. Rasul was a good guy. Rasul was honed.

After our meal, we returned to our tents to pack up before getting underway, which everyone did at their own pace. This would become the norm each morning. I was the first one out of camp and on the trail and, as the trip progressed, I would be off first virtually every day. I wasn't trying to be anti-social, but I was ready to leave so I did.

Some people take a bit more time to get going, but I have never been one of them. Neither has Rob, but I know as the expedition leader, he felt compelled to remain in camp to see that everything and everyone departed in good order, or at least make some kind of visible effort not to just eat and bolt out of camp. I also know if it would have been just the two of us, I would be trailing him out of camp each morning. Besides, over the course of the day there was plenty of time to take a break, enjoy the scenery and hook up with my brother or other members of the group.

In the day's first rays of sunlight, I followed the trail as it wound gently along the river bank. I was out in front of the porters, enjoying the solitude of the Karakoram early morning. The only sounds were the crunching of gravel beneath my feet and the rushing of the river. Today was the day, according to Rob, that we would actually get to see K2.

I didn't really notice, but the trail rose from the river bottom to traverse the lower flank of the canyon walls. The casual, gentle trail was gone, replaced by a twisting and steepening path through a seemingly endless jumble of rocks and boulders. At first, I had to periodically climb over one obstructing the way, but I soon found myself in a maze, with no clear way to go but up.

I pushed myself to keep a fast pace and was soon drenched in sweat. I knew the day's hike was 12 miles and I sincerely hoped it would not be like this the whole way. It was a true "slog." Mercifully, after about a mile I crested a particularly steep section and saw spread before me a vast expanse of the Braldu river bottom, minus a hideous mess like the one from which I had just emerged.

"A good place for a break," I said to myself, finding a nice seat on a rock. Though still early in the morning, the sun was rising through another crystal-clear sky, portending a beautiful but scorching day. From my comfortable perch, I surveyed the section of the valley I had just ascended. Slowly, I began to detect movement below amid the heinous rock pile. One by one, I could distinguish porters and other members of our group, slowly working their way towards me.

Then I saw Rob, moving fast, as usual. I could tell it was him by his nimble movement along the trail. He made quick work of the difficult section and soon appeared before me, grinning.

"That sucked, didn't it?" I asked, expecting him to respond in the affirmative.

"We're gonna see K2 today, Junior," he replied instead.

"Yeah, I can't wait," I said.

Rob and I took off together, with him in the lead. We cruised along the gently winding trail above the riverbed as the last vestiges of morning coolness were overwhelmed by the sun as it rose above the towering peaks flanking us on all sides. Gradually, we neared the end of the 12-mile hike to the next camp site at Paiyu.

Suddenly, as we rounded a bend in the trail, we saw it. We both stopped dead in our tracks. Through a gap in the mountains to the north-east toward the 23,860 foot Mustagh Tower, the massive pyramid of K2 towered into the clear blue sky. It was still more than 60 miles away but dominated the mountain skyline, a towering island amid a vast sea of white caps comprised of peaks each more than 20,000 feet high.

For a few moments we were silent as we stared, me in awe and Rob in reverence. Majestic was the word that came to my mind. It was as if we had entered the presence of some higher power or being. We had just peeked our heads into the Throne Room of the Mountain Gods. Another word – one of my favorites – came to Rob's mind.

"That's so hellacious," he said, turning directly toward me. His eyes were wide and wild, just like the moment before he parachuted off the Royal Gorge Bridge. A huge grin covered his face.

"I'm gonna climb it," he proclaimed, turning back to the mountain.

We started up the trail. As I followed directly behind my twin, I could see his head repeatedly raise and turn towards K2. Over the last couple of miles heading into Paiyu, K2 periodically came back into view as we rounded bends in the trail. There seemed to be an extra spring in Rob's step, as if he were a traveler finally approaching home after a long journey.

Paiyu sits just below the leading edge of the Baltoro Glacier at an elevation slightly under 11,000 feet. It couldn't by any stretch be called a town, or even be considered a village. It was more akin to an interchange along the highway, though in this case the highway happened to be a centuries-old trading route between Kashmir and China. In what could be considered a historical precedent to modern American interstate highway travel, Paiyu consisted of only one structure: a mini mart.

The Paiyu Mini Mart, however, had no bright lights, gas pumps, any ice machine for preparing an icy cold Super Swig, no nacho cheese dispenser and no hot dogs available 3-for-99 cents. The store at Paiyu looked like a Stone Age hovel dug into the hillside. A few scraggly bushes grew nearby, around which porters gathered to socialize and gossip. It was just like at home, except for the view.

Inside, on a couple of makeshift shelves, an array of crackers, cookies, cigarettes and warm sodas were displayed to tempt. I bought some K2 cigarettes as a souvenir.

"I'll take a picture of you smoking one at base camp," Rob promised me.

"Hopefully I'll still have some," I said.

After our stop at the Paiyu Mini Mart, we hooked up with Scott and Celsi, who had also arrived. We set up our tents on the bench overlooking the beginnings of the Biaho River and settled in to enjoy the view and wait for the afternoon to cool off. We didn't have a thermometer, but it felt like it must have been at least 100 degrees.

"It's not nearly as dirty as last time," Rob remarked, "but it's certainly as hot."

Hanging out with the group, the mood was upbeat. The fact that we could now at least see our objective lifted our spirits. The conversation, of course, focused on K2.

"K2! K2! Cecil B. DeMille. The spectacle, the panorama," Rob exclaimed. It was way funny, I thought, but tempered only by the fact that Rob was so excited.

As we reclined, I stared across the peaks to K2. It was so far away from us and we were so far away from home, civilization and family. I thought about what we had gone through just to see it from over 60 miles away. I was overwhelmed by its remoteness, but also knew I had only begun to appreciate its immense scale.

I looked at Rob as he studied the summit and the ridge on which he would soon be climbing. His narrowed eyes and pursed lips reminded me of his face as he studied the Teton peaks when we were kids. But now he was a man, his wild brown mane beginning to thin above his forehead, with a week-old beard partially obscuring his weather-beaten face and an intensity that far surpassed that of a boy's longing wonderment. I hadn't seen a look quite like that since years ago at the Exum climbing school.

"How are you ever going to climb that thing?" I asked almost rhetorically.

"Getting up will be the easy part," Rob responded quickly, "it's getting down that will be hard."

There was a long pause. K2 wasn't called the Savage Mountain for nothing. Throughout its history, roughly a quarter of those strong enough and lucky enough to reach the summit died trying to get down. The cold, hard, high altitude facts of K2, whether it was sheer exhaustion, rapidly deteriorating weather, or simple lack of focus after the summit, had instantaneously turned the greatest day of many a climbers' life into their last. These facts combine to make a safe return from the summit of K2 perhaps the most perilous and deadly feat in all of sport. I wasn't sure if Rob was considering the gravity of his own words or waiting for them, along with any other inkling of doubt, to float off and be enveloped by the mountain air.

"K2 was visible at last! K2-will climb it soon. It was a thrill to see it again – at last," Rob recorded in his journal.

The next day was a rest day, so we slept in a bit, then ate some breakfast cereal and took a leisurely down to the riverbed with Celsi, where we found some running water and a place to wash our clothes and ourselves.

The water was really cold but we got our shirts, hair, feet and most of our bodies clean. After rinsing out our clothes and spreading them on the rocks to dry, we worked briefly on our full-body tans. There was a contest among us to see who could go the longest without changing clothes and, technically speaking, taking a bath should have at least violated the spirit of the contest rules, but it sure was refreshing.

Rob and I were both really getting to like Richard Celsi. He was totally unpretentious and had a great dry sense of humor. It was a good day and Rob was feeling physically much better. We all went to sleep early, knowing the next day's trail to Urdukas was long and ever-tougher as we climbed higher in altitude.

The Baltoro glacier is another of the longest and biggest on earth cutting through the Karakoram. As it grinds its way for 39 miles, it is fed by no less than a dozen tributary glaciers, all of which reinforce its snaking path. Its leading edge, encountered a mile out of Paiyu rounding a bend in the valley, was a natural example of shock and awe. More than ten stories high and two miles wide, the mass of rock, ice and snow it was unstoppable by even the giant peaks. From its base, the Braldu River is born as a gushing torrent that eventually ends up in the Indian Ocean.

The next day, we crossed the Baltoro Glacier and went to Urdukas, with a stop in a spot named Liliwa for a snack. All of the named places along the way, with the exception of Paiyu, were merely campsites. The trail was for the most part easy to follow and we only lost it a few times early on. Rob pointed out to me how the glacier had changed since his last visit. The spot he crossed in 1992 under the Trango Towers, for example, was now completely unrecognizable. Rob hiked with Celsi and Scott and arrived at noon to find a few porters and me waiting. Rob and I picked our spot and waited for the rest of the porters. Rasul arrived and dinner was soon on the way. Rob remarked that the place was much cleaner than last time. The weather was still flawless. We hoped it stayed that way all summer.

Being on the trip with Rob was in many ways similar to the summer time climbing excursions we had made since we were young. We were together, beneath the overarching canopy of the magnificent mountain gods, exhilarated by the surrounding, pervasive-to-us spirits of the wild. Rob was the *de facto* leader, tolerating distractions but always keeping his eyes squarely fixed on the prize. In the middle of one of the most remote spots on the planet, I was able to bury the mundane worries of career responsibilities and adulthood.

But it was also decidedly different in one significant way. This was the real deal. We *were* in one of the most remote and dangerous realms of the mountain gods. We had porters and outsiders with us, along with the personalities and politics they brought, and Rob was at the center of the storm. Despite my position as a pansy trekker, I was with Rob all the way, and of course had a relationship with him that no one else had. I knew that to jump out in front with him and take everyone on who disagreed with him on any matter would have dragged the expedition straight into chaos. If they thought Rob was pushy, I had no doubt what would happen if they got a load of both of us at the same time. But that wouldn't serve my brother in the long run over in his quest for the K2 summit, so I held my tongue.

Urdukas sits above the south side of the Baltoro Glacier on the base of a 20,890-foot peak of the same name. It's a campsite at 13,000 feet on the steep slopes across the glacier from the Trango Towers group. Rob pointed out where he had been on the Nameless Tower. As he stared across the glacier up at the sheer faces, I was struck by the almost disinterested look on his face – at least compared to how he looked when he gazed at K2.

The towers rose between the Dunge and Trango glaciers, which join the Baltoro on either side. Their immense sheer rock faces caught the late day sun, changing color from brilliant orange through deep red before disappearing into the blackness of the Karakorum night.

Urdukas also marked the last spot of grass on the icy, rocky road to the K2 base camp. From this point forward was the realm of the Ibex, a native mountain goat that dances on its toes on the smooth cliffs, and the snow leopard, a creature so elusive and beautiful it has taken on mystical status. We luxuriated in lying on our backs in the soft vegetation, staring across the valley at the Trango spires, studying the cracks and crags on the off chance of glimpsing one of these magical beasts.

Urdukas was also the home of mountain spirits. Walter Bonatti was a member of the 1954 Italian expedition that led to the first conquest of K2. Bonatti and a Hunza high-altitude porter, Mahdi, were shuttling oxygen canisters for the next day's summit attempt to their Camp IX, established at over 26,000 feet. As darkness enveloped them, they found themselves at an icy section too difficult to climb in the dark. Bonatti also realized it would be impossible to attempt a descent on a moonless night without oxygen. Adding to the predicament, Bonatti further understood that if they used the oxygen they were attempting to haul to the summit party above, their endeavor would be for naught. They were at 26,000 feet, without proper gear to spend the night. As Bonatti dug a platform in the snow, Mahdi railed and shook his ice axe against the blackness. Mahdi was beginning to lose control over his faculties. Bonatti, uncharacteristically, was truly afraid. Eventually, Mahdi was able to calm himself, resigned to the will of Allah.

"Like shipwrecked men in a stormy sea, we hung on to life with every fiber of our being so as not to be overwhelmed," Bonatti later recalled. "The struggle became more and more desperate and unequal and we no longer knew if we were fighting for our lives or if we continued to live at all."

Only Herman Buhl, during his solo of Nanga Parbat the year prior, had ever survived a night in the open at that altitude. Coincidentally, the frostbitten Buhl was carried off the mountain by Mahdi. All night, Bonatti and his companion huddled together, waiting for the dawn. Before sunrise, Mahdi could stand it no longer and set off down the mountain, crouched over in pain from the cold. Bonatti waited for light, then began his own descent. The night had not been clear or calm, but one of storms. Mahdi, like Buhl, was severely frostbitten and ended up having several fingers and half of both his feet amputated. Bonatti arrived at the lower camp completely free of any ill effect of his ordeal.

Huge boulders, resting in near inconceivable positions after their tumble from the heights above, dotted the grassy landscape. Near our camp on a large, rounded rock slab, there is a famous off-width crack renowned in the Karakoram called the "Bonatti Crack." It's about 35 feet in length and had a difficulty rating 5.9. Rob climbed it solo in his sandals and made it look easy. At first he said he wasn't going to do it but then decided, since it was part of history and for good luck, to solo it. The other climbers in the group watched, pretending either to be disinterested or unimpressed. I could tell they were sizing Rob up, but after he made the top, though, none followed.

Watching the others watch Rob was extremely satisfying for me. After all the whining about our pace of travel, deficiencies of our diet, videotaping the bridge, and the like, Rob made a subtle statement that I hoped would remind the complainers of why they had supposedly come. In a twisted sort of way, it was like watching Rob about to get in a fight: I immediately wanted to jump in just because they had the audacity to mess with my brother, while at the same time knowing that he didn't need any help from me. When no one followed Rob up the Bonatti Crack, I wanted to loudly point it out to everyone but, thanks to Rob, I didn't have to. Neither did he.

"It felt really good to do the Bonatti Crack," Rob told me later.

"I know what you mean," I replied, and that was the end of it.

Afterwards Rob and I walked over to a small porter graveyard with five unmarked graves. We stood quietly as we pondered who the graves contained and what stories might have led the anonymous souls to such a final resting place.

"There are a lot of worse places to end up," Rob said solemnly. I took that to mean he would be satisfied with such a spot. I had to agree.

After dinner, the climbers had another discussion about the pace of our march to the base camp. One said he needed a rest day and that "the majority" of the team thought Rob was pushing too fast to get to base camp. The trekkers were not included in this conversation, but I had no doubt that their various opinions were being channeled in, mine included. Rob tried to be diplomatic, but privately to me dismissed such talk as "whining."

"I didn't know Whinehold Messner was a part of our expedition," I offered in support.

It had become clear to me early during the trip that no one else on the team shared Rob's all-consuming drive to summit K2. I listened and tried to be supportive of my twin, but figured I should share my opinions with him only. As Rob said, the mountain would sort them out.

The next day on the trail was casual and relaxing. We spent 4 ½ hours on the glacier, easily following the trail once we got going past Urdukas. Celsi, Scott, Rob and I all hiked together to our next camp. We arrived to find some of our porters and some from another K2 expedition waiting. Nearby was an army camp which was horrendously filthy and full of mule manure and other garbage. Rob and I selected what we considered to be the best spot available as the others slowly trickled in. Rob got out the GPS and determined that our tent was placed exactly at 14,000 feet. It was like camping on the top of Longs Peak, but when we looked around there was no interstate or signs of civilization to be seen, with the exception of the army camp.

Pakistan, with its 97 percent Muslim population, was founded in 1947 to provide a home for India's Muslims. Its neighbor to the west, Afghanistan, was convulsed at the time by a bloody civil war that would be won the next year by the fundamentalist Islamic Taliban, who ruled until the U.S. toppled them in October 2001. Next door in Iran, Muslim clerics took over after a 1979 revolution and eventually waged an eight-year war with Saddam Hussein's Iraq. The Persians fought for control of the Khyber Pass in the fifth century B.C., as did Alexander the Great two centuries later. Genghis Khan led his armies through the region in the 13th century.

Needless to say, people have been fighting there since people have been there, so it was a little discouraging but not surprising to see a military base halfway up the Baltoro Glacier at 14,000 feet above sea level. In truth, it wasn't much of a military base, consisting of an old wagon of the sort used by sheepherders in Wyoming and a couple of guys sitting around, ostensibly on "guard duty." As part of the years-old dispute with China over the exact location of the border between the two countries running through the Karakoram, they were Pakistan's first line of defense. They were also clearly bored with not much to do but eat and feed their mangy mules. Next to their wagon stood a huge pile of mule manure and a mound of butter tins. For the sake of the mules and the soldiers, we all hoped the hostilities would be brought to a speedy conclusion.

Just as countries don't always get along, neither do members of climbing expeditions. Although sharing a common goal, disagreements arose over means. In our group, it was evident that the shared goal of climbing K2 was sought with greatly differing degrees of passion. From my position as an outsider, it seemed to me that for some of the climbers it was just a trip to *a* mountain, while for Rob it was the trip to *the* mountain – the Great Mountain, the Savage Mountain, the Ultimate Mountain. I didn't really think about it at the time, but there's an old climbers' mantra that says, "Come back alive, come back friends, come back successful." I believed the last two may sometimes get switched, but I never considered that the first one was negotiable for anyone.

There was another meeting and it turned out to be Rob, Celsi and Scott on one side and Jack and Toubbeh on the other. The latter group thought Rob was being inaccessible and only concerned with getting to the summit. Rob tried to clear the air by saying he wasn't ignoring them but rather under the assumption that they wanted to spend time with their trekkers.

"We'll try to humor them and let the mountain sort us out," Rob said that night in our tent. "I have a feeling it will be me, Celsi and Scott doing the front work. If the others get behind, the problem will disappear as the strongest take over."

I figured he was right, and I could see Rob's frustration in having to continually deal with what he and I both viewed to be petty issues. Everyone had made a huge commitment of money and time, not to mention their potential safety, to try and climb the ultimate mountain. We were 50 miles onto a glacier, completely cut off from civilization. We slept on the ground, ate beans and wore the same clothes every day (at least Rob and I did). What did they expect?

Frankly, I was impressed by how well my twin his cool. On the mountain, talk would indeed become cheap. In the meantime, Rob would have to bide his time. I'd just stay out of it publicly, as far as the others were concerned, but squarely behind my brother in private, as both supporter and sounding board.

On a lighter and much more welcome note, the weather had remained absolutely perfect. The next day we would reach the snow and hopefully get what Rob said would be our first "real" view of K2.

The next morning, Rob and I got up later, at 5:00 a.m., in an effort to see the others off and hopefully ease some of the residual tension from the previous night. But this really didn't work because everyone was so slow in starting. I took off with Celsi and, after waiting another 20 minutes, Scott, Maureen and Rob left as well. Later in the morning, we ended up hiking more or less as a group, casually working our way up the glacier towards Concordia. It was basically the first hiking I had done with anyone other than Rob. Maureen, Scott and Celsi were good hikers and pleasant companions.

The day was perfect again, so the snow quickly became a mess. The last mile to Concordia we post-holed through thigh-deep snow. The top was crusty and we fell through every single step. It would have been a great arrival had we been wearing snow shoes or even pants but, as we were all wearing shorts, there was blood on our legs. We were all wet, tired and sore as we arrived bloody in Concordia before noon on June 10.

I'm not sure who, but somebody had the great foresight to stash some hard-boiled eggs, which were brought out for lunch. There we sat, spread among the rocks sticking up from the snow, drying our shoes and socks while enjoying peanut butter and jelly on chapattis and the eggs. Everyone was smiling. Rob had hoped the sight of our objective would improve morale and bring the group closer together and Rob was right. With K2 in front of us, our spirits did in fact lift considerably.

Just like Rob had said, the view was unbelievable. The mountain looked so huge and steep and remote and the scale was overwhelming – to me, at least. To Rob, it was also a puzzle to be solved.

"I have to take it one step at a time," he intoned.

Concordia is the doorway to the Throne Room of the Gods, where the Upper Baltoro and Godwin-Austen glaciers converge to form the Baltoro Glacier. To the east stands the Gasherbrum Group, over 26,000 feet, highlighted by G IV, a symmetrical pyramid that could have been the model for the Mayan temples to the Sun God in ancient Meso-America. To the south-east, the confluence of the Duke of Abruzzi Glacier and the upper reaches of the Upper Baltoro are flanked by Baltoro Kangri, the Golden Throne, at 23,983 feet and Chogolisa, or Bride Peak, at 25,110 feet.

North out of Concordia begins the final approach to K2. To the west, or left, stand Marble Peak and Crystal Peak, both over 20,000 feet, along with an unnamed companion, also over 20,000 feet. The right wall of this grand gallery is comprised of Broad Peak, a behemoth of a mountain, the world's fourth tallest, standing 26,400 feet high. At the end of the gallery stands the throne of the mountain gods itself, the stairway to heaven, the Dream Mountain: K2.

In terms of the scale and breathtaking quality of one's first real view, K2 is hard to adequately describe. The Tetons in Jackson, Wyoming, are said to be the most photographed mountains in the world, due to their spectacular beauty and the fact that there are no foothills. The peaks thrust straight up from the floor of the broad Snake River Valley. The valley floor is 6,000 feet, with the Grand Teton rising to 13,769, creating the stunning view of nearly 8,000 vertical feet of mountain.

The Grand Canyon descends more than 5,000 feet from its rim to the Colorado River below. From the base camp of K2 at 16,000 feet, which is half a mile above the summit of the Grand Teton, the summit of K2 looms more than 12,000 feet further above.

"It's so bad-ass," Rob used to say, and that's as good a description as any to describe the immensity of K2. It's bigger than the entire Grand Tetons range – and twice as high. It's like digging the Grand Canyon more than five times as deep as it is now, filling it with rock, coating it with ice and snow, then flipping it over and sticking it in the most remote spot on earth outside of Antarctica.

For me it was a bit scary looking up at the summit ridge miles above and imaging myself up there. I also smiled at the thought because that was what my twin lived for and thrived on – and where he belonged.

Since the snow was thigh-deep, wet and very sloppy, we enjoyed the view while letting many of the porters pass by to beat down the trail. Celsi and Scott followed on snowshoes, Rob wore snow boots and I changed into hiking boots. This proved to be a wise move indeed as we now hiked on a snow-packed trail with the added luxury of dry feet. Once again as a group, we were all excited as we picked our way around the crevasses onto the strip of the Godwin-Austen Glacier.

During the early part of the afternoon, we reached our camp in the shadow of Broad Peak, aptly named as it nearly blotted out the sky. Immense and imposing, its size was second in impressiveness only to K2, now standing only a few miles directly to the north. Our base camp destination was just a short march away.

Rob and I began a platform for our tent. Some of the others camped on the snow and Celsi and Scott decided to sleep outside. The porters, like an experienced, well-disciplined construction crew, worked like mad and made many stone walls, one right next to Celsi and only a few feet from our tent.

That night, the deep rumbling of avalanches could be heard

above with unnerving regularity, their descending white clouds sometimes visible on the surrounding giants. In our tent, Rob and I listened for the recurring thunder.

"If one of those swept across here, we'd be gone in a second," he said.

"We should have slept outside," I suggested. Rob agreed.

The next morning, it seemed like a short distance to the base of K2 from our camp at the foot of Broad Peak but that, like many aspects of the Karakoram, was deceptive. The immensity of the surrounding giants skewed everyone's sense of scale. From Concordia, the Godwin-Austen Glacier snakes due north before sweeping northeast past the 22,490-foot Angelus which flanks K2 to the southwest, framed by the Negrotto and De Filippi glaciers. As the glacier flows past the southern ramparts of K2, it forms a long moraine-like strip along which expeditions since the Duke of the Abruzzi have based themselves.

The weather continued to cooperate and the sky was crystal clear, except for a big cloud hanging below the shoulder on the Abruzzi Ridge. As we approached K2, it clouded up and the glacier took on a different character, as cracks and crevasses began to appear. At first it was a simple step across, and then an easy jump as they widened as we further ascended the glacier. Rob and I roped up and, stopping to peer into the blackness of one particularly deep crevasse. We couldn't help but be struck by the sinister presence of K2's true danger and deadliness and, as we saw in those dark depths, not confined to its windswept upper slopes.

We arrived at base camp on the strip of the moraine at 9:00 a.m., June 11, 1995. The Dutch and the Spanish expeditions were already there, both camped well up the strip.

Rob wanted to camp where his friend Charley Mace did in 1992, and he quickly selected a spot for our tent. Rasul arrived soon after and began directing the porters where to drop their loads. It snowed briefly as we set up, but stopped just as quickly as it started.

Everyone arrived in good order and the mood was better than it had been since we left L.A. Rob and I got our own tent up and then helped set up the mess tent. The weather cleared as everyone sorted gear and relaxed.

Later in the afternoon Rob, Scott, Maureen and I went to the Gilkey Memorial, a rock cairn built in honor of American Art

Gilkey, who died during his descent of the Abruzzi Ridge in 1953. Since then, it's been covered with the names and mementoes of those who have perished on K2.

We stood silently, staring at the crowded congregation of spirits who would never leave their beloved mountain. Rob remarked that it was a sober reminder of the risks involved. High above us on the Great Mountain, a miles-long plume of snow trailed horizontally off the upper reaches of the Abruzzi Ridge into the deep blue sky, in stark testament to the utter ferocity of the winds, wildness and danger of K2.

Rich in the village of Askole

Porters along the glacier

K2 base camp

Chapter XIII

"Summit or plummet"
            –Rob Slater

"A new high in lows"
            –Rich Slater

We awoke June 12 under the giant, looming face of K2 for the group's first and the trekkers' only full day at base camp. Since we had arrived at our destination and didn't have to break camp and set out on another hike, we slept in until 6:30 a.m. Rasul made everyone breakfast, during which the excitement of being in the shadow of K2 was palpable. There was a discussion about the mess and kitchen tents and the climbers agreed to buy the LO Bhaig's kitchen tent for Rasul. That decided, we built a table out of stones for communal use.

The climbers then had a long meeting during which everyone got a chance to get everything off their chests. The other trekkers and I didn't participate, but we thought it was a good idea for them to clear the air now that we had reached base camp.

"Scott really said some good things and Jack may be finally coming around," Rob told me afterward. Their discussion had covered the topics which had given rise to bad feelings on the way in: Rob pushing the group, logistical and dietary issues, expedition finances, supplies and the like.

There was no such faith or confidence in Toubbeh, however, but the expedition had needed a doctor to list on the forms. As far as Rob was concerned, Toubbeh wouldn't be a factor on the mountain anyway.

"I want to focus on the mountain and not have to spend a lot of time in encounter sessions, Rob added.

Rob was optimistic that things would fall into a better rhythm when the actual climb started the next day. I hoped he was right, both for his sake and for the success of the climb itself – both of which were inextricably intertwined.

That afternoon, Rob and I walked up the moraine strip to get a closer look at the mountain. I set a new personal altitude record at our highest point, which we estimated to be a bit over 16,000 feet. To mark the occasion, Rob took a picture of me smoking one of the K2 cigarettes I'd bought at the Paiyu mini-mart.

"Here's my twin brother Richie pounding a K2 nail into his coffin at 16,000 feet," Rob narrated as I puffed.

"A new high in lows," I proclaimed. My previous altitude record was 14,256 feet on the top of Longs Peak in Colorado. There, Rob and I shared some Pop Tarts and I topped off the meal on the mountaintop with a smoke. Or, as I also liked to say, "it was so bad it was good."

K2 was so huge around us that it nearly filled the sky. The summit appeared so far off that it actually seemed to touch outer space, where the brilliant blue melded to black. It was like you could actually see the cold and smell the fierce wind.

As we lounged about on the rocks, staring at the mountain, we saw wind scouring the summit ridge. For me, it was scary just thinking about being up there in that place that was so violent, dangerous and implacably hostile, even on a beautiful day.

For Rob, of course, it was different. He had that look on his face and in his eyes that I recognized as total longing and total determination. It wasn't just a place of violence and danger for him but one of opportunity, elation and triumph as well. It was a place where he could face and overcome all his demons of doubt and inadequacy, but also a place where he could attain his loftiest goals and achieve his most passionate dreams.

Rob pointed out to me the different routes, including Reinhold Messner's Magic Line, with an easy familiarity that belied the fact that he'd never been there before but reminded me of the countless hours Rob had spent studying it from afar.

When we rose to leave Rob, perhaps sensing my need for some sort of explanation, offered me one in usual succinct Rob fashion.

"Summit or plummet," he said, as we started back to base camp. I never thought to ask "what about summit *and* plummet?" given the fact that most K2 deaths happened on the way down, not on the way up. If I had, he probably would have said "as long as it's summit *before* plummet." Rob had come to conquer K2, or die trying.

The spot where we stopped was still about two miles from the foot of the Abruzzi Ridge. From base camp, it looked like a casual hike along the moraine to the beginning of the route but, as I had learned during the previous week of hiking, the immensity of the Karakoram was deceiving.

K2 is not a mountain you just cruise up to and began climbing. Between us and the Abruzzi was an icefall of tangled blocks and crevasses. I had silently harbored the unrealistic fantasy of perhaps actually stepping onto the Abruzzi, if even only for a few feet, but navigating the icefall would require being roped up. Since Rob didn't offer, I didn't press it. For one thing, if we'd gone further, it may have led to more tension back at camp because it could have been argued that Rob and I were being disrespectful of the others. Since Rob had to spend the summer climbing with these guys, it wasn't worth offending them. Besides, I really liked Celsi, Scott and Jack, and I didn't want to stir up anything new the afternoon before I left. Rob already had enough personnel management issues on his plate.

Still, it would have been cool to go up on the ridge regardless of what the others said – and we might well have decided to go for it except for the fact that we were totally unprepared to do so: we had no rope, no clothes and no gear for anything more than a casual hike to check out the face of K2 and there is absolutely, positively nothing even remotely casual about any part of climbing K2. Even the "approach" is a serious technical climb for all but the most hard-core and experienced climbers. So while I would have loved to go higher, I was at the same time completely satisfied to have been able to hike above base camp alone with my brother and stand on the very doorstep of the Great Mountain.

We hiked back to camp for dinner with the group, after which everyone sort of drifted apart. The trekkers had to pack to leave the next day and the climbers had to prepare for their first day on the mountain. Richard Celsi and I joked about how we both missed Mini Mart chili dogs, and I promised him I would have one when I returned to civilization in honor of his summit of K2.

The night before I left base camp to return to the real world was in some ways like so many others Rob and I had spent together in a tent in the wild. I couldn't help but mention that, while on the glacier, I'd slept better than I had in years. I know it wasn't the softness of my bed, so I figured it had something to do with peace of mind. As kids with our Dad, we listened to stories of the silliness of The Earl of Alta Vista. As teenagers, the stories involved us and our friends from school and the neighborhood. As men, the realities of adulthood inevitably inserted themselves into our otherwise jovial discourse. We talked long into the night, as avalanches thundered down the giants from the mountain gods who surrounded us.

"I was thinking about getting a tattoo, but, you know, being a lawyer that might not be appropriate. What do you think about that?" I asked, seeking the sage advice of my soon-to-be-a K2-summitter twin brother.

"Fuck them. Go ahead; what are they going to do about it?" Rob spat out. I loved it when Rob backed me up on any insignificantly foolish or otherwise inconsequential matter. It was only a small act of defiance, I concluded, but having Rob's blessing always meant a lot to me.

My twin and I had been confidants since we were young. We had always shared the same kind of irreverent and defiant world view. I think it had less to do with arrogance than with the confidence we derived from each other. Part of me wanted to stay at base camp, not because I could climb K2 with Rob, but just to be there with him and support him during his ultimate quest. I wanted to be a part of it, but I had a law practice and clients I'd told I would return. I thought about staying anyway, but, for once, the call of duty was louder than the voice of adventure, and the thought disappeared into the darkness and the rumbling avalanches.

In many ways, I saw in Rob the best of what I could be, or could have been. I saw the leanness of horrendous physical conditioning and discipline to which I could only aspire. My twin had an incredible, pithy, irreverent sense of humor and world view that people, even if they disagreed with him, found refreshing and intriguing. When I tried to emulate it, I could only summon the crassness of going too far. When Rob gazed upon mountain peaks or talked about the K2 summit, I saw a purity of purpose that I, as a short-sighted hedonist, could only dream of approaching.

I also saw in my twin fear of the same inadequacies and failures I saw in myself. The grades, touchdowns, ribbons, trophies and state championships had come easy, perhaps too easy. It would always be like that, I figured, to the extent I ever even thought about it. Now, as an educated, self-employed professional, I wondered if it was enough, or if it should be enough. Most importantly, I wondered if I had made the most of my good fortune and opportunities. Was I an overachiever or an underachiever?

Rob wrestled with the same questions. He had conquered the Grand Teton, the Fisher Towers, Wyoming Sheep Ranch and virtually everything significant on El Cap and at Eldo. Now, after all that, would K2 be enough, or should it be enough? Was climbing mountains and cliffs in search of the ultimate high more important than a conventional career and family? Should he be focusing on the market instead of a mountain? Was Rob an overachiever or underachiever?

"When I get back I'll have no money, no job and no house," Rob said, as if picking up on my unvoiced thoughts. "I'll have to get another job – but I'll have climbed K2."

"So what, you can always get a job," I remarked, continuing out loud the conversation I'd been having with myself, "and you can always get a house for that matter."

We looked at each other, considering paths taken – and not

taken. The look on Rob's face changed as his thoughts shifted from what might have been to what he hoped would be.

"Richie, I have to climb this thing," he said. "I know I can make it."

"You will," I replied, as certain of him as he was of himself.

"Do you think Mom and Dad are scared?" he asked.

"I think they're concerned as parents, but they really just want you to be happy and to follow your dreams," I told him. "They know you're not gonna be some ham 'n egger, slogging to some job in a suit every day, watching sports on the idiot box every weekend and getting fat. They'd never want you to give up climbing. They want you to climb K2 at least as much as you want it for yourself. More than anything, though, they just want you to come back – just like I do."

"We are so lucky to have the parents we do," Rob said, stating the obvious, "and I'm so glad that you came here with me."

"Me too," I said, as silence filled the tent as it all sank in.

During Rob's several talks with Mom and Dad before he left for K2, they never told him he shouldn't go. The family knew how important K2 was to Rob and no one tried to dissuade him. For the most part, a mountain climb, even if it was K2, didn't seem as dangerous as parachuting off a building or into a narrow chasm.

Dad and Mom had also talked to Rob many times about him finding something in life to be interested in besides climbing, but he had no real interest in working at Goldman Sachs or some bank. Rob wanted to climb and, most importantly, he wanted to climb K2. Mom and Dad recognized this and realized they couldn't stop him.

I also realized Rob wanted to climb K2 more than anything. I recognized it was dangerous and even life threatening, but I never tried to dissuade him. For one thing, there was never any doubt in my mind Rob would make it. Even after reading the Savage Mountain's deadly history, even after being there at the mountain's mighty foot and seeing its horrific ferocity for myself, I didn't change my mind. Everything Rob did with climbing and parachuting was life threateningly dangerous, but I didn't see it that way. I always believed Rob was so skilled, so courageous, so honed and so calculated in his daring that it was a given he'd overcome every risk and obstacle. I never considered trying to talk him out of climbing

K2. In fact, whenever the subject came up, I encouraged him.

Second, and perhaps selfishly, I wanted Rob's pursuit of the ultimate challenge and ultimate thrill to continue. For my twin to not only have such a horrendously ambitious goal, but then to actually achieve it was real inspiration to me. Rob showed me that summits really did exist and could be identified. More importantly, he showed me they were attainable. If Rob could figure out his summit and then marshal the requisite discipline and desire to achieve it, maybe I could too. Vicariously at least, Rob's search was mine as well. Deep inside me, I always figured he had chosen the better path. His quest was pure.

The next morning, the air was filled with a wide array of emotions. For the rest of the trekkers and me, it was time to say goodbye and begin the long hike out of the Karakoram. We were sad that our time at base camp was ending, but we felt privileged that we'd been able to make the trip and be a part of our friends' and loved ones' quest for K2.

We also knew that, while we had reached our destination, the climbers had not. Their destination was still more than two miles above us on the windswept summit pyramid. Whether it was their destiny remained to be seen.

When Pam Roberts said goodbye to her husband Jack, tears flowed down her face. She clearly understood the potential danger of her husband's endeavor. Over the course of the trip, my initial impression of Pam proved to be correct. She was genuine and totally unpretentious. As I watched her sob, I felt bad for her, knowing as she did that she might be hugging and kissing her husband for the last time.

Rob and I embraced. I told him I knew he'd make it and to have fun on the top. Rob told me again how glad he was that I had come along.

"Remember, there are a lot of people who love you and care about you coming back more than they care about you climbing K2" were my last words to my brother.

"I love you, too. Say hi to Mom and Dad," were his last words to me.

We were both tearing up. The thing that stood out in my mind, above the intense emotion of our goodbye, was the incredible look of excitement on Rob's face. He absolutely beamed. I knew he couldn't wait to get on the mountain. As he turned away from me, I saw his eyes dart immediately to the summit of K2. I couldn't identify it specifically, but I sensed there was something up on K2 for me also. I hoped my twin would find it.

Neither of us, though, gave any thought to the idea our communications henceforth would only be through dreams and the mountain wind. As Rob wrote in his journal after I left:

"Felt very emotional saying bye to Richie. I need to come home!"

Last look back...

Rob beneath his Dream Mountain

Chapter XIV

"Got to push. Got to summit. This is the chance of a lifetime."
–Rob Slater

June 13

Shortly after the trekkers and I left base camp, Rob's K2 climb finally began. As soon as I turned and began my walk back down the glacier, I lost my ringside seat at the captain's table next to the driving force behind the 1995 American K2 Expedition. I also lost my tent mate and my eyes and ears for the events which were about to unfold above me on the great mountain of my twin brother's dreams. I knew Rob was keeping a journal, in which he wrote diligently each night. I also knew my family and I would receive mail and at least a couple of updates from Rob via the satellite phone over the course of the summer. In addition, the world-wide climbing grapevine might provide some further news. But in any event, Rob would be home in a few months to tell us all about it and show us the pictures. In fact, knowing Rob had his camera and was documenting the whole trip, I hadn't even brought one.

At first light, just after 5:00 a.m., with 35 pounds of gear in their packs, Rob, Celsi and Scott started their first of many trudges up the strip. They roped up at the end of the strip, where Rob and I had been the day before. From there, the walk out to the icefall was long and basically flat. As they hiked, the south face of K2 crept slowly by. They saw an avalanche in a chute to the left of the Abruzzi Ridge that didn't even make it to the ground.

They skirted the first few crevasses and entered the icefall. The trail was poorly marked but they were able to follow it, which was fine for that first day, but they knew when it snowed they would have to start all over again. Scott led, and at times it was hard for Rob and Celsi to keep up with him, but the three moved well together. After about 30 minutes, they emerged from the icefall, where they took a short break to unrope and eat some energy gel packets. After 15 minutes, they started up the scree toward the spot for their advanced base camp, which they had decided to set at the foot of the Abruzzi Ridge.

There were already a dozen Dutch expedition members and porters there when they arrived. Rob and his climbing partners stashed the loads they had carried, which included ropes, their ice axes and gear, to establish the camp. It had taken an hour and 50 minutes to advanced base camp, which they all agreed was very good for a first time. After some hot milk, all were in very high spirits to finally be on the mountain itself. As they rested, they surveyed the route, which consisted of a long snow slope leading up to the gullies and rocks below House's Chimney. It looked just like the photos in the many books Rob had studied all the years prior. Because they felt good and were all so excited, they decided to climb the snow slope above for acclimatization.

They started up the slope without crampons, but that was clearly not the way to go, so Celsi went back and got them. Though they had no ice axes, the snow was firm and since the incline was only about 35 degrees, they cruised up rapidly, fueled by adrenaline, to the base of a buttress at 17,500 feet. Looking up, they could see where the Dutch had placed fixed ropes to aid climbers on the lower portion of the ridge. When they returned to the advanced base camp, the Dutch asked Rob and his group to fix 200 meters of rope below the lowest lines, which they said they would do the next day.

Then Rob, Celsi and Scott literally ran down the slope, making fast work of the altitude they had just gained. The return trip through the icefall went smoothly as they picked their way without a rope. Plodding along the flat glacier seemed to take forever, but Rob, Scott and Celsi walked down the strip in high spirits and arrived back in camp by 10:00 a.m., where they excitedly detailed their trip and the condition of the route to Jack and Toubbeh, who had stayed behind and arranged food in two-day/two-man bundles.

By dinner time, everyone was packed and excited to carry a load of gear up the mountain the next day. Scott, Celsi and Rob planned to fix the 200 meters of rope the Dutch had requested while Jack and Toubbeh carried the next loads to advanced base camp.

When the climbers retired to their tents at 8:00 p.m., it was snowing heavily, but by 9:00 p.m. it stopped. Rob wrote that night in his journal that the feeling of actually being on the Abruzzi Ridge that first time was nearly indescribable as he gazed up at the snow, the ice, the rocks and the sky. It almost caused him to lose his balance as the immensity of the moment and his surroundings enveloped and almost overcame him. He was on K2. He would climb it.

"The sky looks very nasty – I'm skeptical we'll get to climb tomorrow," he continued. "I've got to push – got to summit – this is the chance of a lifetime. I felt strong on the Ridge today. I need to pace myself, though. I should have no problems keeping up with Scott and Celsi, who make a good team – I hope so much we summit together. That would be so fabulous. I'll get up at 4:00 a.m. and hopefully we can push. I have to keep motivated. I really feel we can make it. I feel strong... This mountain is huge but climbable – one step at a time!" his entry concluded.

As darkness fell, shortly after 8:30 p.m., Rob went to sleep confident, yet realistic. Scott and Celsi had shown themselves to be fit, serious and determined climbers, demonstrated by Rob's comment about keeping pace. He knew he needed teammates who were honed to have any serious chance for the summit and initially at least, Scott and Celsi seemed up to the task.

That same night, several miles down the glacier beneath the

massive face of Broad Peak, I had my own tent. Alone, I thought about Rob as I listened to the rumbling of avalanches on the surrounding peaks. I knew he had only planned to carry a load of gear up to the advanced base camp at the foot of the Abruzzi Ridge, but I wondered if he'd the chance to go any higher.

It made me happy to think of my brother finally up on his mountain. I was glad I came to K2. It was great getting the chance to be with him and to be there for him over the past several weeks. I had a lot of stories to tell back home about what I'd seen. I got to go with Rob deep into his world and, hopefully, had played some small support role at the beginning of his quest. I thought about the stories Rob would come home to tell at the end of the summer. I couldn't wait to hear them. My journey to K2 had been a success. I fell asleep content.

June 14

Back at the Great Mountain, it snowed on and off that night, but the accumulation was very small. At 3:40 a.m., there was some clear sky and a cloud band at the Camp II level, which over the summer the climbers came to see as usual. Rob wanted to climb, as did the others, so they all got up for a quick breakfast. Rob left first at 5:00 a.m., about five minutes ahead of the others, plodding along in his Gore-Tex suit. At the rope-up spot, Scott, Celsi and Rob tied on one rope while Toubbeh and Jack used the other. Proceeding through the glacier, they marked the way with little flags and reached advanced base camp at 7:30 a.m.

As they prepared to climb the ridge, they uncoiled a 200-meter rope and tied into it, with_one climber on either end and one in the middle. Each made a coil of the slack, which allowed them to remain roped together, yet still move up the slope in unison. Celsi led off but said he was very tired, so Rob took over and tried to pace himself as he led them up the snowfield past their high point of the day before. They stopped at 18,600, feet and rested on a natural rock bench.

By then, the day had warmed far enough above freezing that the snow was soft and balled up under their crampons, but in no way detracted from the view or exhilaration they felt as they inched their way up the ridge

After their break, Scott led off about 200 feet to another

bench, where he dropped the rope. Celsi and Scott climbed another 100 feet to the fixed lines placed by the Dutch. While Celsi and Scott placed an anchor for the top of the new fixed line, Rob futilely tried to untangle his section of the rope. Scott had no better luck when he returned, so they cut the rope to untangle the last bit and Scott continued down to fix the pieces below.

While Rob waited, the wind came up and the temperature immediately dropped. Rob was well aware of how, in the mountains, the temperature difference between being in the sun and shade was accentuated. It seemed even more so at higher altitudes. Everything about K2 was more intense.

Soon after, Rob was joined by the Dutch team descending from higher up.
Together, they reached the bottom of the ropes and easily ran down the last 500 feet to the advanced base camp, tired but stoked to have reached 18,800 feet on schedule.

On the way back to base camp, Rob, Celsi and Scott stopped to fix the grave of Mrowka Wolf, a member of the 1986 Polish expedition, who died high on the mountain with three others during a desperate attempt to descend in a blizzard after reaching the summit via the Abruzzi Ridge. Japanese climbers had found her body the next year, still attached to fixed ropes below Camp IV, and her body had been brought down the mountain to its present location.

"Her grave was very sad," Rob wrote later. "There were some rocks piled around with a ratty tarp over her, but we could see her harness and jacket, though not any of her body."

They decided that it was better to wrap her in the tarp and then completely cover her with stones so she wouldn't be seen or bothered again.

As they piled rocks onto Mrowka, Celsi made a startling discovery – Mrowka's head! She still had her hair and teeth, but no eyes or much skin. Celsi said he'd heard that her head had fallen off when she was moved off the Ridge in 1987, and they surmised some birds must have gotten to her. Rob placed Mrowka's head inside the tarp with her body, along with a finger he'd found. The three climbers then covered her with so many rocks that the tarp was no longer visible.

"Rest in peace, fellow climber," Rob said as they left. The climbers felt they had done something decent to make Mrowka's grave permanent and private, and that no person or other creature would ever disturb her grave again. They all felt sad for Mrowka but were fascinated by what they had found.

"Every year, something turns up," said Celsi. "This year it was us who found it."

As Rob, Celsi and Scott approached base, they met Jack and Toubbeh, who were on the way to visit the Dutch camp. They stopped to talk about plans for the next day. Scott said he might take a rest day. Celsi said he was going up.

Later that night, Rob wrote about how the conversation had sorted itself out: "I'm inclined to go up because I want this mountain so badly and I really need to push. During dinner we decided to go to Camp I in the morning. Scott, Celsi and I will carry nothing to advanced base camp and then light loads above. Then a rest day."

He concluded on a less administrative note: "Today I learned of the awesome size of this mountain as well as my absolute conviction that I will climb it. I'm glad the team seems to be getting on better and now that everyone is on the mountain spirits are up."

That day, as Rob made his way above 18,000 feet, I rounded Concordia to head down the Baltoro Glacier on the long trek home. I paused for a last close-up view of my twin's Dream Mountain. I studied the mountain's right skyline, which I knew was the Abruzzi Ridge. I knew I wouldn't be able to actually see anyone on the ridge, but I looked for Rob anyway.

"I know you're up there," I said quietly, smiling to myself before resuming my march.

June 15

The next day, as he did every morning he would go up the mountain, Rob awoke to Rasul's whistle. It was 4:00 a.m. on a perfect, cloudless day. Even K2 was without the usual cloudbank between Camps II and IV. He took off with Scott at 5:00 a.m., followed shortly after by the others and arrived at advanced base camp in an hour and 20 minutes. Rob and Scott took a short break before Celsi arrived, then the three readied themselves and headed for Camp I.

They left together but Scott quickly pulled ahead. He was carrying no gear because he was tasked with picking up the fixed rope above. Rob fell into a rhythm and moved well, pulling away from Celsi and eventually catching Scott at the start of the fixed ropes. Rob broke trail on the rope – "fun actually, and I enjoyed getting higher," he wrote later. The sun shone brilliantly and again softened the snow that it again balled up under their crampons. Scott led the last 200 meters to Camp I, 3,000 feet above base camp, 19,000 feet above sea level, where they arrived at 9:50 a.m.

There was only one possible spot for a tent at the camp site, so Scott and Rob just rested in the sun enjoying the fabulous view.

"I'm finally on K2!" Rob exclaimed to Scott, wearing his huge grin. Celsi arrived about 20 minutes later, and they all worked together to prepare a platform in the snow for the tent – and they all got headaches whenever they bent over in the rarified air. They moved the gear onto their new platform and got ready to head down at 11:20 a.m.

The route above Camp I looked like a lot of rock climbing, but with the fixed rope Rob figured it would not be too bad. Suddenly, neither House's Chimney, nor the summit itself, looked so far away to Rob, who wrote that night: "I felt really strong today and am more confident than ever that I am strong enough to summit."

Having reached their day's goal, they quickly and effortlessly descended down the ropes, but slowed down on the lower slopes below because the snow again balled up on their crampons. Near the bottom, they saved energy and had a great time by glissading – a controlled sitting slide – using their ice axes to check their speed on the steep slope.

They rested briefly at the bottom, before trudging through the icefall and across the glacier to base camp. Along the way, they all agreed it was a monumental waste of time to continually hike between base and advanced base, so they decided to start for Camp II from advanced base camp.

Jack and Toubbeh carried to advanced base that day, but were still two steps behind Rob and Scott in acclimatization. Celsi was very gung-ho, but he was still a step behind Rob and Scott. Rob confided to his journal that "Scott is the one to be aligned with and will work for Camp II with him... (Celsi) is a great guy and I hope we three get to the summit together... It's a big mountain but we got our first stab at it today." With continued good weather, they hoped to reach Camp II on June 19th.

Just as Rob had learned of the awesome size of K2 on his

first day up the mountain, the reality of the awesome size of the Karakoram hit me my second night. We were camped by the military outpost with its bored soldiers and mangy mules. Seeing them again reminded me how, in some respects, time stands still in the Karakoram. Without Rob, I suddenly felt completely isolated.

The other trekkers and I were now two days from base camp, but had several more just to get back to the trail head at Askole. Then Maureen, Pam, Ruth and I had the jeep ride to Skardu and the totally unappealing prospect of a bus ride back to Islamabad in front of us. Needless to say, the excitement and anticipation of the way in was lacking on the way out. Also missing was the feel of a "big" expedition. We had only a handful, as opposed to a long train of porters. Collectively, we were closer to being one group rather than two large organizations – one of porters and one of climbers and trekkers - working their way through the splendid desolation of the Karakoram.

June 16

A rest day. Rob woke about 7:00 a.m. when the sun began heating up the tent. The day was perfect. Rob assembled all the gear, including sleeping bags, pads and everything else that needed to go up the mountain. Their new plan called for Celsi and Rob to go to Camp I the next day and then shoot for Camp II the day after that. Scott and Jack would then go for Camp II the day after while Celsi and Rob descended to advanced base to then make another carry to Camp I. After that, they would all descend to base for another break.

During their rest day, they visited the Dutch base camp, where they heard a spotty radio message that the Dutch climbers had failed to reach Camp II, or even House's Chimney.

"Maybe we'll end up passing them," Rob wrote, "though we like just jumaring the fixed ropes. It really saves us a lot of work. Hopefully they will fix ropes all the way to Camp III and we can attempt the summit together. We like the idea of their help breaking the trail and fixing ropes to the Bottleneck. At any rate, we will continue to push hard and if we pass them, so be it... I hope the weather holds. I am really getting excited about getting high on the mountain – and my first night on K2!"

While Rob and his team rested, my trekker companions and I made our way further down the glacier. We stopped to camp under the Trango Towers at our same camp site at Urdukas.

It was nice to see grass and vegetation again, but it reminded me that I was leaving the wild desolation of K2 and would, inexorably, have to rejoin civilization and the real world. I thought of Rob, who was not only still in the wild, but actually just getting started on his great adventure. I wondered how high he had made it up on the mountain so far.

Our group was small, especially compared to the human train we accompanied on the way in. In addition to the three trekker gals and me, we had a few porters and a designee of Rasul who was in charge of cooking and seemed to also be in charge of personnel. We were relegated to the same menu we had enjoyed since the first day of our trek. Taco Johns or a Mini Mart chili dog sounded mighty appealing, but I was still way too far from civilization to start agonizing over junk food.

Unlike the trip to base camp with all the climbers, no one had an agenda and we had succeeded in reaching our destination of the K2 base camp. There was now no pressure or expectations. The only concern was going home. I had occasion, the first actually, to talk a little with Ruth, who I found to be quite engaging, pleasant and sincere. I was disappointed with myself for perhaps prejudging her earlier on during the trip by association.

June 17

Rob awoke at 4:00 a.m. in great anticipation of spending his first night on K2, but the day started out contentiously.

"At breakfast," Rob recorded in his journal, "Jack started picking on Celsi for not carrying enough weight! He hasn't done shit but whine and he's off on Celsi! Scott, Celsi and I all stomped out of Base expecting Jack and Toubbeh to leave the expedition." With heavy packs and much conversation, it took them an hour and 35 minutes to reach advanced base camp.

"At advanced base we were packing and eating, preparing for the long slog up the snow slope when Jack arrived," Rob's journal entry continued. "Scott lit into him and it all came out, finally. How Jack's done nothing but whine, his 'protein deficiency' at Urdukas, etc. Scott tore him apart. I put my two cents in also. So did Celsi. Jack broke down and cried and apologized. I started up the snow slope tired of all this third-grade nonsense. Hopefully this clears the air."

Celsi, Scott and Rob began climbing again on mushy snow under a hot sun, feeling very lethargic. Rob had a headache and could barely move. After a while, though, he got his rhythm and quickened his pace. At 5,700 meters, Rob and Celsi "picked up," or clipped onto, the fixed rope. Scott arrived shortly thereafter and took over the lead. On that day, they had no idea of how many times they would have to climb what would become an all-too-familiar route to Camp I.

Arriving at the Camp I site, a small notch in the ridge at 6,000 meters, Rob, Celsi and Scott took a 30-minute break and then set up the tent. But first, they had to shovel out a platform in the wind-packed drift on which to place the tent. This exertion, coupled with the thin air, made Rob dizzy and he had to sit down. There really was something to be said for acclimatization. Eventually, he felt better and the three climbers crowded into the tent and began making dinner. First, though, they had to melt enough snow to fill all five of their water bottles, which took almost two hours. This was called "brewing." They ate various items from the food bags but both craved fatty foods – of which they had none. An Arby's Beef 'n Cheddar, or something comparable, would have been great, but those kinds of foods won't keep unrefrigerated for any period of time. It was a tedious process, but the end result was right on target.

"Dinner was instant mashed potatoes – plain but good," Rob wrote of his first night on K2. "I felt warm and relaxed and ready to push to Camp II."

Meanwhile, my trekker gal companions and I continued to inch our way toward civilization. In the early part of what would surely be a blistering afternoon, I rounded a bend in the trail and caught sight of a friendly, familiar sight: the Paiyu Mini Mart. As I approached, I could tell it was a lot more crowded than the last time. I hoped it was because they had just got in a big shipment of ice and were having a Super Swig sale. Instead, a trekking expedition headed for Concordia was coming up the glacier, just as we had done more than a week prior.

I headed over anyways, hoping they got a shipment of something I might want. They didn't, but amid the crowd milling about I ran into "Mac" McCleery, a retired doctor from Cheyenne and friend of my Dad's. To say the least, it was quite surprising to meet a familiar and friendly face so far from home.

Mac was with the trekker group on its way to Concordia. Maybe because of my shared DNA with Rob, I launched into it about K2 and the hellacious view that awaited him.

"Even though it's still 60 miles away, you can't believe how huge it is until you actually get up there," I proclaimed. I tried to convey that the size and true magnitude of the Great Mountain could not yet truly be appreciated and tried to describe its grandeur, in the most eloquent way I could, without Mac thinking I had lost my mind or my composure.

"It's so bad-ass," or something to that effect, I exclaimed. I might have even thrown in an F bomb for extra accentuation.

Acting like I had some inside information, which I did not, I told Mac that Rob was probably half-way up the Abruzzi Ridge by then, and pointed out the right skyline where he would be.

I also had to warn my fellow Wyomingite of the post-holing fiasco we had experienced on the final approach to Concordia, imploring him to wear pants that day along with some appropriate shoes. I'm sure, more than once, I said, "just wait till you see K2!," although I didn't call Mac "Junior."

The mini mart was out of chili dogs, but Mac gave me some salami and crackers. Just looking at it and thinking about all the fat and grease inside made my mouth water. It had been weeks of nothing but healthy rice, beans and water. I thanked Mac, told him again how great the view of K2 was from Concordia, wished him well on his journey and headed back to camp for my feast. On the way, I saw our porters, sitting together in the shade. I motioned hello to them and recognized immediately they had seen my treats. If it was a treat for me, I wondered, what would it be for them? Without hesitation, and to the porters' great surprise, I handed them the salami and crackers. Even though they spoke no English, I took the way they smiled at me as they shook their heads up and down as a "thanks."

"Enjoy, guys, and thanks for carrying all my stuff," I said as I walked away, my mouth no longer watering.

June 18

Rob slept well his first night on K2. He got up at 5:15 a.m. to start the stove and Celsi and he each had a cup of hot chocolate before packing up. Rob carried only one tent, which was not much of

a load, but he had never climbed that high before. Celsi carried all
the food, water and the radio. Rob's feet hurt initially in the new
boots he was wearing, because he hadn't had a chance to break them
in before going up the mountain, but he felt really strong and soon
was way out in front as he cruised up the ropes feeling better and
better. The Doll House chimney was but a small challenge and soon
he was face-to-face with House's Chimney. The watery ice in the
back of the chimney made for a special treat after weeks of silty
river water and warm snowmelt. With the luxury of the fixed ropes
for protection, he slurped and guzzled his fill.

Rob topped out of the chimney to an incredible view of the
strip far below and the Masherbrum Group to the south across a vast
expanse of space and sky.

"I felt like I was really on K2 – I also felt strong and knew
the summit was another step closer," he described in his journal.

At the notch in the Abruzzi Ridge that would become Camp
II at 6,700 meters, or 22,000 feet, it was extremely cold and windy,
with a wind chill factor far below zero, unlike the wind-protected
narrow chimney he had just climbed. Rob quickly stashed the tent
and donned another pair of gloves, then headed down without delay.

Rob warmed up and began feeling more comfortable below
House's Chimney and by the time he'd descended through the Doll
House Chimney, he began meeting Dutch porters on their way up to
stock the Dutch camp. "Farther down the Ridge," Rob later wrote in
his journal, he met Celsi and told him it was "really cold up there"
and that "he was about halfway to Camp II."

Celsi decided to turn around and Rob and he shot back to
Camp I in a quick 20 minutes. There they found Scott amid a
growing thunder of rocks and boulders that rained down the
mountain, freed by the melting snow, thudding loudly as they
bounded down the ridge and ice fields in long arcs. It was more than
unnerving; it was downright frightening so Rob and Celsi decided to
head down to base camp, where Rasul made lunch. Toubbeh
informed them that one of the Dutch climbers had been hit in the
face with a rock just above Camp I. Scott and Jack were helping
evacuate him to base.

Rob wrote later that they needed "to avoid Camp I – way too
much rock fall danger. Besides, if I can't climb from base to Camp

II I am not even in the game. I'm hoping I'll be able to climb all the way to Camp III. Inshallah... I felt great today at 6,700 meters. I need to stay healthy, focus on the mountain and be smart about preserving my power. So far so good... What a day!"

For those of us on the outbound journey, following the trail and using the same campsites as we had done on the way in was, as Rob would say, "a casual hike with a light pack." For one thing, whether or not we were willing to admit it, at the end of the trail each night it felt a little closer to home and the creature comforts of civilization. For another, it was downhill.

Someone – I'm not sure who – proposed the idea that we do the last three day's hike in two days. It would mean a couple of longer days, but a new campsite. We hadn't been taking rest days and, after all, it really was downhill all the way. In addition, it made little sense to get up early and be done with the day's hike well before noon. I liked having the rest of the day to look around, relax and take in the scenery and basically enjoy not having to do anything. It was good work if I could get it, as Rob would say. Nevertheless, I was all for it if that's what everyone else wanted to do. I let my position be known and thereafter pretty much stayed out of it. I have never claimed to be an expert on women, but I knew enough to not make an issue out of it one way or the other, especially if any of the gals disagreed. To me, it was a decision which could be made in a matter of seconds, but if the ladies wanted to discuss it they could. In the end, it was agreed.

June 19

Celsi, Toubbeh and Rob rose at 4:00 a.m., but they all felt tired and groggy. Owing to an ongoing problem with the fit of his left boot, Rob's feet hurt enough that he was not too interested in going to Camp I that day, but he went anyway.

They left base camp at 5:10 a.m. Rob slowly waddled to the ice fall, promising himself that he'd attend to the boot the next day. The weather deteriorated steadily and it was already snowing at 6:00 a.m. when they radioed Scott and Jack at Camp I, who they learned were coming down to help another Dutch climber, this one who had his arm broken via rock fall above Camp I. With the temperature dropping and visibility dropping by the minute, Toubbeh decided go to advanced base camp and wait for Scott and Jack while Celsi and Rob gratefully turned around and plodded home through the growing snowstorm.

The snow continued while the climbers talked and played cards until 5: 00 p.m., when they all went to the Dutch Base Camp to make calls on the Euro team's satellite phone. Rob talked to Dad for four minutes and excitedly told him how he'd been up on the mountain and how overwhelmingly big it was.

After the phone calls, the team revised their plan again for when the weather cleared. The next time up Scott and Rob would go straight to Camp II, spend two nights there and then climb to Camp III before coming down. This, they believed, would put the team in an ideal position for its summit bid. They had also learned that the Spanish expedition was ready for its summit attempts on the South Spur – a route that merged with the Abruzzi Ridge route at the Shoulder - as soon as the weather allowed. That night, Rob wrote:

"It felt great to get in touch with people back home. I'll call again after we touch Camp III, which should be within the next week. Then the summit wait begins...

"Maybe the Spanish will fix the ropes for us – that would be a godsend... I feel really strong. I want to sleep in Camp II and touch Camp III before going down for a rest. Then I want to go all the way back up to Camp III and sleep, leaving the summit gear before returning to Base to wait for the summit push...

"It's getting closer – I can hardly believe it! I just feel it – I will summit. What a thrill that will be. I will be rested and ready to sleep in Camp II and carry on to Camp III. I'm half-way there. I've got to keep moving and stay in focus."

My companions and I were also moving, though we didn't have any snow to worry about. For us, the weather issue was the heat as we descended further from the high heart of the Karakoram. It had now been weeks since our last showers and, as we tramped along in the heat on the dusty trail, thoughts of the first bath back in civilization occurred more often to all of us.

As we got farther from our friends and loved ones at the K2 base camp in the physical sense, they remained close in our thoughts. As we broiled in the sun, it never occurred to us that it might have been snowing on K2. We did realize, however, as we walked out of the Karakoram, that Rob, Jack, Toubbeh, Scott and Celsi were, literally, in their own world.

In my group, it was much the same way. Although by this time we had been together for many weeks, we were still, in some ways, just a collection of individuals. As the reality of separation sank in, we each had a different "other half" in our respective relationships.

Pam had a spouse on the Savage Mountain and, judging by the emotion displayed during their goodbye, each seemed well aware of the potential for danger. I thought Pam, probably like the rest of us at this point, was anxious to complete this stage of the outward journey. Maybe closer proximity to Jack without the ability for contact made it harder. Maybe she was simply anxious to begin in earnest the waiting process. I certainly didn't bring it up with her.

Ruth, in contrast, only had a boyfriend on the mountain. I did not know and did not feel it was any of my business to find out about the depth of their relationship. Their outward appearances gave me no strong indication one way or another and, without diminishing or belittling the nature of their connection, I didn't equate the same emotionalism of Jack and Pam's separation to that of Ruth and Toubbeh. Ruth played it close to the vest with me and I gave it little thought.

In further contrast, I had an identical twin brother on K2. But as far as separation anxiety was concerned, and notwithstanding the strong emotion present in our own goodbyes, I honestly wasn't thinking about any potential danger facing my twin. I knew Rob would summit and be back in Cheyenne, with pictures to prove it, soon enough.

In yet further contrast was Maureen, who had no spouse, sibling or boyfriend unit on the Abruzzi Ridge. I had no doubt Maureen, as a caring person, appreciated some danger involved for the climbing team, but, again, it wasn't something she dwelled on outwardly.

June 20

Another rest day. Everyone slept in until 7:00 a.m., which wasn't hard considering it was still snowing lightly. Rob and Toubbeh spent about two hours trying to fix his left boot, but there were already raw spots on his foot, which prompted a frustrated Rob to write in his journal that "time will heal it but it's a nuisance to be slowed down by something that shouldn't happen at all."

There was still light snow at bedtime so they would definitely not be climbing the next day. Instead, they would pack up and make final plans for the push to occupy Camp II and fix to Camp III. Rob, Scott and Celsi would push the route. Scott was indeed showing himself to be "The Man" as Rob had initially suspected – "so strong," he marveled in his journal. Celsi was living up to Rob's expectations as well, putting forth maximum effort for the team.

Jack and Toubbeh, on the other hand, were clearly not impressing Rob or, from the tone of his journal entries, anyone else. As Rob had said many times, K2 would sort them out and it did. Jack and Toubbeh could stock Camp I, and that was valuable, but they were not acclimatized to carry or sleep higher.

And then there was the weather. Everyone hoped it would start cooperating again, but of course no one knew for sure.

"I'd hate to get bogged down here for a week," Rob wrote that night. "A few days are OK – I need a rest so my foot can heal and my legs can rest. I want to keep the upward momentum intact."

Early that afternoon, under a scorching sun, I hiked alone into view of the welcome shade of the large grove of trees at the trailhead. It was both a welcome relief and a disappointment. I had successfully completed the hiking part of the trek, covering many miles through one of the most desolate corners of the planet with relative ease. Physically, I could have turned around and gone back to base camp, but it still felt good to be done with the walk. On the other hand, seeing the camp, with the people milling about and the tell-tale signs of civilization - like the garbage that inevitably accumulates anywhere humans linger, was a first dose of the reality that my grand K2 adventure would have to end at some point. There were a few jeeps present at the site and although I wasn't sure if they were there to take us to Skardu, others would arrive and it was quite a stark reminder that our time of "getting away from it all" was done.

Over the course of the day's hike, the girls and I had become separated, so I sat down on a log to wait, enjoying being out of the direct rays of the sun. Nearby, a couple of porters were sharing what appeared to be a watermelon. It sure looked good and, despite my attempt to be nonchalant, they noticed my interest. One of them cut off a large slab and held it up, motioning me to take it. I didn't think I'd been that obvious, but I got up and accepted their offering. I told them thanks, and they smiled and nodded their heads, just like the guys I gave the salami and crackers to at Paiyu.

Back on my log, I bit into the melon, expecting it to melt in my mouth in a cascade of cool wetness. Instead, all I got was a mouthful of seeds. I started to spit them out, individually, hoping to retain the liquid portion of my treat. I noticed the two porters watching me, kind of laughing and shaking their heads as if to say, "Man, what a gumby; he spits out the seeds." Realizing it was not deemed appropriate to spit out the seeds, I finished my melon honoring local custom, hoping I wouldn't later sprout a vine.

June 21

The weather was still bad, so another rest day was declared. Rob had lunch with the LO from a Broad Peak expedition, who told him that Alison, Kevin Cooney and Alan Hinkes were in Concordia, along with their own group of trekkers. If that was the case, Rob wanted to be in base camp the next day when they arrived. Besides, he figured, another rest day wouldn't hurt. Then he would "be ready to shoot to Camp III."

That evening, Rob saw a huge avalanche off the south face of K2. Weather wise, he believed that, if it didn't snow that night, one more day to settle the mountain could work to their advantage – and maybe the Dutch would clear the trail to Camp II again and fix some more ropes above. On top of that, he was still dealing with the aftermath of his sore foot from the ill-fitting boot as well as chapped lips from the high, dry, cold wind. As he wrote in his journal:

"It just didn't seem right to go today – tomorrow seems right. My foot and lips are healing. Besides, I need to write a few postcards – then on to Camp III on the 23rd."

Meanwhile, the ladies and I enjoyed another beautiful morning as we prepared for our jeep ride through the lower gorge and back to Skardu. I looked for John-John, but it was evident he was not a part of our small caravan. We quickly loaded up and were soon winding our way down through the gateway to the Karakoram. Compared to the ride in, the collective mood was more somber. Slowly but surely, our grand trekking adventure was reaching its end as we continued our inexorable march back to "civilized" humankind. Perhaps the starkest reminder was the noise from the jeep engines and the smell of exhaust fumes. I didn't know about the girls, but that first foul whiff of pollutants brought me back to the Islamabad bazaar. It made the wild remoteness and majesty of the

Throne Room of the Mountain Gods seem so far away. I think my companions may have experienced some of the same feelings. We rode much of the way down the gorge in silence, as we each took in our last views of what had become, at least for me, a place of strong personal meaning. I thought of Rob, so far away.

As we rumbled along the last miles into Skardu, I paused to consider my companions. Like me, they were sun-baked, weather-beaten and grimy. They had hiked over 100 miles through some of the planet's most awe-inspiring but desolate country, forded streams and slogged through glaciers. In my assessment, they had comported themselves admirably. In truth, they were all pretty honed.

June 22

Rob got up at 4:00 a.m. to a cloudy sky and a low barometer that signaled deteriorating weather. Scott was also up, but nobody wanted to go anywhere, so Rob gladly went back to sleep until 7:00 a.m. After breakfast, they decided to wait for the arrival of Alison, Alan, Kevin and their trekkers and focus on getting ready for the next day's climb to Camp II and then Camp III.

Scott and Rob talked to the Dutch about their plans. Everyone committed to go up the next day, weather permitting – but by 3:15 p.m. the weather was as bad as it had been all trip: sub-zero temperatures, cloudy and snowy with a 30-knot wind. Still, everyone agreed to go up the mountain the following day if at all possible. Rob described the plan this way in his journal:

"Even if it's marginal, I want to at least carry to Camp II. This will help the acclimatization process if nothing else and get some more gear up the mountain. Our plan calls for two or three nights up and Scott and me fixing to Camp III with all in support. We'll see what the weather does. I want to get back on the mountain ASAP. Hopefully we'll be up two nights and then back down preparing for a surge to sleep in Camp III – then its' summit time!"

For me, it was time to reenter the civilized world, so to speak. Back at Skardu's K2 Hotel, I checked into my room wearing the same shorts and t-shirt I had worn when I checked out weeks before. My beard, which had even stopped itching after a week or so, was as dirty as my laundry.

Before a much-needed shower, I leaned over the small bathroom sink to shave and, also for the first time in weeks, faced myself in the mirror. I saw Rob – or I saw myself as I remember seeing Rob for the last time, but with one exception. My matted, thinning hair outlined my sunburned, weather-beaten face. I had never gone so long without shaving and my beard was actually pretty full, just like Rob's at base camp. The only difference was my face wasn't lit up with excitement in the massive shadow of K2. It was more a look of resignation. Was it the last time I would see him?

As I tediously and laboriously pulled, scraped and nicked away at my face, my old at-least-somewhat-civilized-appearing self emerged. The water cascading over me in the shower ran brown with the dust and dirt of the Karakoram. As I stepped out of the shower, symbolically it seemed I also stepped out of my grand adventure with my twin.

June 23

Rob spent the one-month anniversary of his departure from Boulder to K2 as his fifth "rest" day in a row in base camp, in bad weather, in very low visibility, with lots of snow and many avalanches thundering in the hallowed heights above. He lounged in the mess tent until 3:00 p.m. before taking a nap, then spent the rest of the day frustrated again.

"How worthless," he wrote that night. "Tomorrow we will try again. I am tired of sitting and want to get back on the mountain and finish fixing. Now at 8:40 p.m. there are stars out and the barometer is slowly rising – I go to bed hopeful once again."

Back in Skardu, my companions and I now presented ourselves in relative civilized, newly-scrubbed refinement. My hotel bed was no more comfortable than my sleeping spots over the previous weeks and, upon arising, I decided to forego shaving. I didn't want to overdo the civilized or refinement thing. I did, after all, have some modicum of self-respect. After our second trip to the airport in as many days, we managed to catch the flight to Islamabad and avoid a repeat of the Ride from Hell with the Marshmellow Sheik. Through the plane's window I scanned the endless ocean of snow-capped peaks for the Karakoram, the Baltoro, K2 and my brother. I knew my chances of spotting them were slim, but I looked anyway.

June 24

The weather finally cleared. The China Wind, as everyone called wind out of the north, from the direction of China that could clear the Karakoram of weather, was blowing at 4:00 a.m. and by 5:00 a.m., everyone was packed and under way. Scott, Celsi and Rob went first; Jack and Toubbeh followed. With the new snow, it took 2 ½ hours to reach advanced base camp, and they didn't get onto the snow slope until 8:00 a.m., which was very late as the sun beat down on the snow and made it sloppy. The Dutch were nowhere to be seen.

Just as Scott, Celsi and Rob rounded the first buttress, Rob saw a huge wet avalanche coming their way. He yelled and they all ran left. Rob got away by a mere four feet, narrowly avoiding being swept away and possibly buried on his mountain forever. Two more big slides went by before they hastily traversed left and got onto the rocks. After 45 minutes and several radio calls to Toubbeh and Jack, who had retreated to base camp, they began picking their way up the rocky ridge. As Rob later wrote:

"...the climbing wasn't necessarily hard-some easy mixed rock and lots of snow-except we had to traverse a scary slope, which Scott led and, while doing so, started many avalanches as he crossed."

It took until 1:00 p.m. to reach 5,700 meters, where they stashed their gear and quickly headed down. It was one of those days where it was a huge relief to just get off the mountain safely.

Back at advanced base camp Rob, Celsi and Scott cooked, brewed up and rehydrated. By 4:00 p.m. they were all in the tent, but realized they only had two sleeping bags, so Scott slept opposite Celsi with Rob in the middle. They used the sleeping bags and their coats to create a cozy nest of down. Conversation centered on the rest of the team. All were concerned about Toubbeh and Jack, especially after their fast retreat today; if they really wanted to climb, they wouldn't have run back to base camp so easily. Over the radio, they heard that the trekkers and climbers had arrived in base camp while they were on the mountain. They looked forward to the new blood in the expedition.

In Islamabad at the Shalamar, Maureen and I were set to begin our long plane ride home. Ruth and Pam, as I understood it, would be doing some further travelling in Pakistan before heading back to the states. For them, the adventure would continue. I thought again of Pam being a teacher and how it would be nice to have the summer off. Good for her, I concluded. Pam departed with the same smile on her face she wore almost the entire trip. We parted company with Ruth as well, who looked rejuvenated and eager for the next leg of her journey through the Fifth World. I concluded Ruth was indeed a cool customer. They were both true trekkers. For Maureen and me, our itinerary again called for a marathon series of flights, countries, airports, customs and layovers. The first stop was Karachi, Pakistan, then on to Dubai in the United Arab Emirates.

June 25

"After a comfortable and pretty fun night, thanks to Scott's stories, we got up at 4:30 a.m.," Rob wrote of their night in advanced base camp. "The day was great so we ate some Pop Tarts, drank some hot chocolate and took off at 5:50 a.m."

That early in the day, the snow slope was solid and safe, so they made good progress to the gear they had stashed on their two prior trips up the mountain, but the fixed ropes were buried, so pulling them out and cutting new steps was a chore. When they reached Camp I at 9:30 a.m., the tent was buried, so they had to dig it out before they could start the stove. After lunch, they began a carry to Camp II. Rob started out, feeling great breaking trail, before Scott took over the lead up to a point about 100 meters below the Doll House Chimney. There, a 40-knot-plus wind and fine, blowing and swirling snow called spindrift caused a 2:00 p.m. halt. They cached the gear they had hauled and descended until they met the still-climbing Celsi a short distance below. In the ensuing discussion, Scott decided to wait at Camp I and go to Camp II the next morning. Rob and Celsi wanted to go down, as they were anxious to greet the new climbers.

Back at base camp, Rob was glad to see all the new faces. British climbers Alison Hargreaves, Alan Hinkes and fellow Boulderite Kevin Cooney had arrived along with their group of trekkers. Rob hoped that the three veteran climbers – the Brits had climbed Everest earlier that summer – would breathe new life into the expedition.

"We need some real climbers who will work for us and the summit," Rob confided to his journal that night. "Alison and Alan are great! They're a very positive addition both as fun new faces and as strong climbers who won't whine."

Although they never met prior to the K2 base camp, Rob and Alison hit it off immediately. Alison, like Rob, was "desperately keen" to go to Antarctica some day after K2. They were kindred spirits, united by a shared passion.

"(Rob and Alison) worked well together," an expedition member observed.

Alison Hargreaves wanted K2 very badly as well, although she lived and pursued her own version of the dream with more subtlety and a refreshing degree of femininity not normally expected on the 8,000-meter giants Everest, K2 and Kangchenjunga. Womanliness combined with her wry sense of humor, determination and nerves of steel was a unique and inspirational addition to the expedition. With a husband, Jim Ballard and their children – six-year-old Tom and four-year-old Kate – waiting at home for her in England, she was torn between her longing as a mother to cradle her children in her arms and heeding her own inner call that coaxed her higher up the Abruzzi Ridge. In 1988, while six months pregnant, Alison climbed the North Face of the Eiger. Two months before she reached K2 base camp, she became the first woman to solo Mount Everest without the supplementary oxygen. With the goal of becoming the first woman to climb the world's three highest peaks, after conquering Everest she had set her sights on the far more dangerous challenge of K2. Alison, like Rob, set the bar extremely high for herself and was not easily deterred. She summed up her view of life by frequently quoting a Tibetan saying:

"It is better to have lived one day as a tiger than a thousand years as a sheep."

Meanwhile, Maureen and I were slowly moving westward across the globe. We found ourselves in the Dubai airport late that afternoon, but our next flight, to London, didn't take off until the following morning.

"These guys have lots of dough," I said to Maureen, referring to the country in general, and to Emirates Air in particular. "Let's just ask them if they can take care of us."

I explained our situation to the lady at the airline counter and, just a few minutes later, we were riding in a Mercedes on our way to a fancy hotel. A car would be sent the next morning to bring us back to the airport. In the meantime, we were to help ourselves at the hotel, including its restaurant.

"These guys do have a lot of dough," we joked. So, just by asking, we got the VIP treatment.

After a nice dinner and a shower, I lay down on clean sheets. My mind went to Rob and I had to chuckle when I thought of myself, riding in a Mercedes and staying at a fancy hotel in the Middle East while Rob was still in a tent and still without a shower or shave. Rob was toughing it out on the Savage Mountain. I had just lucked out.

June 26

The next morning, Rob was up at 4:00 a.m. with Celsi and Alison to make a run to Camp II, but it started snow. The big breakfast with all the trekkers grew longer and more relaxed until it became another rest day, which Rob admitted he needed. They would try again for Camp II the next day – and Rob was indeed energized by the new team members. He'd spent too much emotional capital dealing with expedition personnel issues. With the addition of Alison, Alan Hinkes and Kevin Cooney, those issues essentially became moot. As he wrote that night:

"We had a real fun meal with Alison, Alan and Celsi. I am really glad they're here. Toubbeh is leaving with the trekkers. Jack is trying to go to Camp II also. We'll see what happens."

When Mike Toubbeh departed base camp, there was no emotional goodbye with Rob. They were simply two vastly different people. Toubbeh was a guy who knew his limits and, in Rob's view, had no interest in approaching them. This was a mindset that was antithetical to my twin brother. Toubbeh likely viewed Rob in the same manner. As Mike turned to head back down the glacier and Rob turned up toward K2, I doubt either of them looked back.

June 27

Rob finally got back on the Great Mountain. After the usual 4:00 a.m. whistle from Rasul and a quick breakfast, Celsi, Alison, Alan, Kevin, Jack and Rob headed for the mountain, arriving in advanced base camp at 7:00 a.m. Rob took off up the snow slope with a relatively light pack. He quickly out-distanced Celsi, blazed past Jack at 5,700 meters, then fellow Boulderite Cooney at the bottom of the fixed ropes, and reached Camp I at 9:40 a.m. Everyone else arrived within half an hour and they started the stove and refilled their water bottles. As they brewed, they discussed the weather above them. Camp I was warm but Camp II was in the clouds and it was obvious that the wind was blowing at least 30-40 knots. Alison, Alan, and Kevin didn't think they should go any higher that day, but Rob and Celsi wanted to press on.

"I wasn't in the mood for arguing so I said I was going regardless – if it was too bad to establish Camp II I would come back down to Camp I," Rob wrote later.

At noon, as Alison, Scott and Kevin remained at advanced base, Rob headed up in his Gore-tex suit with a sleeping bag, pad, stove gas and personal gear. Although he initially made good time, the weather worsened and by the Doll House Chimney it was basically a blizzard. Rob pressed on through House's Chimney, but even though he took only one hour and 45 minutes to reach House's Chimney, it took two more hours to reach Camp II. Above it, Rob saw some blue sky and the Black Pyramid. Then he crawled into a Dutch tent, where two climbers inside gave him some hot soup. Rob left his sleeping pad with the Dutch climbers, secured the rest of his gear outside, put on his down coat and started down at 4:45 p.m.

The wind was less strong below House's Chimney and off the ridge. Just above the Doll House Chimney, Rob came upon Celsi, who said he was going to "bivy," or camp without a tent, below House's and he continued up while Rob continued descending until he arrived in Camp I at 6:00 p.m. Jack was there with hot chocolate, which Rob greatly appreciated. From their tent, they monitored the radio call from Scott and Alison in advanced base camp, who suggested to Celsi that he return to Camp I. He agreed and started down slowly while Jack and Rob got settled and waited. Just as night fell, a tired Celsi arrived in camp. Rob and Jack gave him hot chocolate and soup and he went off to the Dutch tent to sleep. That night, Rob recorded:

"The wind and snow were horrible plus I think I ran out of gas. I think the weather really stopped me… I'm getting frustrated at our seeming lack of progress. We need to get Camp II and Camp III put in ASAP. I feel strong and know I can reach the top but we need some help. If the weather is good, which it looks great now at 8:00 p.m., I'm going back to Camp II."

Maureen and I spent most of this day on an airplane. We were supposed to have had a direct flight to London from Dubai, but had to stop in Vienna, Austria, with plane trouble. We ended up just sitting on the tarmac, staring out the window at a less-than-postcard-quality view. I tried to distinguish something "Austrian" that I could identify or relate to enough to claim later as a legitimate basis for saying I had been to Austria. They didn't even let us off the aircraft to get our passports stamped or enjoy a quick schnitzel and stein of brew. It was being back in civilization in the worst respect. I thought of the folks back in Askole who never had to deal with the hassles of being big-time international travelers.

At Heathrow, it finally started to feel like we were nearing home. The place was swarming with people, but I didn't see a single pastel leisure suit. I could also understand the language, and the honed British accents made up for the phrases I couldn't get. Most of all, there was no gut-churning smell. There were numerous bars complete with high stools, draft beer and signs advertising hot dogs. I remembered Celsi and I had a running joke about missing mini mart chili dogs, so I took a stool and ordered a cold beer and a dog. When it arrived, I asked the barkeep if he had any chili, onions or hot sauce. He looked at me like I was from another planet and, being from Wyoming, with an affinity for meals from convenience stores, I suppose I was. Alas, I was still a long way from a real mini mart and home.

June 28

After a good sleep, Rob and Jack woke at 5:00 a.m. to a very grey, snowy, windy day. They decided to go down as the weather was bad and Rob wanted to get on the same schedule as Scott because, as he later wrote, "I've got to align myself with the strongest for the best summit chances... I want to climb this mountain." Rob made it to advanced base camp in less than an hour and waited for Celsi and Jack to arrive. They talked for awhile and agreed that they needed a more structured plan for people and gear.

Scott, Cooney, Celsi and Rob had a meeting and drew up plans for all to abide by to stock Camp I, II and start to work on Camp III. Rob believed that the team would get a second wind and start to make some progress. They had been in base camp 17 days and hadn't even slept in Camp II yet but with the "new blood this will happen soon." It was decided that Scott and Rob would establish Camp II in three days and begin work on Camp III. In the meantime, they would take a day to rest.

"I need it after a day of 13 hours going. I know I'm strong enough to climb this mountain," Rob wrote self-encouragingly that night. "The weather is not great but it doesn't have to be to fix to Camp III. We've got to get moving."

Maureen and I had a long day as well. Unlike our outward flight, which didn't have a single empty seat, the return trip from London to Los Angeles offered many vacant rows. With the help of a couple sleeping tablets washed down with a couple cold ones, I stretched out and snoozed peacefully over the north Atlantic and Canada until final approach into LAX.

We each had one more flight, with Maureen going up the west coast and me over the Rockies to Denver. Before the trip, we had lived in opposite parts of the country and known absolutely nothing about each other. We lived in different worlds, but we had now crossed the globe together. On our way we had seen, enjoyed or endured just about every mode of travel. We had also crossed through a wide spectrum of the human condition, from the fabulous oil wealth of the Middle Eastern deserts to the fetid squalor of the Islamabad inner city. In the process, Maureen showed me how women could be bright, irreverent and tough without sacrificing the quality of femininity. That night, at the airport where we had met at the outset of our journey, I parted ways with a lady who, as a travelling companion, fellow trekker and friend had proven to be quite honed.

June 29

I arrived in Denver at about 4:00 a.m., having taken a late flight out of Los Angeles and losing an hour across a time zone. The only thing open was a 24-hour Burger King. With ice in my soda and catsup for my salty, greasy fries, I celebrated my successful return to the Rocky Mountains and a place I knew well. A couple of hours later I arrived home, marking the official end to my grand K2 adventure.

While it was a rest day at base camp, Kevin Cooney, Alison and Alan Hinkes were in Camp I, planning to carry rope to Camp II before heading down. Jack, Scott, Celsi and Rob planned to go to Camp I the next day. The Dutch were close to Camp III and, hopefully, Scott and Rob would finish fixing to Camp III on the next go-round.

"This will make us in a good position – then only one more trip to Camp III for final gear loads and then the summit!" Rob wrote that day. "I'm really looking forward to sleeping in Camp II and establishing Camp III – I want to climb this mountain so bad. I know I can summit – we need some settled weather. I'd like to get out of here by the end of July...

"I can't wait to take more mountain trips and be close to home. I feel like I'm missing out on a major portion of life – hopefully things will get better after I summit K2. The truth is I know it won't change anything. But it will be an important event in my life. There are limits to dreams I guess but if I can do this I can do anything."

Rich beneath his twin's Dream Mountain

Rob self-portrait on the Abruzzi Ridge

Chapter XV

> "The summit will be one of life's greatest moments."
> –Rob Slater

June 30

Rob spent the night in agony with stomach cramps. When Rasul blew the 4:00 a.m. whistle, he decided to take the day to rest and heal, then climb directly to Camp II on July 1. After sleeping from 5:30 a.m. to 8:30 a.m. he woke feeling much better. At noon, Rob had lunch with Jack, who for some reason didn't go up with Scott and Celsi, prompting Rob to later write: "The team continues to narrow."

The weather was so-so. Camp II was visible but there were lots of clouds. Rob really wanted to hit Camp III this go-round so the team could start thinking about a summit attempt if the weather ever cleared. Then the wind started picking up and it began snowing – again, so Rob spent the day reading and attending to his journal.

"I hope tomorrow I can go up. God, I want to climb this and feel strong enough," Rob wrote, repeating his personal mantra. "I'm trying to get through some new books but can't get real motivated. Not motivated at all to write post cards. I feel very isolated from the world back home. I want to climb this mountain in July. I must be patient and ready to push upwards at all times."

Later that day, he declared to Celsi that "I'm not going home until I summit, but I hope to be home by Thanksgiving!" Celsi wasn't quite sure if he was serious, but knew for certain that Rob was determined to remain and wait for his chance, mirroring the attitude and approach of his new friend Alison, who once said. "If you're given opportunities, and there are two options, always take the harder one. If I choose the harder one, and succeed, I'll be really happy. If I fail, at least it was trying the harder one."

By 8:00 p.m., as darkness began to descend on the Karakoram, the weather was calm and clear. Rob felt better and looked forward to sleeping in Camp II the next night and then pushing through the Black Pyramid.

"May the weather hold – I feel great things are about to happen these next three days," he wrote before retiring that night.

If I would have been keeping a journal, I would have written "First day back." Although it was a work day, I didn't go in to the office. It could wait over the weekend and, judging from the fact that the town was still standing and apparently functioning, it wouldn't matter.

K2 and the Karakoram magnificence, Rasul, John-John, the Marshmallow Sheik and the heat and stench of the Pakistani urban landscape all of a sudden seemed so far away, almost like from a dream. The one thing that maintained its vividness was the look on Rob's face as he gazed upon his Dream Mountain. I figured he would be well on his way to the top by now.

July 1

Saturday. Rob made the long carry from base camp to Camp II, covering over 6,000 vertical feet in altitude. He left at 4:45 a.m. with Jack and climbed to advanced base camp by 6:15 a.m. After a half-hour rest, he started for Camp I. The snow was firm, the steps clear, and it wasn't too hot. Rob arrived at Camp I at 9:15 a.m., drank two quarts of water, rested for an hour, then left for Camp II.

He met Celsi and Alison below House's Chimney and Alan above, and arrived feeling good at 1:30 p.m. Scott was already there, so they got into the tent to brew up. Rehydrated, they made a good meal of Alison's food packets, which were a welcome change from their own supplies.

Rob was also stoked because he'd just climbed from base camp to Camp II, thereby confirming to himself that he was definitely "in the game." He and Scott went to sleep excited, ready to start up the Black Pyramid the next morning on their way to Camp III.

I, on the other hand, spent the day doing yard work. I had moved into a new house a couple of months before the K2 trip. I decided to throw a house-warming party and asked Rob if he wanted to come up from Boulder to check out the new place. It was on a Friday night and Rob showed up. Standing in the kitchen, he had virtually every guest around him as he recounted the story of his Slipstream climb a couple of months prior. He was the life of the party. Then, in true Rob form, he retired early as he planned to get up at 2:00 a.m. to drive to the desert to climb.

It's funny, I thought. One day you're in the shadow of K2, the next you're staying at a fancy hotel in Dubai and then you're laying sod in Cheyenne, Wyoming. I thought of how long of a trip Rob had to get home after he summited the Savage Mountain.

July 2

Somewhat surprisingly, Rob didn't sleep well. He got up twice and had strange dreams. It must be the altitude he thought, as he got up and did the stove work. Scott and he left at 7:30 a.m. with light packs containing personal gear, water and one coiled rope each. The route started on snow but ended with many rock steps which were almost vertical, separated by snowy ramps. Rob even recognized a few places from photos he'd seen.

They climbed mostly on rock but some was on slopes loaded with new snow. The going was weinous – way more strenuous than the Camp I to Camp II climb – and higher in altitude. At one spot, they stopped to rearrange some rope by a step in the ridge. They also cleared away several sections of old ropes from previous expeditions, cutting more than a dozen and throwing them off the ridge. As he worked, Rob thought fleetingly of his comments about Mount Everest being covered by garbage and wished he had a choice other than to himself litter the great K2.

In the early afternoon, Rob and Scott reached the top of the Dutch ropes at 7,000 meters, or 25,000 feet. They stashed their own ropes and gear and headed down, reaching Camp II at 2:30pm. This time, they made an extra effort to rehydrate, drinking as much as they could and refilling all the bottles.

"We need to keep tons of Gatorade on hand to make the dreadful snow melt tolerable," he wrote of the process.

Rob knew sleeping in Camp II was good for acclimatization and that each night should feel better than the last. His sleeping spot was passable but not very good, so they planned to set up a new tent the next day, then try again for Camp III.

"This mountain is big," Rob recorded, "1,000 meters more to go and only half-way to Camp III."

I have always liked going to see my parents on Sundays, spending the afternoon catching up and hearing the latest news from the rest of the family. It was also a good way to mooch a home-cooked meal. This day's conversation was dominated by my K2 trip. It made me kind of feel like Rob, getting to tell of a great climbing adventure. Unfortunately, I didn't have any pictures, but I once again tried to convey the immense scale of the Karakoram and K2. I was asked for my assessment of the mountain itself and the climb. All I could report was it looked horrendous-so high and so big-with the winds blowing a huge plume of snow off the summit ridge across the sky. I told them about the other climbers I met and how, in my estimation, Rob would definitely lead them to the top. I didn't know about the others, including Alison Hargreaves, who was to join them later, but it was clearly the real deal when it came to big-time expedition climbing. To the extent my folks may have been looking for reassurance about Rob, I tried to give it, and I think they got it by the fact I had been all the way to base camp and back. But in truth, I didn't have to exaggerate how I felt he would make the summit and come home with quite a tale to tell. I got no indication my parents felt any different. As usual, we took it as a given that Rob would be successful.

July 3

Rob slept better, most likely because he was better hydrated. He got up once during the night, which created a memorable moment.

"The stars are incredible," he wrote later. "Too bad I'll never have the chance to really enjoy them. The cold makes me get back into the bag ASAP."

Still, he was thirsty when he awoke at 4:50 a.m. and got the stove going. By 6:30 a.m., Scott and he were fed and watered but it was still too cold to go outside. The China Wind had been blowing, however, promising better weather soon, so they simply lounged around for a few hours while the stove heated the tent and the sun warmed the Great Mountain.

They dug a second tent platform about 9:30 a.m., then took a break to enjoy the now-perfect weather. They were sitting around doing nothing when Jack showed up carrying a rope. Rob and Scott were glad to see him make it to Camp II.

Jack stayed for half an hour and then headed back to base camp as Scott and Rob pitched the second tent, a dome tent Alison had brought which set up without much trouble. They moved in their gear and got ready for more brewing, but Scott didn't feel well so Rob ran the stove and ate a Wayfarer meal. Scott declined; he wasn't hungry. The radio call from base camp told them Cooney would be up the next day, possibly with Alison.

The army duffel bag I brought as luggage on my K2 trip was delivered today. I wasn't sure how it made it or the route it took, but was nice to have it, even though it was smeared with some kind of black grease and full of filthy clothes. I wondered if Rob had changed his shirt yet.

July 4

Rob slept soundly, owing again to better hydration and to his new and improved spot, but woke up with a bad headache. Fortunately, it dissipated after he got outside and started moving around. Scott and he set out to survey the scene up the ropes but turned back after only 100 feet because of freezing toes, fingers, faces and no motivation. They decided to call it quits and left for base camp at 7:00 a.m. About half way down the rock ridge below House's Chimney, they met Kevin Cooney, carrying a heavy load. They stopped briefly in Camp I, then continued down. They met Alison at the bottom of the fixed ropes, who told them she'd try to hit Camp II the following day.

"Hopefully only three more trips up here and I'll be done.

We slogged back to base camp very tired and hot," Rob wrote after they returned.

During their absence, two more expeditions had arrived on the strip, one from New Zealand, one from Spain. The New Zealand group included Peter Hillary, son of Sir Edmund, with a phone Rob hoped to try out. The Spanish team would be attempting the same South Spur route as the other Spanish team already on the mountain.

The strip now had its full complement of six groups for the summer: Rob's group, the Dutch and the Kiwis on Abruzzi; the two Spanish teams on the South Spur and an American group on the North-West Ridge.

The first Spanish team was already on the Shoulder, intending to try for the summit the next day, weather permitting. There was always the weather. Spirits rose and crashed on wind speed, snowfall and temperature.

"The Spaniards plowed up there yesterday and are taking a break today," Rob recorded that day. "I hope the weather holds.

"Scott and I will probably be here four days. By then Camp III should be fixed so we can go to Camp II, establish Camp III and return. Then one more trip to Camp III, hopefully on the same go, and sleep there for the night. Then we descend to base camp to wait for summit weather."

"This is the month – July – I need to summit K2. I am acclimatizing well and am going to summit. Got to stay focused and keep working to keep my body ready for the summit push. Everything is coming along. I have to keep pushing for the summit."

In my book, the 4th of July is one of the most important holidays. Being schooled as I am in history and political science from my days at UW, I have great appreciation for the foresight and bravery of the founding patriots of our nation. In consequence, I believe the 4th should be appropriately commemorated, and there is no better way to do so than with hot dogs nearly burned on the grill. If chili dogs are possible, it's even better. For this 4th of July, I toasted Richard Celsi with several. I also couldn't help but think of Rasul and Rob and his team's menu as I surveyed the choices of an All-American cookout. I knew it was too early to reasonably expect them to be at the top, but I hoped for Rob, Richard and the rest of their team's progress.

July 5

A rest day for Rob and Scott. Rob "slept until 6:00 a.m. and tried to listen to the AM radio call. He caught parts of it and learned Kevin Cooney was going up alone to fix ropes and Celsi and Alison are going to Camp II." The day was nice and warm and mostly clear, so Rob sat in the sun, listening to the Scorpions, enjoying the incredible avalanches coming off of Broad Peak and writing postcards – a time-honored K2 tradition.

Throughout the summer, trekkers, climbers, expedition support people and porters coming and going from the various base camps along the strip acted as intrepid mail carriers. It was amazing how efficiently this casual-but-serious system actually worked for Rob and the other climbers, who "mailed" their missives regularly throughout their stay. Rob liked especially to send postcards to the young daughters of his old friend and Boulder climbing partner Hammer. Along with greetings and progress reports, they always included a standard message: "Tell your Dad when I get back we're going to the desert."

Unfortunately, Rob also spent his rest day dealing with the return of the diarrhea and stomach cramps that had slowed him a while back. Meanwhile, Celsi and Alison went to Camp II while Cooney fixed ropes alone along the route. But the day's big drama was that two Spanish climbers tried to summit – and came up short by less than 250 meters. They left Camp III the night before at 11:00 p.m. and reached 8,400 meters by noon – but radioed down that the snow was terribly deep and, in the Bottleneck, it took them five hours to go 90 meters. Clouds shrouded the upper mountain all afternoon, but by 7:30 p.m. Jack radioed that the Spanish climbers had all made it back to Camp II.

"I can't believe how grim it is up there," Rob wrote after he heard the news. "They must be shattered – so close. I hope they make it down OK. (Making it to Camp II) means they are mostly safe and at least out of the clouds. I feel for them – I hope we get better conditions and can push on through to the top… I am starting to get Summit Fever. I want this mountain!"

Rob then weighed in on his diarrhea and its causes and consequences: "It must be the water here. I can't afford to be sick. No more cold water from here. Anyway, I'll rest a few more days and be ready for the climax of this and hope it ends successfully in

July. I'm already looking forward to Home. God, I hope I feel better."

As for me, I was trying to get back into the daily grind of practicing law and working for a living. During our long march to the K2 base camp, I had started to get used to living in the mountains, without a care of the outside world to bother me. Sitting in my office, I could look out the window and see the blue Wyoming summer sky and think back to the magnificent ceiling of the Karakoram. I hoped that Rob, high on the Abruzzi Ridge, was looking at the same kind of crystal sky.

July 6

During breakfast, the team learned that a Spanish climber had died the night before below the lowest fixed ropes after falling 2,000 feet. His body was in the Spanish base camp waiting to be flown out. Rob wrote later about this somber news that "we all talked about it and agreed lamely that it is inevitable someone will die on K2 this year. I hope it won't be one of us. I have to keep things in perspective and get home. There is so much to look forward to."

Scott and Rob decided they would wait two more days before going up again, in part because they believed the group needed another meeting to plan the establishment of Camp III and prepare for the summit. They also knew they would need some better weather to get beyond Camp III. "The Spanish apparently had really warm weather on the Shoulder and above," Rob observed. "An olive branch granted by the mountain before it slams the door shut on the summit."

By that evening, the weather looked to be possibly breaking down and getting worse. It dipped below freezing, colder than it had been in quite a while and the wind picked up but, on the other hand, lots of blue sky remained. "I'm not too psyched to sit out a long storm but it is inevitable and maybe it will clear out the crud and allow us to reach the top. I want to get on with it and get the summit and go home," Rob wrote that night.

I had made my summit, meaning the K2 base camp and then gone home. I was now, as they say, "back in the real world." It meant shaving and putting on a suit and tie every morning. It also meant I couldn't go weeks at a time without a shower or change of clothes. This is not to say I'm the kind of guy who doesn't bathe or change his socks; it's just that, at first, it took a while to get back into real person/real life mode. The whole epic Karakoram and K2 experience was still fresh in my mind. As always, you don't appreciate something enough until it's gone.

July 7

It was an absolutely perfect day, with a slight China Wind and not a cloud in sight, as the climbers met to discuss upcoming plans. They decided that Alison, Jack, Scott and Rob would go to Camp I, then Camp II, then Camp III before coming down for the summit push. A few days later Cooney, and maybe Hinkes and Celsi, would bring loads to Camp III and sleep there also. All the climbers would carry personal gear, food and equipment to stock Camps II and III. Then they would be ready.

For Rob, going to Camp I then Camp II would be easy, even with some weight; he'd been doing it for weeks now. "All is going well," Rob wrote, then added emphatically, "I talked to Alison and Cooney today and feel very confident we will summit. The team is very strong and gets along well. Hopefully the big day will be around July 18th or 19th. I am totally gripped with Summit Fever! I have to make it – I feel I will. Cooney and Alison are confident as well. This is the best possible combo for us to succeed. I can't wait – will it happen – It has to – I know it will."

In his enthusiasm, Rob continued, "We will sleep in our down suits in Camp I and carry on to Camp II for a better night. Then we'll really be on the mountain. I called Dad today. All is well. He seemed happy to hear from me. I told him again 'I have a mountain to climb.' I'll call again after I summit, which should be on July 18th or 19$^{th.}$ It will be one of life's greatest moments. I need to relax and conserve strength on this trip up. It will be good to climb with Alison. She is very positive."

Rob, like the rest of the team, needed to rest for the last surge to Camp III to have a good chance for a successful run at the top. They decided their best bet was to keep well-hydrated, relax, try to take a lot of photos and take good care of themselves.

"The summit draws closer," Rob wrote, reflecting the shared optimism of the group after they agreed on what they hoped would be their final plans. He concluded with a reflection on the perfect day they'd all enjoyed. "We need summit weather like this."

I, of course, was unaware Rob wrote he was gripped with

Summit Fever this day. To me, since that first day at Exum so long ago, Rob had *always* been gripped with some kind of summit fever.

July 8

After a 4:00 a.m. breakfast, Scott, Alison, Jack and Rob went to advanced base camp in an hour and a half. Scott and Rob wore tennis shoes, which they had discovered were simply the lightest, most comfortable option for times when the route was packed. After making the hike so many times already, they believed it was clearly the way to go and sure saved a lot of energy. Rob led everyone but Scott, and reached Camp I in 2 ½ hours, then started brewing under a sky full of building thin, wispy cirrus clouds that usually mean fair weather. A big cloud bank could also be seen behind the Masherbrum group to the south.

As they packed for their carry to Camp II, they hoped the next day's weather would be good enough for them to push to Camp III. They departed sluggishly for Camp II, but once Rob got going, he felt good and pushed on to the camp in 2 ½ hours, again trailing only Scott. They settled into their tents, Jack with Scott and Rob with his new pal Alison, with whom he cooked a good meal and had many drinks to rehydrate.

"Scott was really moving. He is the man," Rob wrote admiringly. "Alison is quite funny. It's nice to spend some time with her finally. We had a lot of laughs about many different things."

July 9

When the climbers got up at 5:30 a.m., the weather looked like it had the night before, with high cirrus over them and clouds behind the Masherbrum group. But the cirrus had lied and a storm hit before 6:00 a.m., with strong winds and swirling, driving snow. They decided to sit tight until the next morning and then either carry to Camp III or retreat to base camp. The hours were spent brewing, cooking, resting and chatting as the wind blew fast and the day passed slowly.

By now for me, the initial excitement of being back had long since been immersed in the daily grind. As I met with clients, whether new or already established, I was reminded how running one's own business was a long-term, ongoing endeavor. It was something that was carried around at all times. It made me think back to being on the glacier with Rob. No worries about clients, overhead or deadlines. Good work if you can get it was right. I wasn't being asked about my trip as much, so was no longer getting to retell the tale. When I talked to Mom and Dad, we could do little more than figure Rob was climbing the mountain and, after he made the top, he would come home.

July 10

Rob tossed and turned all night as he heard snow fall harder and build up against the tent fabric. When everyone awoke early in the morning the weather was still bad, but the storm lessened and visibility improved to about 75 feet so, at 5:30 a.m., Scott said he was going down. Alison and Rob reluctantly followed suit at 6:30 a.m., reaching Camp I easily, where Scott was waiting. "Jack was nowhere in sight. He was brewing up at Camp II when we left," Rob recorded later. "I know the mountain now," Rob thought to himself as Scott and he, followed by Alison, descended into the warmer air below the clouds. "This will be a help when we come down from the summit," he concluded, remembering what he had said repeatedly to his brother and family: "Getting up will be the easy part..."

As they made their usual plod through the icefall and glacier, Rob and Scott stopped to put on tennis shoes on the moraine and reached base camp by mid-morning.

Back at camp, Rob discovered that "apparently Jack has tried to move to the Northwest Ridge expedition!" Rob was exasperated – more trials and tribulations for the expedition leader – but he had more important things to worry about.

"Our team is well functioning so I can't devote any energy to these lame 'pro climbers.'"

At dinner, they adjusted their plan to stock Camp III. The next day, they would all rest, then Kevin, Scott, Alison and Rob would go to Camp I. The day after that, they would fix to Camp III and sleep. The following day, Celsi, Jack and Alan would switch places with the first four. Then, once again, they would be ready for a summit push.

The weather began clearing later in the day and they all hoped it would settle. That night, the moon was nearly full and cast a beautiful glow across the Karakoram. By 8:30 p.m., Rob was glad to be warm in bed with a rest day waiting.

"Kevin has loaned me his CD player," Rob journaled. "This sounds great – I have two candles burning and I will perhaps read a bit and enjoy the music.

"Now we are at least on schedule with Kevin... he is a good man; he's smart about how to climb the mountain and a real 'upper' to talk to. He's very positive and knows how to go about getting us to the summit. I'm glad us four are working together. We have a great chance. Kevin thinks less than 10 days. The summit is getting closer."

July 11

Rest day. That morning, all were present for eggs. Rob had five, over easy. "I'm eating so much and am such a slob – I haven't lost an ounce. I need to get up to the summit to shiver off about 15 pounds," he wrote of his appetite. They now set July 21 as Summit Day so Kevin, Scott, Alison and Rob all wanted to establish Camp III the next day regardless of the weather.

Dinner was especially fun that night, with everyone singing Deep Purple songs. Before retiring, Rob recorded:

"I really like our group – such a good crowd. This time we'll make it. The full moon is out on Broad Peak. The Karakoram looks incredible in the moonlight. Of course K2 is in a cloud. What a mountain. We don't even get to see it often but usually just enough to keep us looking up and wondering – just like women's clothes ought to be."

Part of the allure for me wanting to go to K2 was the excitement and anticipation of a new experience. The same was true for Rob concerning the summit of K2. I wondered again if it would it be enough to satisfy him and would it bring him close enough to the edge.

July 12

"Happy Birthday Sissy!" Rob began this day's journal entry. Despite his optimism the night before, Rob awoke at 4:00 a.m. feeling poorly. After breakfast, the group decided to wait another day and Rob was glad to stay in bed. Poor Rasul was sick as well, so they had to cook for themselves that day.

Rob moved his tent and was very pleased with the result, as his floor space increased drastically and his bed was once again flat. He called Sissy from the Kiwi camp to wish her happy birthday, then stayed to talk with Peter Hillary and some of the Dutch climbers, amusing them with tales of his BASE jumping exploits. Everyone who knew Rob knew he was a great story teller. His BASE jumping tales always drew a crowd no matter where he was, and the same was true on the moraine strip at the base of the Great Mountain.

Rob went to bed that night cheerful and hopeful, as he almost always was.

"We had a very fun dinner and had many laughs," Rob journaled. "Alison is really funny. Our group is a good one.

"Tomorrow the weather looks good so we're off to Camp II. We will put in Camp III but will not be attempting the top because we won't have enough gear. No one has slept in Camp III yet so we're just not quite ready. I got all set for the summit. When I go, all my stuff will be on the mountain.

"I feel good and hope this will all be wrapped up in 10 days or so. I can feel it – it's going to happen – I'd like to think I could go now but we're not set yet. I need to sleep in Camp III once I get all my gear up. Then the summit team will sort itself out and I can finally reach the summit of K2."

Sis told me the excitement in Rob's voice about being on K2 was palpable.

"Richie," she told me, "I could see his face when he told me about how big and amazing the mountain was."

I also wished Sis a happy birthday and we agreed it will be great to hear Rob's tale and see his pictures from the top of K2.

July 13

The weather was good, so Kevin, Scott, Alison and Rob took off for Camp II as planned. It was Rob's seventh trip to the 22,000-foot level and, at six hours, the fastest.

"If anyone were to ever read this it would sound like a broken record," he journaled, "up at 4:00 a.m. to Rasul's whistle. We ate and left at 5:00 a.m. in tennis shoes for advanced base camp. We didn't rope up this time and made it in one hour and 30 minutes. The hideous snow field was soft and warm and there were no real good tracks to follow. Scott blasted away as usual. Two hours and 15 minutes later we were at Camp I where we melted snow before taking about three hours to Camp II.

"We all feel good and are resting comfortably. Once again I am rooming with Alison. The Kiwis are now next door with two tents. I like that group. All are friendly, especially Peter Hillary. I feel much acclimatized to here now. On to Camp III!"

July 14

Their acclimatization plan was really starting to take hold and after a restful night, the group packed very heavy, 35 pounds or so each, and at 8:00 a.m. started in nice weather to establish Camp III. They reached their highest point – 7,000 meters, or 23,000 feet – in only two hours. They continued up some interesting and very steep mixed climbing and reached a snow face below a huge serac barrier, where they waited until two Dutch porters surmounted the serac. Then, they slogged up an endless slope in thigh-deep snow until at 2:00 p.m. they too reached the top of the serac barrier, occupied by one Dutch tent.

The team brimmed with confidence, as it took only six hours with full packs, they all felt good and the site was surprisingly accommodating. The two Dutch porters dropped their loads and descended as Rob, Scott, Alison and Kevin quickly set up two tents in a safe spot secure from the wind and spindrift.

Unlike the Dutch, Rob's team did not use porters to ferry loads up the mountain to the higher camps. For one thing, the expedition would have to feed and pay them which, given the already-tight budget situation, wasn't feasible. More importantly, to Rob, just like using supplemental oxygen, having others do the legwork for the expedition was poor style which would only detract from the purity of the experience and accomplishment.

"I felt good today and had a healthy appetite – I'll never lose any weight," Rob wrote before retiring. The group all slept in their down suits and bags that night. Rob fell asleep easily, but woke before 9:30 p.m. with very irregular breathing, unable to catch his breath. He wasn't cold, but he just couldn't relax and slow down his breathing. Having something some more to drink made him feel better and he fell a back to sleep again, not awakening until 5:30 a.m.

July 15

The morning was warm and sunny, with no wind and only a few clouds. Everyone sat outside for an hour while their things dried out. Eventually, they generated the necessary energy to get dressed and head up the route towards the serac to survey the route above. The snow was deep and avalanche-prone and Rob was absolutely without energy. Every step was an effort requiring many breaths.

Clouds came and went as ice crystals floated in the air. Rob couldn't help but to note the stunning beauty, despite how poorly he felt.

Scott led and eventually got to the exposed ridge crest above the serac to the remains of someone else's old Camp III. High above, the beginning of the Shoulder could be seen. The way was riddled with serac and crevasses. It didn't look easy at all.

The ridge formed their skyline to the left. Everything else was miles below. All the Gasherbrums were visible, with G II, in Rob's opinion, looking the best. To the north lay China, desolate and uninhabited with hundreds of miles of glaciers carving through countless 7,000-meter peaks. "I felt like we were finally on the mountain, even though the top is a mile above," Rob wrote later.

The group was growing closer, all working well together and getting along. It seemed that the mountain had brought them together. "Scott and Kevin's judgment I really trust," Rob confided to his journal. "This is the best possible alignment for the summit."

They established Camp III by leaving almost all the clothes, food and equipment they'd brought with them. Now set for the summit push their next time up, they rested and soaked in the splendor of the surroundings, enjoying the fruits of their labor.

Rob and his team departed Camp III at 9:00 a.m. and blasted down the ropes effortlessly; they got back to Camp II in about two hours. During their descent, they passed the Dutch on their way up for a summit attempt and Celsi and Alan Hinkes on their way up to Camp III.

"Good luck and blaze a trail for us!" Rob exclaimed to the Dutch, but evidently regretted his less friendly treatment of his ascending teammates. "I should have been more polite but it was cold waiting for them so we left as soon as possible."

Rob and his companions walked in single file through the icefall, with Scott and Rob in tennis shoes and reached base camp at 3:00 p.m. Rasul greeted them with his warm, familiar smile, recovered from his bout of sickness and glad to see them.

That evening, Rob recorded the local news in his journal: "Eleven summited on Broad Peak with one death. The Americans on the North-West Ridge of K2 are leaving in two days for the top. We leave in three days for the top." Death, it seemed, warranted but a matter-of-fact mention in the shadows of the giant mountains, especially now that they were finally ready for a summit push. As

Rob wrote:

"NOW the weather is flawless. NO clouds and only a slight China breeze. Will it last? I feel lucky – I feel it will happen. So does Kevin. "It's finally so close. We are all in strong shape and want to summit. If the weather holds we will climb K2 – imagine that. I've thought about it for so long and now it will happen. I can hardly wait. I look forward to the ultimate trip to the mountain of all mountains."

Word of the death in the Throne Room of the Mountain Gods failed to reach Cheyenne. Even if it had, it would have made little difference to me. I knew people got killed climbing-especially on the 8,000-meter giants like K2 and Broad Peak. I had slept in the shadow of both, after all. But without diminishing the seriousness or sadness of any death, I always knew when the Reaper came for a mountain climber; it would be for someone other than my brother.

July 16

Another perfect day. The day before, the weather and pressure had really picked up and all night and day the sky was flawless. At 3:00 p.m., the sky in all directions was still perfect, so Scott, Kevin, Alison and Rob planned to head to Camp II the next day with no loads. Then it was on to Camp III and the summit. The Dutch, with two porters and Alan Hinkes, were on their way to Camp III. They had spent the previous night in Camp II and would try for the top the next day. Two other Dutch climbers and two porters were also ready to try in the next couple of days.

Rob washed his clothes and hair so as to be as light and comfortable as possible for the summit. Everyone, including Rasul and the LO, were almost giddy with anticipation.

"This is it," Rob wrote. "I feel calm but very excited. I can't believe our time has finally come. I feel good. Four days should see us through. Will the weather last for three more days? I don't even care about the fourth day as we will hopefully be in Camp III and on the ropes.

"How do the others feel? Alison is itchy and wants to take advantage of the good skies. Kevin and Scott inspire confidence. Both are excited I think. We all feel our plan is good and with the weather and the others ahead to break trail, plus the fact that we've spent a night at Camp III and have all our gear up there, we feel the stars are party to the top and the gods are screaming 'go, luck is with you – you'll reach the top!'"

Rob's acclimatization had been steady and conservative. Going to Camp III from Camp II would be good and only require one night at Camp IV and one at Camp III on the way back. For Rob, Camp II was now casual and would provide a good sleep before going to Camp III.

"I can't wait," he wrote. "I hope /know my next entries in this book will be about how we summited K2!"

July 17

Rob awoke at 4:00 a.m., just before Rasul's whistle, for what he hoped would be his last trip up the mountain. They were off by 5:00 a.m., but just as he started through the icefall, Rob saw a human torso sticking out of the ice. He figured it was most likely one of the porters from 1939 who had tried to rescue Dudley Wolfe. The body was clothed in wool and had a piece of hemp rope tied around its waist. The whole spine and back were intact, but the head, arms and legs were gone. Rob surmised they might show up as more ice melted. "Another piece of history emerges from the glacier," he wrote.

Checking out the body slowed them a little, but they arrived in advanced base camp at 6:40 a.m., which was still very fast. Kevin, however, decided to go back because of a bad cough. Rob and Scott felt tired but decided to go on. Alison was raring to go and took off first. Once on the slope, it became apparent to Rob and Scott that they had no gas. Scott said he was going down, but then decided to try for Camp II and see how it went, so Rob went with him.

By the time they neared a rock island about halfway up, however, Rob realized he was way too tired to continue. They were up there a day too early. He wrestled with the idea of resting in Camp I, but decided that wouldn't do him any good, so he and Scott hung their packs on the rock island and headed down at 9:00 a.m., hoping to catch up with Alison the next day if possible. Back in his base camp tent, Rob wrote:

"I was sad to see Kevin go as he is a good man and very strong. I know I did the right thing by coming down. I got to base camp before 11:00 a.m. early enough to still have a good rest day. The big drama of the day is the Dutch and Alan Hinkes who summited at 6:15 p.m. God, I want to summit... I envy those who summited – but they deserve it because they pressed on. So we'll see how this goes – I feel this is the time. I'll write again in four days after I've been to the summit."

On the other side of the world, I had no way of knowing about Rob's progress or frustrations. I just kept feeling, like Rob, that the summit was close at hand.

July 18

Rob got up at 3:00 a.m. in order to beat the sun for what he once again hoped would be his last trip up the mountain. He ate in the cook tent with Rasul and left at 3:45 a.m. under clear skies and a brilliant moon. "Crossing the glacier alone in the dark was actually nice and the scenery was beautiful," Rob wrote later. He made it onto the trail, through the icefall and into advanced base camp in one hour and 15 minutes, his best time ever.

The snow slope above advanced base was firm and Rob felt so good that he made it to 5,700 meters (18,500 feet) in 50 minutes and Camp I in two hours and 15 minutes. After a short break, he was off to Camp II, arriving at 10:45 a.m., seven hours after leaving base camp. Alison was there to greet Rob before she took off for Camp IV. "Had I known she would go from Camp II to Camp IV in six and a half hours I would have gone with her. She only took two hours and 45 minutes to go to Camp IV from Camp III," Rob recorded approvingly, but he didn't try to follow her. To him, the weather appeared to be deteriorating again, so he decided to save himself, as he was already a bit tired. Rob brewed up and spent a comfortable night at Camp II.

July 19

The weather did in fact get worse during the night and it was obvious to everyone that they weren't going up. Alison came back from Camp IV about 7:30 a.m.; Scott and Kevin arrived from base camp shortly after. All in the same tent, they brewed and talked until 11:00 a.m. before deciding to descend. They arrived at advanced base camp around noon, packed some extra gear for the next trip up and got back to base camp at 3:00 p.m.

"What a disappointment," Rob journaled. "The weather is breaking down and people are talking about home."

July 20

The weather remained unsettled, with most of K2 above

Camp II shrouded in clouds. It rained throughout the day at base camp, an unusual but not unheard of event on the 16,000-foot-high strip.

"I hope this not a long storm," was all Rob had to say about it in his journal.

When I was asked back in Cheyenne about my brother on K2, all I could tell them was "I'm sure he's close and I'm certain he's going to climb it. I expect him home within a month." Of course no one, including me, knew exactly what would happen and when, but I believed my prediction was at least as good as anyone else's.

July 21

The weather was improving but still unsettled. Two months earlier, when I was still with him during the trek to base camp, our group had taken a rest day at Paiyu. It was from there that we'd first seen K2, still more than 50 miles away. Full of excitement, Rob had discussed the summer's timetable and anticipated summit dates with me.

"The Dutch are pulling out July 27," he said. "I'm not pulling out until I summit – even if it's December 27 – though I hope to be home for Thanksgiving."

In his tent now, Rob's thoughts turned rueful: "The Dutch are getting ready to leave. If we had waited and pushed on we would be on our way to the summit. I want a chance."

July 22

More of the same old dreary weather, but a much clearer picture formed in Rob's mind as they hunkered down for another day in base camp.

"If we could get through the band of clouds between 7,000 and 8,000 meters we could summit," he wrote. "We are going to have to risk it. Kevin and I are itching to go back up ASAP. I'm thinking of Charley Mace waiting in Camp IV for three nights – I'll risk it if it means I will have a chance for the summit."

Rob, however, was soon to learn that he wasn't going anywhere for a long time.

When I thought of Rob on the Great Mountain on the other side of the world, it always brought back memories of the horrendous size, scope and scale of K2 and the Karakoram. With that in mind, I gave no further thought to how long it might take. In the meantime, I believed, Rob was having the time of his life on his ultimate mountain. Rob would be home after he summited.

Rob digging out on the Abruzzi Ridge

With Richard Celsi, Scott Johnston in the K2 base camp mess tent

Chapter XVI

"In the spaces between awareness
We dream
In the spaces between the dreams
We dare
And in the spaces between the daring dreams lives
Sport Death"

–Robin Heid,
Sport Death: A Computer Age Odyssey

July 23

Rob arose at 2:45 a.m. on this Sunday morning to see about going up the mountain, but the weather gods denied him. K2, Broad Peak, and all surrounding peaks were socked in by a cloud layer that extended all the way to Camp II. Rob mulled the dreary situation and declared to his journal. "If everyone leaves I'll have to either team up with the Kiwis or solo. The weather is getting worse."

July 24

Monday brought very heavy snow – a real storm that

appeared could last quite a while. Rob began to worry about their tents and gear up on the mountain. There were also avalanches and low morale to boot. It snowed all day and dumped two feet onto the humans clustered at the bottom of the Great Mountain. As the Dutch got ready to leave, they gave away some food, so Rob's group now had more crackers and cereal.

No one was on the mountain as everyone waited for the storm to end. Rob sent out a couple postcards, finished "The Crossing" about George Washington and started reading "Angle of Repose." After so many weeks away from civilization, nearly every book brought to the mountain had been passed around and read by everyone.

July 25

The storm continued as the snow and wind seemed without end. It was by far the worst weather of the entire trip.

After breakfast, Rob spent several hours and lunch talking to Jeff Lakes of the Kiwi team about Canadian ice routes. "I need to get really honed on ice," Rob wrote later in his journal. "I can't wait-I have to do those routes ASAP. I am also looking forward to getting to the desert."

Avalanches rumbled through the clouds all around camp. Visibility was about 100 meters. The cold and wind were brutal as the storm raged with no let-up in sight. There was nothing to do but east, sleep, talk and write.

"Jack said he'd leave his down suit in case mine was lost. We're so close," he journaled. "We have all the legwork in and all we need is the weather. I will stay as long as it takes – I'm not going home empty-handed. Even if it clears we will be in base camp two days so the snow can settle, so my wait in base camp will be several more days minimum. We've been here six weeks now. I really want to get this done and go home, but we are light years from going home. I can only focus on the summit."

July 26

The third day in a row of heavy snow. There was now about 10 feet on the ground and still it fell with no let-up in sight. The snow was really getting old, but it was only the third day, so they would just have to wait. Kevin and Jack, however, were set to leave on August 4, so it was entirely possible that the weather wouldn't clear until after two of their team members had left.

The previous night, Rob had read until 1:30 a.m. and was still awake an hour later when Scott came over to ask him to clear the mess tent if he got up. Rob was thinking about the desert.

"When I get home I'm going straight to the Res to climb a few towers. I can't wait to get back-Eldo and desert towers! Then on to the big Canadian ice routes. I guess it will never end.

"I've got to finish this off – a chance of a lifetime. I wish the snow would end. Until then I'll read and try to stay patient and healthy."

That night, after he finished with his journal, Rob read until 9:30 p.m. and slept until the alarm woke him at 1:00 a.m.

Back in my office each day, I continued my work on the various business-related projects I had going. At that time, I was also doing a bit of personal injury and criminal defense work. I was trying, though, to build up a bigger base of regular business and corporate clients so I wouldn't have to be continually drumming up new, short term cases and clients. I was tired, as a district court judge once said, of "processing low grade ore."

"There's got to be more to it than this," I hoped.

From my desk, I could gaze out the window into the Wyoming sky. With its near-constant wind and long, brutal winters, Wyoming may not have the nicest weather in the country, but it certainly, in my opinion, has the best sky. I think this arises from my days at Exum in Jackson, staring into the immense blue cauldron above the Teton summits with Robbie. I know he had always felt the same way. I could only imagine his view from the K2 summit, which I continued to believe, was close at hand for my twin.

July 27

Rob got up and dressed, then spent an hour and a half shoveling snow from the mess tent. The snow was falling hard as ever, which he found to be so depressing that it kept him awake.

"I couldn't sleep and eventually lit a candle at 3:00 a.m. and read until 4:00 a.m.," he wrote later that day. "The Angle of Repose is quite a good book, a historical novel about an American frontier family. I slept until 7:30 a.m. and the sound was gone – no snow! Alas, once I cleared the snow from my tent the sound was as pervasive as ever."

During that morning's extended breakfast, the snow stopped

and the clouds began to lift. "What a relief," Rob recorded, echoing the sentiments of all. The sun shone through the clouds and it was instantly hot. Everyone dried out and enjoyed the lack of snow. The whole of K2 reappeared. The tents at Camp II were visible and, even better yet, the Shoulder was blown absolutely bare. This did a lot to recover everyone's' spirits.

"Now I know we can summit with a little weather," Rob journaled.

Although the lifting of the weather lifted the spirits of the group, there were still clouds of doubt and defeat in the air. Rob was "sick of people talking about going home. Kevin and Jack will probably leave first. Luckily Alison and possibly Scott will be here for the duration. I want this so bad. It really depresses me to talk of going home without the summit – unthinkable."

Before lunch, they built a huge dragon of snow and sacrificed Tony Rigatoni to appease the mountain gods. Apparently they did not approve of his outfit. Word arrived that the American North-West Ridge group would pull out the next day if the weather didn't improve. It looked grim for them, Rob admitted, but to him it seemed a little early to throw in the towel. Of Rob's group, it looked like no one would leave before August 4 at the earliest. Celsi and maybe Scott would be off on the 11th to catch their planes.

"Not me," said Rob, "I'm going to climb this mountain. Hopefully this will pass soon so we can get on with it."

July 28

For the fifth day in a row, the group again awoke to the sound of falling snow. It was totally socked in and snowed without let-up all day. Everyone's spirits sank again, especially after yesterday's teasing glimpse of the storm's possible end. There was more talk about getting porters and going home. Alison and Rob left for the Broad Peak base camp, located less than an hour's walk down the glacier towards Concordia, in late morning, but ended up spending two hours at the North-West Ridge expedition base camp, which they passed on the way, before actually getting on the trail. An hour later they arrived at the Broad Peak camp, where Scott Fischer was leading a commercial expedition on Broad Peak. Jeff Lakes, Peter Hillary and Celsi were already there, and it was fun for Rob to hang out and trade insults with some new faces. Rob gave

Fischer a letter for Mom and Dad to be mailed, then he and Alison walked back, glad to be getting some exercise after hiding out for days in their tents. They were not so glad, however, to reach base camp at 5:00 p.m. and find there were more discussions of plans to leave.

The LO and Jack were going to Skardu the next day to order porters for August 8th for Kevin, Scott, and maybe Celsi. Alison and Rob would go out the 20th.

"Maybe we can stay longer if I can talk Alison into it," Rob confided to his journal. "Hopefully we won't need to. If the weather clears we will all go for the summit in two days, allowing for avalanches. The North-West Ridge team is also on the verge of leaving. I want every chance possible – I'm going to the summit. I will have Jack call home for me when he gets to Skardu. That way Mom and Dad hopefully won't worry. I'm going to climb this mountain – whatever it takes I'll risk it."

When I thought of risks involved in mountain climbing, I always thought of something happening to someone else. To the extent I contemplated the risks to Rob on K2; I considered those risks to be less a factor of danger and more a just part of the allure and excitement of the endeavor.

July 29

Rob's 48th day in base camp turned out to be the best day in a long time. He awoke at 7:30 a.m. to the nicest morning in more than a week. There were clouds about with a westerly flow, but also blue sky and sun, with K2 and Broad Peak mostly visible. Kevin and Scott made day trips to Concordia and the Broad Peak base camp, respectively.

Jack and the LO left for Askole. There was a group photo before everyone departed. The Great Mountain, as Rob was fond of saying, continued to "sort" them out. Although Rob and Jack had had a tempestuous relationship over the summer, Jack had made numerous trips ferrying supplies up the mountain. Jack's effort, Rob realized, was ultimately to his benefit in his quest for the summit. Under the giant looming face of K2, Jack had stood up. Jack's effort was not irrelevant. Jack was honed.

Snow fell intermittently during the afternoon as Celsi and Rob hung out and talked while Rob again washed his shirt and socks for his summit push. Rob watched the clouds change constantly around Broad Peak and K2.

After dinner and just before dark, around 7:35 p.m., the group emerged from the mess tent to a beautiful dusk. Chogolisa was absolutely clear and glowing white. The China Wind was blowing and Broad Peak had a trail of clouds coming off it to the south. K2, of course, was wreathed in clouds above Camp II.

The sky looked to be improving and the forecast was good. If the weather held next day, they would make a summit bid the day after.

"I feel really good this time." Rob wrote again. "It's got to work. The mountain will sort it all out I think. I wish I had the desert rock – there are so many towers I want to do."

July 30

A Sunday, slated to be the last day of forced inactivity. The remaining members of the 1995 American K2 Expedition – Rob, Richard Celsi and Scott Johnston, plus the later arrivals Alison Hargreaves, Kevin Cooney and Alan Hinkes – awoke to a beautiful morning with the sun bathing K2 in crystal sharp light. The weather seemed to be reverting to its normal pattern of clouds between Camps II and IV and a clear summit, which was certainly good enough to climb the mountain. It was actually quite hot, meaning well above freezing. The intense sun and reflection off the melting snow made everyone feel lethargic. They were all set to go to Camp II at 2:00 a.m. the next morning. The weather seemed to be perking up and they hoped to top out on August 3$^{rd.}$ Then they could get porters and all leave by the 10th. That night Rob wrote:

"This would be brilliant and allow us to reach our flights on time. Imagine that. I hope this isn't another false start but it seems different. This time we will all be together, which gives me much confidence. Also, we are climbing into hopefully clearing weather instead of trying to beat the oncoming change. I feel good – I think it will happen this time. Luck is with us. I will write again in five days or so about how we climbed K2."

July 31

Instead, he wrote again the very next day. "Once again back in Base Camp. This is really getting old." That morning, they were up as planned at 2:00 a.m. and off an hour later by headlamp. Getting to the glacier was difficult in the new snow because they kept punching through the top layer. The glacier itself, though, was much easier and the climbers arrived at advanced base camp at 5:00 a.m. It took a while to dig out the buried gear, but within a half-hour Rob was off up the first snow slope. It had some new snow and lots of avalanche debris, but it was mostly ice. They got to 5,700 meters in an hour, then moved slowly up the fixed ropes as Scott pulled the ropes clear of the snow and ice and broke trail all the way to Camp I, which they reached at 8:30 a.m.

After brewing for about three hours, Rob headed up to Camp II behind the others at 11:45 a.m. The going was slow, even though he was following tracks, and he didn't have much energy. As he plodded, he guessed that he didn't have many more trips up the mountain left in him. All he needed was one more, though.

At 1:30 p.m., however, they dejectedly turned around just short of the snow arête because they were clearly not going to make Camp II that day. Kevin had been shoveling the ropes out of three feet of snow and it was taking forever, and they were just standing around getting cold in the wind.

Back at Camp I, the climbers debated what to do. Initially, Kevin and Celsi were going to stay and then break trail to Camp III while Alison, Scott and Rob went to base camp to rest and return when the trail was in. Then Scott decided to stay. Rob felt like he would possibly miss out on a summit bid so he also wanted to stay, as did Alison. They only had three sleeping bags and one tent, so Alison and Rob decided to bivouac so as to avoid going down. Kevin and Scott then objected and a long discussion ensued. Finally, to placate all, Alison and Rob returned to base camp, arriving to Rasul's waiting dinner at 7:30 p.m.

Rob also felt like he wouldn't miss a summit bid by coming down because he'd decided that Kevin had been sincere when he said on the mountain he had no summit hopes himself – that he was only trying to help by breaking trail. In the end, it had been decided Kevin, Celsi and Scott would break trail to Camp II the next day, then wait for Alison and Rob the following day.

"Hope the weather holds, as this is getting old," Rob wrote dejectedly.

August 1

Rob slept well in his tent and got up at 6:00 a.m. for the radio call from above. Celsi reported that it was really windy and that they would go to Camp II and then take a rest day, allowing Alison and Rob to catch up. The China Wind was very strong and quite cold, but gave Rob hope that they could summit. He was glad not to have spent a horrible night at Camp I and instead would now be ready to blast to Camp II the next day. Everyone hoped that the Kiwis would reach Camp III and be ready to go for the top with them. Rob tried to remain positive.

"I can't take too many more false starts," he journaled. "This will be it I feel – the China Wind is strong and the route to Camp III will be plowed."

I had now been back in the world for about a month. Cheyenne Frontier Days, "The Daddy of them All," as it is billed, is a rodeo and western celebration that draws many thousands of visitors to town each year during the last week in July. It's a week for which a large group of volunteers spend the other 51 weeks of the year preparing. Whether or not one likes the horse and cowboy thing, to the economy and community of Cheyenne, Frontier Days is a big deal. Once it's over, though, I start to feel the summer has passed its zenith and is now winding down. My family and I were beginning to feel the same about Rob being in the Karakoram. The summer climbing season was winding down and he would soon be on his way back.

August 2

Rob was up at 2:00 a.m. and off in less than an hour. The glacier and ice were good, but it was very windy at Camp I, so he didn't stop to brew up and went straight to Camp II. He arrived around 10:00 a.m. to find that all of the Kiwis were there. Jeff Lakes made Rob a cup of coffee and told him Scott and Kevin were up in Camp III.

"Are they going for the top? Rob asked, but no one had an answer until 7:30 p.m., when Scott and Kevin appeared and reported that Camp III was buried. They did manage, however, to collect their personal gear, two sleeping bags and the stove. Rob offered his opinion that the sleeping bags and stove should not have been taken, as they would just have to be carried back up. Maybe it didn't occur to him that this might be a sign that Scott and Kevin were throwing in the towel and salvaging as much as they could before they went home – without summiting.

August 3

The next morning, Rob carried a 30-pound load from Camp II to Camp III in about 5 ½ hours, which was not bad considering that he took a one-hour break at 7,000 meters. He felt good when he arrived as the others began digging down to their camp. Alison arrived 15 minutes later and Rob and she commenced to search for their tent. They found it 4 ½ hours later but, luckily, all the gear was inside and dry.

A very tired Celsi arrived about 5:00 p.m. Alison and Rob convinced him to descend to Camp II ASAP, which he did about a half an hour later.

"I felt bad for him," Rob journaled about his friend. "He tried harder than most."

Rob and Alison got their tent sorted out by 8:00 p.m. and were warm and excited. The Spanish were going for the summit the next day and three Kiwis were going with Rob's group. This seemed to be a perfect plan – except for the fact that the weather appeared to be deteriorating again.

"Just two more days is all we need," Rob recorded hopefully, though even as he wrote he knew that Kevin and Scott were due to leave the next day.

August 4

"How much more can I take?" Rob asked on of no one in particular other than the mountain gods and his journal. After a somewhat difficult night due to excessive spindrift and no comfortable pillow, he awoke to find that the weather had indeed closed in again and by early morning it was very windy and cloudy. A deluge of spindrift coming off the serac above covered everything in the tent.

They got up at 6:30 a.m. and looked despondently at the clouds. "Why can't we have a break?" muttered Rob, again to no one in particular. At the 7:00 a.m. radio call, Scott said that he and Kevin would leave that day if the porters came from Concordia. The Kiwis dug in one tent and let Rob and Alison store gear inside. "Too bad I have to come up here again,' Rob lamented, but the Kiwis were happy to go down – and happy to have Rob join them when they pushed for the top next time up.

Rob tried to convince Alison to either stay and wait, or go up now, but she said there was no way two people could reach the top because of the snow. Rob argued that they should at least try, but apparently lost the argument because at 9:00 a.m. they headed down and reached Camp I at noon. Alison was loaded down with all her personal gear so she was slow and it took them a long time to cross the glacier.

Rob arrived at base camp at 3:30 p.m. under mostly cloudy skies. Alison came in 20 minutes later. Celsi was back safely as well. "He's a good man – the best of the lot," Rob opined. Scott, Kevin and Alan were set to leave as soon as the porters arrived. Celsi would probably go on the 10th or so. Rob decided to wait with the Kiwis and make one more summit attempt.

"I still want this peak badly and cringe at the thought of not making it," Rob declared, but he returned to the positive outlook in which he had so long took refuge. "A few days rest and the Kiwis and I will give it a go and summit. Then I can go home. What a fun trip home it will be after summiting."

After that entry, Rob stayed up late writing the first 16 appendices to his journal. "I don't know what these mean – but maybe someday I will," he concluded.

August 5

Rob was awakened by rain at 7:00 a.m., so he prepared to just relax and sort out gear and food. During gear sorting, he had an argument with Scott about gear, breaking trail, and all the things that come to a head when people are frustrated. After a while, they apologized and had a long talk that really cleared the air. Rob thought they would leave as friends and things seemed much more settled and comfortable. "I like Scott a lot and hope all can work out. I guess I misread Scott and Kevin in Camp I the other day," Rob later wrote, disappointed with himself for doubting his teammates over their loyalty to the overall success of the expedition.

Alison, Scott, Celsi and Rob sorted all the food and made several porter loads for the next day. Rasul went to Concordia to get 14 porters. They were to leave with Kevin the next morning. The mess tent was looking empty. For dinner, they ate with the Kiwis, which meant excellent food and a fun time with Rob's new climbing partners.

"The moon is getting quite bright and will be full in six days – a good omen for the summit," Rob wrote for his final thoughts of the day. "God I hope I make it. It would be a great way to end the trip. I am anxious to leave but want the top. I still have some juice left so if the weather clears I hopefully will be out in a week or so."

August 6

The day began on a positive note for Rob when Alison woke him at 6:00 a.m. and declared that she was staying. 'I am really glad to hear this for two reasons. First, it will be fun to have someone around in Base Camp as well as the trek out. Secondly, it increases my chance to summit dramatically," Rob confessed.

The plan was to wait four or five days for a change in the weather, then try to go with the Kiwis to have more manpower to break trail. They hoped the current storm wouldn't dump too much new snow on the mountain. "Even if it does, this time I'm going to summit. I just have to make it. I know we're strong enough," Rob vowed. There was little doubt Alison felt the same.

After breakfast, they got the porter loads together and said goodbyes. It was emotional for Rob to bid farewell to Celsi and Scott. They were "both solid gold," according to Rob. In other words, they were honed. Alison cried. A porter stole Tony Rigatoni, but it seemed to Rob a good omen that in his new home Tony would be loved by some little Balti girl.

Rob took in the scene and considered his situation. "So hopefully four days rest and four days on the summit climb and we are on the road home. It will be great fun to hike out after summiting with Alison. I feel really good about this attempt. No more distractions. The strip seems a bit empty and lonely now. Only our two tents spread far apart and the cook tent remain. The American North-West Ridge team is leaving on the 10th after having reached 8,000 meters. They were in Camp III 10 days."

More to the point, Rob continued, "We really need to push on this trip; no more turning around because the weather is marginal. If Charley Mace can sit in Camp IV for three nights and summit in a storm, then we can summit in less than perfect conditions also. Now is the time to get really tough about pushing through. I know we can do it."

August 7

Rob may have been confident and determined when it came to his prospects on the mountain, but when he awoke to Rasul's whistle he again saw nothing but gray. The cloud ceiling was low and ice coated the ground. He went back to sleep and woke up at 8:00 a.m. feeling tired, but he felt better after breakfast when he looked up at the sky and saw some blue sky peeking through the clouds. Rob sat around all morning reading. Alison got up at 9:30 a.m., and at noon they went to the Spanish camp for lunch. They found that the olives, pate and venison were hard to eat, but the potatoes and the chorizo were good. It was fun and the language barrier didn't prevent them from having a good time, so they ended up staying until 3:30 p.m.

When they left, Rob walked down the strip and shot a few photos, but the weather turned bad again, so he was back in his tent reading by 4:00 p.m.

After dinner, Alison and Rob walked to the Kiwi's camp and caught a glimpse of Broad Peak through the clouds, but at 8:50 p.m., it started snowing again. It was depressing, but with a glimmer of high-altitude hope: The weather seemed to be better above 7,500 meters than at base camp. One more rest day and they would try to go up one last time. Rob wrapped up his thoughts for the day in his journal.

"The end is near but I have to give it 100 percent. The snow is now stopping so I'll take a peek outside and then maybe listen to some Rush and dream of all my upcoming desert trips before I go to sleep."

August 8

More snow and clouds. There was no blue sky at all; nothing but gray. Rob felt a little better that morning so, after eating his morning wheat germ and doing some reading, he walked up the strip for fun. Poking around the spot where they had earlier discovered the 1939 Sherpa, he found a hand and a jacket sleeve with a bone in it, but no head or other limbs. Rob carefully covered his find with rocks before heading back to camp.

Within two or three days max, they hoped to head up the Great Mountain again. In the meantime, all they could do was hope and wait for the weather to clear. Considering his timetable, Rob wrote that he wanted to "get back for Labor Day and hit the Res! I can't wait except I have to summit K2 first before I can leave."

The Kiwis, Alison and Rob played Frisbee golf with aluminum plates and had a great time. They decided they would play again the next day and include the Spanish. After a dinner of spaghetti and pineapple, Rob found himself in his sleeping bag with his feet slowly warming as he recorded his day.

"The Kiwis are going up the day after tomorrow. I hope it stops snowing but as of now it doesn't look like it yet."

August 9

Yet another day in base camp. The early morning brought a very strong China Wind. Huge waves of cloud swirled off the top of K2 but the whole Abruzzi route was visible and the barometric pressure was also rising.

"If this keeps up we will go to Camp II tomorrow," Rob wrote hopefully. "I am beginning to feel this is our chance. We need to be at least in Camp II when the weather breaks. If there are only a few good days we need them for the summit and not for going back to Camp III. The day has really shaped up and the China Wind still blows. The day gradually cleared and oddly enough K2 was clearer than any other mountain all day."

They decided that everyone would leave for Camp II the next morning at 3:00 a.m. The Spanish were to leave then too. "I feel great – this will be our best chance," Rob wrote, still hopeful. "The pressure is rising so I hope we can do it this time."

Porters were ordered to arrive on the 15th and leave the 16th. Rob said goodbye to the North-West Ridge team, noting that "they really tried and deserve the summit. They are gone tomorrow."

Rob felt very relaxed and ready to push. Alison showed him her video of the Shoulder. "WOW! I can't wait to get there," he exclaimed. For his last journal entry Rob wrote, "I will go all liquid diet and concentrate on staying hydrated. This is the big push. I feel better about this try than the others. It seems like a different expedition now. Hopefully the weather will settle down. I'm psyched, I want it bad. I want to go home with the summit pictures in my camera."

Alison amid the aftermath of another storm

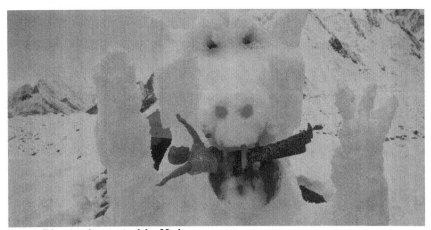

Tony Rigatoni meets his Maker

Looking down on the world from K2

Chapter XVII

"The credit belongs to the man who is actually in the arena, whose face is marred by dust and sweat and blood, who knows the great enthusiasms, the great devotions, and spends himself in a worthy cause; who at best, if he wins, knows the thrills of high achievement, and, if he fails, at least fails daring greatly, so that his place shall never be with those cold and timid souls who know neither victory nor defeat."

–Theodore Roosevelt

"Summit or death, either way I win," Rob proclaimed more than once before his K2 summit day. I had heard it several times, along with "summit or plummet." Those statements did not mean Rob had some kind of death wish. To me, they were simply his unique, provocative way of intimating that he felt some form of ultimate experience awaited him at the top. They further demonstrated something I had long known about Rob, which was that a great part of what he found appealing about mountaineering in general and K2 in particular was the chance to dance another step closer toward that nebulous, undefined Edge. The summit of K2 would be the closest to the Edge Rob had yet danced.

As the rest of the climbers gave up their K2 quest to return to families, jobs and civilization, Rob became more focused and more driven. More accurately perhaps, as Richard Celsi observed, Rob became even more "obsessed" with reaching the top. To Rob, circumstances to that point had denied him his chance. Without that opportunity, the entire trip would be for naught. o go home without having made a summit attempt, without having stayed to the bitter end and taken advantage of every single opportunity would have been, to him, utter failure. The thought of shrinking in any way from his once-in-a-lifetime chance was unthinkable.

With the remnants of the New Zealand group and only Alison Hargreaves from his own expedition, he saw a new team and a final chance to reach the summit.

Rob pondered life after K2 and his self-perceived failure of progress in other areas of life. Without a wife and kids, a home in the suburbs and a career that entailed going to work on a regular basis, he wasn't quite living the American Dream in the conventional sense. Rather, when an opportunity arose to embark on a new climbing expedition, he had no qualms about letting the employment chips fall where they may upon his return. Rob's personal American Dream was founded on taking advantage of the great challenges that mountaineering and the wild places had to offer in seeking the ultimate thrill. In a world which sometimes seemed to steal dreams, Rob was determined to hold on to his. The importance he placed on the K2 summit was a demonstration of the vehemence with which Rob pursued this quest and his dream.

Alone in his tent at the K2 base camp, Rob wondered if there were limits to dreams. While his focused on the summit of K2, he wondered what the realization of his K2 dream would add to his life. Since our first days climbing as kids, clambering about Wyoming's Vedauwoo rocks in cowboy boots with a clothesline for "pro," each time Rob topped out he had immediately set his sights on something harder and higher. Simple climbs in Vedauwoo led to the cliffs of Eldo and, ultimately, to the Big Walls of El Cap and the Wyoming

Sheep Ranch. Winter hikes led to the frozen waterfalls outside Estes Park, Colorado, and eventually to the giant ice routes of the Canadian Rockies. Not surprisingly, Rob was also drawn to the sandstone spires of the desert – Monument Valley, Valley of the Gods, the Fisher Towers. A love for mountain heights and being on the edge of space led from rappelling to BASE jumping. Alpine mountaineering, encompassing all the disciplines of the cliffs, ice, altitude, exposure and endurance, led from the Tetons to the Karakoram. The culmination of Rob's search manifested itself at the top of the summit ridge of the giant, windswept rock and ice massif of K2. Would it be enough?

Following her success as the first woman to solo Mount Everest without supplemental oxygen just a few short weeks before joining the 1995 American K2 Expedition, Alison became probably the best-known female alpine mountaineer in history. A case could probably be made that Alison was also the most skilled female alpine mountaineer in history. With all this going for her, it is probably further safe to argue that Alison could have joined any expedition she wanted.

Over the course of the 1995 summer K2 climbing season, Alison and Rob made many trips up the mountain together, both as team members and tent mates. They spent many long hours together talking, undoubtedly, about the summit high above them in the clouds that they both so desperately wanted. In this shared respect, they were immutably connected. In the end, after the rest of the team departed, it was only Rob and Alison.

"All I need is a few days of clear weather," Alison noted in her journal, with slightly less bravado than her new climbing partner Rob, but indicative of no less determination. Alison and Rob would not be satisfied without at least a chance for the summit.

August 10

At 9:00 p.m., six climbers from the Spanish expedition left in two groups for their final summit attempt from their base camp just above Rob and Alison's tents on the Strip. Their route, the Southeast Spur, fairly paralleled the Abruzzi Ridge to the west before merging with it near the Shoulder. There, Rob and Alison planned to reunite with them on August 11 at their Camp 3.

August 11

The cloudless night of August 10, 1995, passed as a full

moon hung over K2 – the Dream Mountain, the Great Mountain, the Savage Mountain. The winds were calm. At 3:00 a.m., August 11, Rob and Alison left base camp for their long-awaited summit try. A bit later, Kim Logan, Bruce Grant, Peter Hillary, Matt Comeskey and Jeff Lakes of the New Zealand team left Camp II and headed up the mountain.

Rob and Alison made excellent time on the lower part of the mountain, cruising in relaxed fashion up the route they had come to know so well over the previous two months. Between Camp II and Camp III, Rob and Alison came upon New Zealand team member Kim Logan, who had led the way above Camp II, breaking trail and digging out the fixed ropes buried by the recent storm. Together, Rob and Alison, along with Kim and his teammate Bruce Grant, paused at Camp III, which had been once again buried by an avalanche. They spent an hour searching in vain for the tents and ended up waiting several hours more before Peter Hillary, Jeff Lakes and Matt Comeskey joined them.

At that point, the climbers faced a dilemma. The tents and supplies of their former Camp III were nowhere to be found. Did they continue the search or press on to Camp IV, betting that the camp and its supplies would be found intact? It was decided that Rob, Alison, Bruce Grant and Kim Logan would push on under the full moon to Camp IV. Peter Hillary, Jeff Lakes and Matt Comeskey would rehydrate and follow.

Rob and Kim broke trail for three hours before Alison relieved them for an hour. They arrived at the Camp IV site shortly before 9:00 p.m., only to discover that it too was missing. As the temperature dropped to -40 degrees Fahrenheit, they searched for the camp they had so laboriously stocked on prior trips up the mountain. Just before turning back down the mountain, they found it and two tents were set up to house the six climbers. To save weight and conserve warmth, Rob and Alison shared one sleeping bag, Bruce and Kim another. Under the full moon, on the mountain of their collective dreams, the six spent a cold, cramped and uncomfortable night.

August 12

The day dawned beautiful, with perfect weather. Alison and Kim Logan broke trail on the Shoulder, trailed closely by Rob and

Bruce Grant. When they reached the end of the Shoulder, where the snow slope steepens as it rises toward the Bottleneck, they were just above 8,000 meters, or 26,000 feet. They were greeted by one of the most magnificent views on Earth: The sea of massive mountains that is the mighty Karakoram, brilliant in white and blue, stretching beneath them in all directions like frozen 20,000-foot-high whitecaps.

Peter Hillary and Jeff Lakes joined them soon after. Matt Comeskey eventually made it from Camp III as well, despite feeling poorly. Bruce Grant, however, was overcome by fatigue and decided to return to Camp IV.

It was decision time again. From their spot on the Shoulder, they could see the Spanish camp on the Southeast Spur. They knew from radio transmissions that, after the two Spanish climbing teams had reunited the day before at their 7,100-meter-high Camp 3, team member Manuel Anaon had retreated to base camp because he didn't feel strong enough to go on. The remaining members – Jose Garces, Lorenzo Ortas, Javier Oliver, Javier Escartin and Lorenzo Ortiz – had successful climbs of Everest, Hidden Peak and Nanga Parbat between them and planned to try for the summit that night.

Rob and his companions reasoned that their Spanish counterparts would break trail and fix to the Bottleneck, just below the Traverse and the summit ridge. As the sun shone brilliantly and the wind stayed calm, the group spent the day enjoying the view from above the Shoulder as they rehydrated and rested for the next day's summit bid.

One by one, the climbers returned from the Shoulder and huddled in their Camp IV tents as night fell and the temperature plummeted. Again they jammed together in two shared sleeping bags in a sadly inadequate attempt to conserve warmth and stave off the bitter cold. Nobody slept and, as Kim Logan later recalled, they "had a bad time of it." Shivering, they waited for the night to pass, jammed together, but each alone with his or her own thoughts and fears, knowing this was to be their last chance at the summit.

August 13

At midnight, Lorenzo Ortiz, Javier Escartin and Javier Oliver left the Spanish camp for their summit attempt, assuming that they would meet their English-speaking compatriots somewhere below the Bottleneck. One of the remaining members of the Spanish team,

Lorenzo Ortas, did not feel well enough to even begin the climb and stayed behind in camp, abandoning his summit bid.

Alison and Rob took off from their Camp IV around 1:00 a.m. while Kim Logan fixed buddy Bruce Grant a brew and sent him on his way about 2:00 a.m. After Grant left, Kim downed a liter of water and set out himself for the summit. Shortly thereafter, however, Kim became violently ill and was forced to return to Camp IV. Kim's efforts to avoid dehydration produced unintended consequences.

Matt Comeskey had also been feeling unwell, so he and Kim began their slow descent to Camp II. Perhaps prophetically, Kim later wrote, "I feel confident I could have reached the summit but not return."

Under the full moon, the Savage Mountain was silent, though it never slept. The only sound was the crunching of the snow, hardened by the wind of the previous storm and Rob and Alison's breathing. It took a while to calm their excitement as they tried to find their rhythm. As he had done since first laying eyes on K2, Rob marveled to himself at its size. The steep snow slope seemed to go on forever. It was bitter cold, nearly -30 degrees, but there was no wind.

Rob and Alison, climbing together, enjoyed the somewhat easier going afforded by the others breaking trail. Still, the going was tough on the 55-degree slope. A short while out of Camp IV, they came upon Jose Garces, who had turned around because of cold feet. Too bad, Rob probably thought to himself, as they passed in silent acknowledgment, no words being necessary. Jose had come so far and gotten so close. Rob didn't notice if he stopped to talk to Alison. They were all in their own worlds as they moved like plodding shadows through the moonlight.

Through the night Rob and Alison climbed, ever upward, waiting for the dawn but wanting to be as high on the mountain as possible when the sun finally rose. As day broke, they were below the long, steep approach to the Bottleneck. It was the dawn of a great new day; the dawn of *the* great day. The weather looked good, the wind was down and they felt strong. The endless sea of wild peaks spread out beneath them. By day's end, they believed, they would stand on the summit.

Rob and Alison reached the Bottleneck by mid-morning. They were at the threshold of the Traverse and the summit ridge – the final stretch. The remaining Spaniards, Lorenzo Ortiz and the two Javiers, Escartin and Oliver, were already there. Shortly afterwards, Bruce Grant, the final Kiwi, arrived as well.

Meanwhile, back at Camp IV at 8,000 meters, Peter Hillary set off between 9:00 a.m. and 10:00 a.m., following Jeff Lakes, who had departed some time before. It was the impression of the two Spaniards, Garces and Ortas, who abandoned their summit bids earlier, that Hillary had no intention of pushing towards the summit, but rather wanted to get some photos of the Bottleneck area and then go back to base camp.

Up above, the climbers found that three sections of the Bottleneck were already roped. This was good news, as Rob and the others would save time and energy by not having to fix that difficult section or carry the extra ropes. A rope left by an earlier expedition was used for the first section, as each of the six clipped on and began their way up through the maze of cliffs and seracs. The way was so steep it was almost overhanging. As it turned out, another older rope from some forgotten expedition, left exposed and easily accessible by the recent storm, seemed to be the best prospect for the next section. They all agreed, clipped on and continued up.

Between pitches, Rob no doubt reveled at the scene below, grateful that there was no wind and that the weather was holding.

Following a red rope placed earlier by the Dutch expedition, they made their way up the final section of the Bottleneck and by noon everyone was through. One of the Spaniards made a radio call to his teammates below. Rob knew his and his companions' excitement of embarking on the final push was shared below. He was starting to feel that the K2 summit would actually happen. It was quite cold, but what did he expect? At least it wasn't windy. Below, Rob noticed some slight cloud formation in the distance, but nothing out of the ordinary. The mountain gods were indulging them.

On the way down to Camp II, Kim and Matt stopped at Camp III. There the Kiwis discussed what they thought to be the deteriorating state of the weather. At noon, Kim talked to Peter Hillary on the radio. Peter and Jeff Lakes had made it to the base of the Bottleneck. Rob, Alison, Bruce Grant and the three Spaniards were already high above. Hillary was concerned about the weather possibly closing in later in the day and decided to turn around. Jeff Lakes had a decision to make as well.

"I'll kick myself if they get to the top and I don't give it one more try," Jeff said to Hillary. "I've been here twice, mate, and I don't want to come back." Hillary wished his friend well as Jeff decided to continue. Far above him, Peter saw Alison, Rob and the other climbers cross the Traverse and disappear into the gray and white of the K2 summit shroud.

Two hours later, Jeff decided to turn back. He was just above the Bottleneck, but felt it was too late and he was too far from the summit to keep climbing. Over the next two hours, as Rob, Alison, Bruce Grant and the three Spanish climbers worked their way up towards the final pitches below the summit, Jeff worked his way back down to through the Bottleneck. During that same time, far below, Peter Hillary continued his own descent.

Peter arrived at the Spanish Camp IV tents at 4:00 p.m. and called Jeff on the radio borrowed from the Spanish climbers Garces and Ortas. Jeff reported that Rob, Alison, Bruce and the Spaniards were on the summit ridge. The Spaniards gave Peter a drink before he resumed his descent down the Abruzzi Ridge. Earlier that day, after Garces had turned around and began his descent back to Camp IV, he'd passed Rob and Alison on their way up. Rob passed him in silence, alone in his thoughts and effort. Alison looked at him, pausing only to say, "I'm going up."

According to Garces and Ortas, the weather at that stage was no different than the previous day, with the usual build-up of daily clouds temporarily enveloping various parts of the mountain, but clear on the Chinese horizon and perfectly windless. The three Spaniards, Lorenzo Ortiz, Javier Escartin and Javier Oliver, who were climbing with Rob, Alison and Bruce, were carrying a portable radio, via which several messages relaying their progress were exchanged with base camp and Camp IV throughout the day.

That afternoon, Rob and the others worked their way across the Traverse. The going was slow, but steady. They had entered the heart of the death zone, where earth met space and oxygen was scarce, less than a third of that at sea level. Rob never seriously considered bringing oxygen.

As Rob plowed through the snow and ice below the summit ridge, each step was a labor. It was cold and steep, an endless expanse of white and gray against the brilliant dark blue sky. In his effort, he kept his head down except to pause and check his progress against the skyline and periodically gaze into the otherworldly vista around him.

Somewhere above, he knew he would emerge finally on the summit ridge, but he couldn't dwell on that. All his effort was focused on taking the next step. He was going to make it. He was not going to stop and he was not going to turn around.

Rob reached the summit ridge by 4:00 p.m. The adrenalin started to kick in and his mind raced. Rob had to temper his excitement with the fact that he was not yet there, even though he could almost taste the top. His field of vision now included much more blue than white as the mountain finally began giving way to sky. Above, he reasoned, Lorenzo and Bruce must be almost at the top. If they could make it today, so would he. Alison was just above him, deep in her own thoughts of the impending summit. The final meters went by in a tortuously slow procession. Yet again, he couldn't help but marvel at the immensity of his Dream Mountain.

As the afternoon wore on, opposing forces of weather and nature invaded the Karakoram and converged on K2. An anticyclone packing powerful counterclockwise winds began bearing down on the mountain from the north. From the south, warmer, moisture-laden monsoon air rose through the narrow mountain valleys toward Concordia and the Godwin-Austen Glacier. The ensuing collision created a violent maelstrom that shrouded the mountain of dreams from the ground up and transformed it into a mountain of death.

Earlier, across the abyss and further down the Godwin-Austen Glacier on Broad Peak, American guide Scott Fischer was leading a group of climbers. Being at a lower altitude, they were hit by the storm's fury before it reached K2.Throughout the day, Fischer had followed the progress of his fellow climbers, rooting them on as they clawed their way up the Abruzzi Ridge. When the gale struck, Fischer and his team struggled to lash their tents to the mountainside. Shocked, Fischer looked up to discover the six on K2 were still moving up.

The storm started battering the lower part of K2 with 50-knot-plus winds between 5:00 p.m. and 6:00 p.m. Lorenzo Ortiz radioed at 6:00 p.m. that he and Bruce Grant had reached the summit. Alison, Javier Oliver and Javier Escartin had also reached the top, with Rob trailing just a short distance below.

The weather at the summit was reported as extremely cold, but windless. Lorenzo Ortas, who took the call, said he'd been told that the weather was "good, really exceptional. They could have descended easily in the light of the full moon." Garces added, from his own experience, that "...the snow was very firm and ideal for climbing."

A short while past 6:00 p.m., on August 13, 1995, Rob Slater reached the summit of K2. Everything above him was blue. The world filled with nothing but his big grin and pure exaltation. Rob thought of Mom and Dad. They had worried, but would now be relieved and share in his joy. His twin brother knew all along he'd make it. So did his other brothers, Tommy and Paul. His sister Sissy had been scared, like Mom, but she knew it too. It would make for some good stories sitting around Mom and Dad's living room in Cheyenne.

Rob thought of The Team – the people who had over the years been like a second family and helped him develop the skills that brought him to the summit of K2. Hammer and Black Death Heid, Leavitt, Al, Stu and O'Donnell all meant so much to him, as did Cosgriff, Tabin, Kaiser, Matt, Rollo, Bruce and Barbella. It was their victory as well. On top of the world, Rob felt love for them all. The Family and the Team were with him.

The K2 summit is an otherworldly place – and not just in the physical sense. For Rob and his fellow summiteers, it marked also the end of a long, difficult emotional struggle. They had all wrestled with disappointment, doubt, fear and fatigue. Each, without question, had practical, real-world concerns awaiting their return. But all those faded as, one by one, each climber crested the last few meters of the summit ridge. On top, together in their victory but alone, each overcome by the magnitude of the moment. Gazing about, Rob realized how close he was to the presence of the mountain gods. For a fleeting instant, he wished he could keep going up.

Above, the sky was a crystal clear blue, churning imperceptibly as it spanned the short distance into space and the heavens. Below, the cloud bank boiled and billowed, obscuring the lower camps and the sea of peaks surrounding the mountain of their dreams. Imperceptibly, as they enjoyed their brief visit to the K2 summit, the breeze picked up, accentuating the bitter cold. It was the mountain's gentle reminder. The world below had turned into a seething cauldron of gray and purple. They did not tarry. The newest conquerors of K2 began their descent. As Rob had always said, "Getting up will be the easy part. Getting down..."

About the same time, more than a mile and a half below, Peter Hillary made it to Camp II, happy to have lived through 100-knot winds. A radio report soon came from base camp with the news that the six climbers had made the summit. Hillary was hit by a stark realization: "Oh God, it's blowing 100 knots down here at 21,000 feet; what the hell is it doing at 28,000?"

The summit ridge of K2 has no fixed ropes. There are no landmarks by which to navigate or rock outcroppings to provide shelter. The summit ridge is a steep, icy stretch of total exposure to the harshest elements of the planet. On a good day, the benevolent spirits showcase the finest Mother Nature has to offer. On a bad day, the demons of the wild bring forth their worst.

As Rob and the others began their descent, the euphoria of the top was smothered by the bitter reality of the storm erupting toward them from below. In an instant, the breeze became a wind. Rob hastened his pace. Even with gravity now on his side, the slope seemed endless and the relative shelter of the lower mountain light years away. It was still clear above, but the tide of the clouds below was rising. Euphoria was gone, replaced by adrenalin.

At Camp IV, the hurricane-force wind hit the tents occupied by Ortas and Garces, who were awaiting the arrival of the climbers from the summit. In their opinion, "it was a dry-type of wind from the north, the China Wind, with no precipitation at all. It was the sort of wind that repelled the monsoon storms to the south and, eventually, cleared the Karakoram of clouds, leaving crystal-clear skies."

Soon after the first gusts, the tent of Garces started to skid, about to be torn off the mountain. Outside, Ortas clung desperately with his bare hands as the tent slid toward the abyss. In the nick of time, Garces was able to jump out. The two retreated to the remaining tent, where they cut a slit in the windward wall to lessen its resistance to the gale. As the storm's ferocity intensified, they were eventually forced to abandon that tent as well. Reduced to mere survival mode, Garces and Ortas huddled in the small depression where their tents formerly sat. In a single sleeping bag, they clutched each other amid the shrieking winds.

The storm intensified with amazing speed. Rob struggled to keep his balance as the wind rose to gale force. Despite the dire predicament in which Rob had almost instantaneously found himself, he could not help but marvel at the strength, ferocity and awesome power of K2.

Moments later, he was forced to halt his descent as the wind approached 100 miles per hour. At this point, Rob and his fellow climbers could only cling to the summit ridge, hoping the maelstrom would abate soon enough and long enough for them to scramble to set up a bivouac somewhere in the cliffs below.

But the storm did not abate. Instead, it grew more furious.

Observers in base camp scanned the mountain with binoculars as the storm rose to obscure everything above. One reported what, to all, must have been a horrifying sight: the descending climbers pinned to the mountain on the ridge below the summit. A moment later, the climbers disappeared in the clouds.

Rob clawed the summit ridge as the wind roared. He thought of Mom and Dad, his family and the Team. They, and the wild places, were the essence of his being. Rob had always loved and respected the mountain gods and their realm. Even if he had lingered on the mountain, why had they forsaken him?

As the sun set, the barometric pressure fell and the wind speed rose, scouring the summit ridge at more than 150 miles per hour. One by one, Rob Slater, Alison Hargreaves, Javier Escartin, Bruce Grant, Javier Oliver and Lorenzo Ortiz were torn from the mountain and cast into the netherworld beyond earth and sky and roaring wind. Above the wind, not a single sound was heard. As Rob's grip was torn from the great, savage mountain of his dreams, there was no pain and no more cold…

At that moment, across the world, I awoke in a start. It wasn't a nightmare, but a strange feeling of uncertainty laced with weird comfort. It was a feeling I had never had before. I thought of my twin, far away, and experienced an uneasy sense of closeness. Robbie had come, silent in the night, to say goodbye.

As his body plummeted into the whiteness of the abyss, Rob Slater turned back towards the summit of K2. He was wearing his big grin. The mountain gods had not forsaken him; they had made him one of their own. The mountain gods were honed.

The realm of the Mountain Gods

From the upper Abruzzi

Paying homage to my favorite celebrity

Chapter XVIII

Confessions of an Ultra Fool

Interstate 80 spans the United States from San Francisco to New York City. The highest point on this transcontinental route lies at the Summit Rest Area between Cheyenne and Laramie, Wyoming, in the Medicine Bow National Forest. Surveying this scene is an eight-foot bronze bust of Abraham Lincoln perched atop a 20-foot granite pyramid at 8,450 feet above sea level. Through blazing sun, howling wind and raging blizzards, Honest Abe's countenance remains unchanged as he watches over this trail runner's paradise which I fondly call the "Summit."

A marathon is a 26.2-mile long footrace. An ultra-marathon is a run longer than a marathon, the most common distances being 50K (31 miles), 50 miles and100 miles. A trail ultra, as the name implies, is an ultra-marathon run on trails. There's no pavement and it's strictly for those who love the dirt.

Trail running requires more concentration than track or road running. One misstep or inattentive moment can mean a sprain or a broken bone, miles from the nearest human being or Mini Mart nacho cheese fountain. With the ruggedness of the trail, it's not possible to zone out the way you can jogging down a nicely paved path. Trail running does, nevertheless, offer more than ample opportunity to leave it all behind and enter an altered state of mind. Commonly known as "runners high," the body produces chemicals called endorphins that, when a certain threshold is reached, produce feelings of pleasure and euphoria. Some runners become addicted to this high, earning the labels "avid," "compulsive" or "nuts." In extreme cases, the title of "ultra trail runner" is bestowed. It's self-assuring to have at least one healthy addiction. One should not go through life Kool- and Corona-fueled only.

One bright winter day in 2001, I took my two young sons, Robbie II and Chet, out to Crystal Reservoir near the Summit and the rock formations of Vedauwoo. I showed them the cliffs I jumped from with my brothers so long ago. We walked around on the frozen lake as they peered with fascination into the long, deep cracks and fissures. I described for them the Antarctic pack ice I have never seen and how it resembled the ice we were on, only on a tremendously larger scale. I told them how their Uncle Robbie and I had planned to sail the wild Southern Ocean and promised them, with great earnestness, that someday the three of us would.

As we drove home, I recalled Rob's boast that he could hike the 32 miles from Cheyenne to Vedauwoo in less than a day. My brothers and I had scoffed at Rob's notion of someone, even him, hiking that far in a single day without stopping. But it got me thinking and I concluded Rob could have easily covered a distance like that, even if he went at the slow-for-him pace of four miles per hour. Maybe it hadn't been such an outrageous claim after all.

Not long after, I encountered Dr. Brent Weigner. Listening to his tales of ultras through the mountains, jungles and across the polar wastelands, I was struck by the amazingly close similarities between the "Great Ultra One," as I call him, and my brother Rob. Brent talked about ultras in the wild with the same gleam in his eyes as Rob had talked about climbing. A light went on in my brain and I thereupon resolved to do the 52-mile Rocky Mountain Double Marathon the upcoming Memorial Day, 2002, which began at the

Honest Abe statue and wound through the surrounding mountains of Vedauwoo.

The next Saturday morning I was up at sunrise to try my first 10-miler. It was a blizzard, with howling winds. I went out anyway and, by the time I peeled off my ice-encrusted clothes two hours later, I was hooked. Besides, it was about time I had a healthy vice and I needed a positive channel for all the rage and negative energy that had been building up inside me over my loss of Rob. It was a rage and negativity I hadn't yet been able to shake even though almost six years had passed since the day my twin brother summited his dream mountain... and soon after said a dreamworld goodbye to me.

My favorite trail run begins from the Summit. I call it the "Death Crotch Loop." It dives straight into the heart of the wild, winding through forest and alpine meadows bordered by sagebrush and choked with willows. As I begin a planned 20-miler on a Saturday morning in February from my parking spot near Honest Abe, the sun is just beginning to rise. The fact that few others want to do this provides weird gratification during those first cold, stiff steps. Unless the wind is really howling, which is usually the case during the winter months; it only takes about half a mile to get warmed up. With warmth comes exultation, but I stop to walk.

"Rob. Rob, I'm here!" I scream out. I always yelled during the first few years but now, sometimes I just whisper. Then I stop and listen to him in the wind as the snow flies horizontally. Or I hear him in the silence as the snow falls slowly straight down. Or I feel him in the first brightening rays of the new summer day. He is always there and he always answers. It's as though he waits patiently for me to come calling.

As I run, I think back to my first trip up Longs Peak in the winter, without Rob. On snowshoes, I reached at sunrise the stream crossing just before the trail breaks out of the forest into the high alpine tundra. I decided to follow the stream bed straight up and found a small depression surrounded by large snow drifts. There was hardly any wind and almost no sound. I sat down and pulled out a package of Pop Tarts; one for me and one to leave as an offering to Rob and the other mountain gods. Sitting in silence, I was surprised to see that more than a dozen ptarmigans had joined me, their plumage pure white and accented by small patches and thin streaks of brown. Nonchalantly they congregated about, perhaps eyeing my snack.

As I commented to myself and Rob how awesomely wild this place was in the winter, a blast came down the mountain and blindsided me from behind. In an instant, the world was white amid the deafening roar of the wind. Frantically, I crawled about in search of my gloves, which I had unsuspectingly set down minutes before in the calmness. I found one plastered to the windward side of a small tree 20 yards down the slope. I shouldered my pack and stumbled down the mountain toward tree line, knocked to my knees several times by the gale.

Back in the trees, I stopped and looked up into the white. Just 50 yards above me the world was a violent, deadly place. The snow which had been plastered to my face began melting. I had been reminded, lest I had forgotten, of the fickle and sometimes instantaneously deadly nature of the mountain gods. But even in those short moments of anxiety and the terror of total helplessness I had just experienced, I felt Rob there, shaking his head as I floundered on a mountain whose distant top was almost a mile lower than K2 base camp.

I emerge from the trees into the bottomlands, where the Death Crotch Loop enters a broad meadow of knee-high grass sprinkled in the spring with red, yellow and purple wildflowers. Above to the right the ski runs of the old Happy Jack ski area are recognizable only to those who skied there before it closed decades ago. It was before Rob and I had made it to high school, but after Rob had pretty much traded skiing for ice climbing and winter alpine ascents.

The lodge is gone and the pines have gradually reclaimed the slopes bulldozed by an earlier generation, but people still sled on the lower portion of the mountain. I've several times pointed out the best runs and spots of the best jumps to my kids as we've trudged up the hill with our sleds.

From the old ski area, the DC Loop continues along a series of beaver ponds, a number of them boasting some rather impressive lodges. The beavers are quite elusive, but their efforts at house building and dam maintenance provide clear and convincing evidence of their ongoing presence. On occasion, the kids are lucky enough to spot one. I always hope they do, believing for some reason it will help foster in them a fascination and respect for the wild places. As I think about Rob and family, I grind out the first five miles fueled by adrenaline and endorphins.

"Maybe I'll do 30 miles today," I boast to myself.

There is neither a more exhilarating nor a more lonely feeling than travelling through the wild, alone, in the dead of winter. The only sound is the wind. The only colors are the white of the snow drifts, the gray of the sky above, the dark green of pines and brown of the earth not covered by ice or ground blizzards. The only smell is from the biting strength of the mountain weather.

I like being alone-it reminds me of Rob and the spirit he shared with the heroes of polar exploration. Sir Douglas Mawson, a British physicist and geologist, led a 1912 Antarctic expedition to explore and conduct scientific investigations, establishing his base camp at a place he named Cape Denison. During the month of July, the average wind velocity was 63.6 miles per hour. One day, the wind blew at 107 miles per hour for eight hours straight, with gusts up to 200 miles per hour. Cape Denison earned the nickname, "The Home of the Blizzard."

The area around the Summit where I run is my Home of the Blizzard. It's a special place that I prefer to run in bad weather and always alone. There's something about being alone in the wilderness that fosters involuntary critical self-examination. I run the gamut of emotions as well as the trail. In the process, I talk to Rob. I know he already knows what's going on with me, but I tell him about it anyway.

An easy downhill trail, with the wind at mile four and fueled by the initial endorphin rush brings exultation and confidence.

"I am a king. I can go forever. I'm with my brother in the mountains," I proclaim to myself. But as any crack head will tell you, the high never lasts. Lonely hours, brutal uphills and bitter headwinds open the door of doubt. I think back to the countless trips our family took up here when we were growing up. In the car, Mom and Dad told us to stop bickering and look outside at the scenery, hoping we would grow to appreciate the beauty. We had the promise of youth, a feeling of immortality and a sense that time would never run out.

"You boys can do anything you set your minds to," Mom

always said. I think of how Rob took this to heart, especially with his climbing. Rob, like everyone, occasionally lamented paths not taken, but never dwelled on such things for he had found and pursued his passion. Few others are so fortunate.

Ground blizzards race through the trees and across the trail like furious, never-ending wisps pouring horizontally over the landscape. It's like running in the clouds, all white, cold and pure. I am free. I used to curse the wind, the bane of all young Wyoming tennis players. As a boy in the tent with my Dad and brothers, I felt secure as I listened to it flap the rain fly. During my first year after law school, I lived 30 miles outside of Cheyenne in the mountains. I found comfort in its howling as I lay awake, alone at night. I curse it no more. It is now my companion, if not my friend.

In Antarctica, the surface winds create solid waves of snow called sastrugi, creating an ever-shifting sea of whiteness. One of Rob's favorite subjects was Antarctica and his plan to retrace Scott's fatal route to the pole from McMurdo Sound-unassisted.

"Now they have women skiing across Antarctica with radios and GPS's getting airdrops of fresh lettuce," he would sneer.

"We should sneak into their tent some night..." I would offer in response. But no one would go with him on such a trip, he'd complain. No one that is, except me.

"I know you would," Rob would reply. "But we might need an airdrop ourselves..."

"We'll get some Taco Johns and some young models," we agreed.

My spirits lift as I recall such conversations with Rob, which inevitably followed the same pattern. Even serious subjects like crossing Antarctica would ultimately degenerate into absurdity, but always end with a good laugh. Sometimes it was only Rob and I who laughed, but that was always enough for us.

Rounding a bend in the trail, I come upon a deer feeding in the early morning dusk. I stop abruptly as, just off the trail about 20 yards ahead, she looks up. Instead of immediately fleeing, she stares me down. Our eyes lock. As she turns toward the forest, I notice movement around her as several others turn and head into the thick darkness of the trees. In a matter of seconds they all bound gracefully and silently from view. It reminds me of Robbie nimbly ascending a scree field in the Tetons so many years ago.

The trail up into the Death Crotch begins innocuously enough, following a draw in a direct line up the mountainside before entering a thick grove of aspen. Higher up, the aspen give way to a dense pine forest. Approaching the top, the draw continues to narrow as the terrain gets steeper. I am entering the "Death Crotch." I don't know for sure how it came to be called the Death Crotch but, in my opinion, it fits. The last half mile to the top is a killer. I can only dream of running the whole thing. "Lungs up-legs down."

In the winter, climbing the Crotch into the teeth of the wind quickly turns any sweat I have worked up during the downhill into a coating of ice. I zip the blue fleece jacket that used to be Rob's and put on the fleece gloves Rob gave me on the K2 trip. My pace slows and my enthusiasm drops for the first time since I started out.

"What the hell am I doing out here?"

The sun has fully cleared the granite spine of the mountains and casts a brilliant light but provides little warmth against the wind. I pull a package of Pop Tarts out of my waist pack and stuff one in my mouth. I wash it down with Gatorade, chewing and gasping for breath at the same time, but I keep moving. I begin to jog. The mountains are unimpressed. I am a fool. Robbie could have run it, though, "coming off the sofa," as he would say.

Once in a while during the summer months, I encounter a mountain biker, invariably coming down. On a few occasions, I've encountered an unrestrained dog, one of which came at me. I gave him a quick pop on the snout, which sent him whimpering away. The owner, like the parent of supposedly "cute" kid, seemed offended that I wasn't enthralled with his mutt with the bandana tied around its neck.

"Control your animal, asshole. This is a public place," I say as he goes by in his tight shorts and fancy helmet. He mutters something unintelligible but does not stop and quickly disappears in the trees below. The whole event takes only about 15 seconds, but it breaks my solitude and immediately, and perhaps quite irrationally, shifts me into anger mode, much of which usually focuses on my loss of Rob.

At first I'd consoled myself with clichés such as "he died doing something he loved" and mollified myself with the thought that "at least he was coming down from the top instead of dying while still going up." I'd also tell myself it would have been worse had Rob made it off K2 and then got killed in a plane crash on the way home. All these sentiments were true, but masked my deeper feelings at the time.

Years ago, I had stood next to Rob before he dove from the Royal Gorge Bridge and hung on the giant crane with him on top of the Denver City Center. Momentarily at least, I had considered following him into the unknown should something have gone terribly wrong. Now that the unthinkable had happened, should I?

"That's pussy," Rob would have said unequivocally at such a notion-and he was right. The mere thought of what an act of such selfishness would do to my parents snapped me right back to reality. The thought passed more fleetingly than it had on the bridge and the crane.

The anger stage was the easy part. I cursed the world and everything and everyone in it. I was defiant, doing a fairly good job of covering myself with tattoos of death, demons, skulls and malevolent mountain gods which reflected my rage, hoping to at least offend anybody I felt didn't share my pain. How dare they go around with smiles on their faces, enjoying a beautiful day? Didn't they realize the world is a miserable place?

Hating the world was easy, just like placing blame. It all seemed so unfair. It was like Rob, my family and I were being callously selected for torment without good reason. Rob never hurt anyone. Neither did Dad – and definitely never Mom. Seeing them suffer made me seethe with helplessness. But hate and blame don't solve problems, bring people back from the dead, or produce positive energy or results. Still, it was hard not to project and everyone else would just have to bear the brunt.

I've been coming to the DC Loop for several years following the loss of my twin. Here I have fought ferociously with my demons, vanquishing some and leaving them to moan in the cold, dark crevasses. Others remain by my side. I have also encountered mountain spirits, which have helped me along my way. I am not afraid of the mountain gods, despite their sometimes seemingly fickle and unforgiving nature.

When I first heard of the storm that struck K2 on Rob's summit day, my mind began to race. Did he make the top? Did anyone see him fall? What about the others? Given the multitude of questions my family and I had and our appetite for answers, it was extremely frustrating to repeatedly hear "we're not sure yet" in response. New information trickled in at an agonizingly slow pace. While we waited, we rationalized that everything would turn out just fine. We tried to deny even the obvious and unbearable possibility of the inevitable. It was just going to take some time for the information flow to reach Cheyenne from the heart of the Karakoram. Eventually, the information flow did reach Cheyenne and we learned the sad truth. Rob had made the summit, but he had not survived the descent – and he was not coming back.

One Sunday afternoon in the summer of 2004, I went over to Mom and Dad's for a visit and to mooch a home-cooked meal. Sis was up from Denver, so it was also a great opportunity to catch up. Standing around in the kitchen, I could tell something was up by the furtive glances between Mom and Sis.

"Hey Richie, are you dating anybody?" Sis started off, innocently enough.

"My friend's mom knows a girl here in Cheyenne she says you might really like to meet, she continued. "She has a good job and doesn't need anyone to support her and isn't looking to get married."

"Not interested," was my quick response.

"Oh come on, she's really smart, and she's pretty, too."

"Not interested," I repeated, this time more emphatically.

"Now Richie," interjected Mom, "it wouldn't kill you to meet this girl. The worst thing that could happen is you might have lunch with a nice girl."

"Not interested. Everyone tries to set me up. I've already met enough nice girls for one lifetime."

"Come on Richie, just meet her. It's not like your committing to marriage…"

Reluctantly, I agreed to meet this gal. It would happen during the business week, so as to give each of us an easy out. Her name was Mary and she was some kind of insurance executive. She had the professional thing goin' on big-time.

Neither of us wanted to get involved, but we did anyway. I talked her into a run through the summit woods by Honest Abe. Though never having run the trails before, she gamely agreed. On a particularly steep and rocky section, Mary had a nasty fall. Muddied, bloodied and bruised, she never complained, mentioning only she preferred the gentler trails that wound through the aspen.

"Way honed," I thought to myself.

Mary had two little girls, Mattie and Grace, who introduced me to an entirely different, exciting and rewarding aspect of parenthood. Whether I have ever deserved it or not, I got lucky – really lucky. The following year, I raised my glass to my beautiful new bride and daughters.

At some point, with all the anger and hate, something would have to give. Alone in this local throne room of the mountain gods, I wondered about many things. I pondered the gifts bestowed upon me. I was lucky, as the most important gifts such as life, health and family, had arrived through no merit on my part. Though I may have squandered opportunities, through my wife Mary and our children I saw the chance for redemption. They meant everything to me and represented what is good in life and certainly everything good in my life. I could not spend the rest of my life wallowing in a hole of hate and self-pity.

An old buddy of mine, Roger Gill, walked into my office one day with a legal question. Invariably, the conversation turned to Rob, who he had known as we were growing up. Roger had read something about Rob in some climbing publication. Shaking his head with a smile, he repeated,

"Man, that fucker Robbie lived. He fuckin' lived."

My friend may have had a proclivity to toss around the F-bomb, but all I could do was nod in agreement. Roger was right; Rob had lived, on his own terms, and by doing so had made the most of his time. In the process, he deeply touched the lives of those lucky enough to be around him. I had to do the same.

I was done fighting the gods about Robbie. Questions of did he stay too long in the Karakoram and was he foolhardy and approach too close to the edge did not matter. My brother summited K2! Now he was gone-at least in the physical sense, but he was very much with me in the spiritual sense, just as he always has been. I accepted and grew content with this knowledge. It's just like your kids sleeping peacefully in the next room; you don't have to go in and wake them up just so you can hold them in your arms. Closeness is there and that is enough. It's the same with Rob.

As I work my way up the seemingly endless switchbacks of the Death Crotch, the fire in my chest spreads to my legs. Someday, I tell myself, I will run to the top without stopping. Then maybe I'll be honed too. Today I make it to the top of the first of three false summits – further than last time. I suppose if I ever do make it, I'll probably keel over, my heart having vapor-locked.

I think back to mile 47 of the Rocky Mountain Double Marathon. "Come on, Junior, you can make it," I heard Rob saying. Two miles later, the blisters between my toes began to pop. It felt like hot oil being poured over my feet. In my semi-hallucinatory state, I was in a slow-motion dream, only it hurt and I couldn't wake up and make it go away. But I didn't want to wake up and I didn't want the pain to go away.

A bull moose 20 feet off the trail among the trees startles me back to the present. I feel a jolt of adrenaline. The big bull glances up but pays me no further mind. I begin the last climb. My mind returns to when I was about to complete the 52-miler. Dad had been accompanying me as my support team. I told him I wouldn't stop unless I could crawl no further. I took out my 1995 American K2 Expedition t-shirt and put it on for the finish.

"In honor of Rob I'm going to try and show some style at the end," I said.

I do not, and neither did Rob, look to The Father, The Son or The Holy Ghost. I believe in my father, Rob, my family, my wife Mary and my children. I believe in the spirits and demons of the wild, the most honed of which become mountain gods. Spirits are the manifestation of the benevolent forces in the universe. Demons can infiltrate the security and serenity offered by the spirits and deluge your mind like a mountain stream obliterating an abandoned beaver dam. In the wild, I run with them both, feeling neither pride nor fear. I need them both. They represent nature's balance.

The Crotch tops out at one of the highest points of the Summit range. It's barren and quiet except for the wind and the screeching of hawks high above. It is also almost always cold, regardless of the season. It's one of the spots where Rob likes to hang out. I join him, breathless from running the last steep section.

"Summit or death, either way I win" was more than just a provocative Rob Slaterism. It wasn't about death; it was about life.

Rob's summit was taking on challenges and continually pushing and striving. Once a summit was achieved, it shifted upward or outward toward the next edge. Rob's summit was reaching for the sky. He started reaching early and he kept on reaching toward ever-more-extreme limits as he climbed in the mountains and flew through the air. In the end, the only challenges left were K2 – and death. For Rob, it wasn't so much if he could overcome them, but rather that he could meet them both. For me, even if Rob failed, he triumphed spectacularly.

My summit is also reaching for the sky. Like Rob, I have always felt and wanted to be different, but unlike Rob I was not quite sure how. I wanted to be different, but not from my twin. Rob had far more courage than I, but he also had far more courage than anyone I ever knew. I didn't necessarily want to be a lawyer, but I am my own man and I take care of my own. I want to be a good son and brother and I hope I am. I want to be a good father and husband and I will keep trying. I would like to be a good author, but that will be up to the readers. I cannot climb the highest mountains or scale the steepest cliffs and then parachute off into the blackness, but I can run for miles through the teeth of the mountain gods' winter. Someday I will do the Hard Rock 100 with its 33,000 feet of vertical climb and French kiss the Hard Rock at the finish line. I will do Badwater, the 135-miler across Death Valley and up Mt. Whitney. I will hallucinate at mile 95 and scream back at the desert demons. I will fight off the trees as they come alive to ensnare me. I'll eat a couple of cold hotdogs at mile 132 and keep going. And even if I fail it will be of little moment for, like Rob, I will have dared. It will be so great. I want to feel the same way Rob felt the moment before he....

There is no great revelation. The secret is there is no secret. The satisfaction comes from not turning back. Rob knew it – and lived it. He fuckin' *lived*. I believe it and want to live it like Rob. I want to be with my brother again, and not just in spirit. My contemplations in the wild have taught me much about myself and brought me closer to Rob. I've discovered that we weren't so different after all. Summit or death, either way I win too.

From the top of the Crotch, the trail descends gently for several miles along the ridge back toward Honest Abe. I drop into the trees. A canopy of pine and aspen shelter me from the wind and the outside world. My brother is right beside me. It's all downhill from here.

My spirit remains restless, but I am at peace.

Just before going out on the City Center crane (Rob on right)

Mom and Rob

Epilogue

"The lover of life's not a sinner
  The ending is just a beginning
  The closer you get to the meaning
  The sooner you'll know that you're dreaming..."
                    –Black Sabbath, Heaven and Hell

     Mom and Rob had been tight, on a special plane. Though Rob was not one to keep too many secrets, the basis of his determination and the few fears he did not readily divulge to others he shared with Mom. All moms deal with the usual uncertainties experienced by their offspring, but with Rob, his fanatical determination and obsession with feats of death-defying outrageousness was not the sort of matters with which most moms were presented, especially on a regular basis.

     When Rob went off to solo El Cap-and jump off the top, Mom was concerned. As Rob discussed his plans to parachute from skyscrapers, Mom was more than concerned. Both Mom and Dad, despite having been told for years the tales of horror and death surrounding K2, believed Rob would make the summit and come home safe and sound.

Mom and Dad never told Rob he couldn't or shouldn't attempt K2 or any desert tower, ice route, BASE jump, or a trek across Antarctica. That would have been like telling Rob he couldn't pursue his dreams. Worse, it would have been like telling Rob he couldn't have dreams. Instead, they just wanted him to make it back.

A lot has changed since that bitter evening on the K2 summit ridge 16 years ago. At first it seemed as if life was shattered, but time has continued its unrelenting march and it's never ending capacity to heal, or at least ease the pain, and to teach.

The loss of Rob hit Mom hard. As part of the grieving process, she confronted herself with questions of why she hadn't done more to dissuade Rob from K2. Quickly, though, Mom and everybody else in the family realized that any attempt to keep Rob off the mountain of his dreams would have been an exercise in utter futility. In the spring of 2007, Mom's pain over losing Rob ended when her spirit flew to the rainbow and she joined her son. They are now together, laughing as they did so many times on Sunday afternoons.

My wife Mary has proven herself in every respect to be a loving and dedicated wife, partner, confidant and mother of the highest order. The two finest women I have ever known have the same name. The tenacity with which my Mary clings to the dream of the family has refocused her husband on the truly worthwhile aspects of existence. My Mary, like my father's, is a giver of life.

I finally decided to quit smoking. If the mountain gods will take my twin brother, the cancer gods will certainly take me.

A lot has also changed in the climbing world since Rob's day. In a world of internet, reality TV and culture of celebrity worship, climbing has made it onto the radar screen. It's a reflection of how our society has changed, with its focus more on notoriety than character, on "edginess" rather than integrity, where form takes precedence over substance. In keeping with popular culture, true risk is minimized while perceived risk is absurdly inflated. Rob's climbing achievements can be best appreciated in the context of the environment then and now.

Nowadays, hotshot climbers practice difficult routes over and over, with the aid of a top rope or huge boulder pads to cushion any fall. When the route is finally wired, it's time for the big solo. Of course, the cameras are there to record the great feat of daring for the web and for the climbing press. As Rob sat in his apartment staring at the Pacific Ocean Wall topo map taped to his wall, with the words "Solo This Route" scrawled across the top, any thoughts of practicing or top roping the route first or padding the ground were utterly inconceivable. Equally inconceivable was the idea of seeking notoriety in the media after doing so.

Rob would now be Uncle Robbie to seven Slater boys and three Slater girls. He undoubtedly would have loved hanging out with them, and them with him as he enthralled them with his climbing stories and other at-the-Edge adventures. Just as undoubtedly, they would have been amazed by the casually-described dangers that formed the foundation of his tales. Most importantly, they would look within themselves and wonder if they could ever summon such courage, determination and will – and then conclude that, yes, *they could*. Rob had a way of doing that. He inspired the people around him to do more, or at least try more, than they ever thought possible – much like a good parent inspires a child first to dream and then take that first step toward reaching for their own personal sky.

One summer, I was pushing my young son, Robbie II on the swing when he called out, "I want to swing so high I go to Uncle Robbie!" On some level, everyone who knew Rob wanted to be like him. Everyone who knew him lived vicariously through him in some way. Rob was the epitome of courage and daring. Uncle Robbie has inspired the nephews and nieces who never got the chance to meet him. He has inspired me to go on and to try my best to keep his spirit alive in how I live, in my kids and in the wild places where we go to visit him. Rob was totally honed. Now he is a mountain god, but I still miss my brother.

Far away, in the heart of the Karakoram, an icy blast across the K2 summit ridge creates a trail of white extending for miles through an otherwise crystal blue sky. Unheard and unseen, the wind howls, the mountain demons shriek and the resident spirits dance before their gods.

My Mary

APPENDICES

*From Rob's K2 Journal

How to waste a summer? I shouldn't say that because climbing K2 is a very worthwhile goal, especially if/when I make it. Now on August 5th after another summit attempt has been thwarted by the weather, and my whole team is leaving, I thought I'd write down a few things that will occupy my time in the future-climbing-wise that is. More than anything, this trip has taught me (even though I already knew) that the best trips by far are with my best friends to specific objectives, preferably the desert/Res or Canada (on ice). Therefore, in no particular order, is a series of lists of the most appealing "future climbs," as well as things that may or may not be related to climbing.

APPENDIX 1

"Top Ten Reasons to Climb in Eldorado"

10. Mellow Yellow
 9. Le Void Roof
 8. Revelation
 7. Scary canary
 6. Book of Numbers
 5. Rover
 4. Tube-sock Tan Line
 3. Krystal Klyr
 2. To RP Or Not To Be
 1. Perilous Journey

ELDO RULES!

APPENDIX 2

"Canada On Ice"

1. Reality Bath
2. Arctic Dream
3. Riptide
4. Andromeda Strain
5. Kitchener Couloir
6. Deltaform Supercouloir
7. Sea of Vapors
8. French Maid
9. Nemesis
10. North Face Mt. Bryce

*Since four routes listed above are not pure ice routes, honorable mention must be given to Pilsner Pillar, Ice Nine, Takkakaw Falls and Weeping Pillar.

APPENDIX 3

"The Serious Stuff"

1. Right Mitten Thumb
2. North Sister
3. South Sister
4. Sentinel Tower
5. Mitchell Butte
6. Gray Wiskers Butte
7. Shangri-La
8. Yei-bi-Chei
9. Indian Chief
10. Bear and Rabbit

I need to get to work on this list ASAP when I get home.

"Other Serious Stuff"

1. Chinle Spire
2. Angel Wing
3. Candlestick Tower
4. North Sister (to finish off the whole ridge)
5. Aphrodite
6. Block-top
7. Horsethief Tower
8. Sheep Rock
9. Bridger Jack
10. Six-Shooters
11. Everything else not mentioned or already climbed

"Restaurants I Would Like to Eat In"

1. Amigo Café
2. Pasta Jay's in Moab
3. Ye Old Bridge Café (should be #2)
4. Stump and Magpie in Banff
5. The Diner in Mexican Water
6. The Oasis
7. Pablo's
8. Rio
9. Resded in Chicago
10. O'Fame' in Chicago
11. Taco John's in Lander, WY or Glenwood Springs, CO

12. Taco Bell in Grand Junction, CO
13. Roberto's in San Diego
14. La Chispa in Jackson, WY (should be #6)
15. Jackson Hole Golf and Tennis Club

This list is so out of order that I will stop at #15. Obviously, location is an important factor in restaurant quality.

APPENDIX 6

"Longs Peak Diamond Routes I Have Done"

	Partner
1. The Obelisk	Rollo
2. Aryanna	Alan Lester
3. Pervertical Sanctuary	Steve Kaiser
4. Curving Vine	Henry Lester
5. Hidden Diamond	Henry Lester
6. D-Minor 7	Rollo
7. D7	Al Torrisi
8. Black dagger	Rollo
9. Forrest Finish	Mike Gilbert
10. Yellow Wall	Hammer
11. Casual Route	Bruce Hunter

Need to do when next in shape:
-D1
-Erocia
-King of Swords
-Joker

"All the Fisher Towers"

		Partner
1.	River Tower	Stu Ritchie
2.	Dune Rock	Alan Lester
3.	Lizard	Tom Cosgriff, Hammer, Al, Stu, Tom Cotter, Mike O'Donnell
4.	Forming Tower	Tom Cotter, Stu
5.	Dock Rock	Stu
6.	Ancient Art	Sue Wint
7.	Kingfisher	Tom Cosgriff
8.	H.J. Pinnacle	Tom Cotter
9.	Cotton Tail	Stu
10.	Echo Tower	Stu
11.	Gypsy Eyes	Stu
12.	Gypsy Joker	Stu
13.	Sidekick	Stu, Ralph Burns
14.	Broadsword Rock	Stu, Ralph Burns
15.	Titan	Mike O'Donnell, Sue Wint
16.	Oracle	Stu
17.	Hindu	Cosgriff, Sue Wint
18.	Sari	Stu
19.	Mongoose	Stu
20.	Pink Pussycat	Hammer, Al
21.	Gothic Nightmare	John Sherman, O'Donnell, Sue Wint
22.	Citadel	John Sherman
23.	Doric Column	John Sherman

"I LOVE MUD"

APPENDIX 8

"The Best Desert Towers"

1. Left Mitten Thumb
2. Spider Rock
3. Totem Pole
4. Middle Sister
5. Cleopatra's Needle
6. Oracle
7. Citadel
8. Texas Tower
9. Jacob's Ladder
10. Eagle Rock Spire

This list, as I look over it, already seems wrong. Eagle Rock should be higher than #10 probably. What about Shiprock, Agathla or King on a Throne? Common routes like Moses or Sister Superior are not mentioned because they are too commonly climbed; this lessens their appeal. Illegal routes are more satisfying to climb and are thus more prominently featured on the list. Nailing routes are generally better than all free routes. The desert experience requires some nailing!

APPENDIX 9

"Illegal Towers I Have Climbed"

		Partner
1.	Totem Pole	Hammer
2.	Middle Sister	Hammer, Al
3.	Left Mitten	Hammer
4.	Agathla	Hammer, Elroy
5.	Owl Rock	Hammer

6.	Chiastla Butte	Hammer
7.	Jacob's Ladder	Hammer, Al
8.	Eagle Rock Spire	Hammer, Sandy Fleming
9.	King on a Throne	Stu, Brad Bod
10.	Throne	Stu
11.	Mitchell Mesa	Hammer, Al, Elroy
12.	Shiprock	Sue Wint
13.	Spider Rock	Hammer
14.	Venus Needle	Hammer
15.	Cleo's Needle	Hammer, Al

This List is WAY TOO SHORT!

APPENDIX 10

"El Cap Routes I Have Done"

		Partner
1.	Zodiac	Tom Cosgriff
2.	Shortest Straw	Bruce, Sherman
3.	Zenyatta Mondatta	Randy Leavitt
4.	Lost in America	Bruce
5.	Tangerine Trip	Cosgriff
6.	Scorched Earth	Randy Leavitt
7.	Wyoming Sheepranch	John Barbella
8.	Sea of Dreams	Mike O'Donnell
9.	Pacific Ocean Wall	Solo
10.	Dawn Wall	Joy
11.	Mescalito	Jack Collendar
12.	Nose	John Noak
13.	Nose	Hammer
14.	Nose	Rollo
15.	Shield	Steve Kaiser
16.	Aquarian Wall	Rob Kapenta

Aborted attempts on Born Under a Bad Sign (twice), Sunkist, Salathe, Wings of Steel

APPENDIX 11

"My Favorite Eldorado Routes"

1. Naked Edge
2. Le Toit
3. Serpent
4. Diving Board
5. Sidewalk
6. Super Slab
7. Center Route
8. Ariel Book
9. Scotch 'n Soda
10. Anything on the Rotwand

*X-M has to be on this list also. It should probably be #6 and replace S.S.
*Leane's Dream should be #4

APPENDIX 12

"The Classic Eldo Scary Routes"

1. Night,   5.11b X 5.11 crux 30 feet out from protection
2. St. Augustine,   5.11c or 12AR   5.10 moves 35 feet out
3. In Between,   5.11b R stemming above #2 RP's
4. Inner Space, 5.11b crux 40 feet above bad pro
5. Marie Antoinette, 5.10a X   ground fall from 35 feet
6. Love Minus Zero, 5.11c backed off twice!!
7. Leane's Dream, 5.11b   Perfect face pitch
8. Deception Passed, 5.10b   Loose but great!
9. Scary Canary,   5.11d   Loose
10. South Face of T-1, 5.10c Run out

These routes never have chalk except for mine, Gilbert's and Brigg's.

APPENDIX 13

"Tapes I have @ K2 Base Camp"

1. Enya
2. Enigma
3. Cars
4. Cranberries
5. Iron Maiden
6. Scorpions
7. The Wall
8. Hootie and the Blowfish
9. Kate Bush
10. Pearl Jam
11. Rush
12. U2
13. Clannad
14. Morrissey

I'm sick of all of them except Enya.

APPENDIX 14

"Things to Worry About @ K2"

1. Weather
2. Will I make the summit?
3. Weather
4. Getting a job
5. Money to buy expensive books
6. Going home
7. Coming back
8. Will life go on if I don't summit?
9. The next desert tower to do- Rt. Thumb
10. The Mountain
11. Life passing me by
12. Growing old and having no life
13. Chapped lips

APPENDIX 15

"Food I'd Like NOW!"

1. Navajo Taco
2. Manicotti
3. Cap'n Crunch
4. Kate Moss

5. Any Mexican food w/o onions
6. Anything cooked by Al Torrisi except squid
7. Club sandwich and fries
8. Mom's applesauce cake w/ whipped cream
9. Salad from the Oasis
10. Thai food

APPENDIX 16

"Food Cooked By Rasul"

1. Dahl
2. Chapatti
3. Spaghetti
4. Macaroni
5. Tuna
6. Potatoes
7. Rice Pudding
8. Porridge
9. Black beans

BIBLIOGRAPHY

1. Robin Heid, Jump Shots, Westword, Volume 6, Issue 20, June 1-15, 1983
2. Sir Douglas Mawson, The Home of the Blizzard, London: William Heinemann, 1915
3. Galen Rowell, In the Throne Room of the Mountain Gods, Sierra Club Books, 1986
4. Suz Platt, Respectfully Quoted, Barnes & Noble Books, 1993
5. The Illustrated World Atlas, Barnes & Noble Books, 2004
6. Roberta Mantovani, Kurt Diemberger, K2: Challenging the Sky, White Star S.r.l.,1995
7. Jennifer Jordan, Savage Summit, The Life and Death of the First Women of K2, William Morrow, HarperCollins Publishers, 2005
8. Jim Haberl, K2 Dreams and Reality, Tantalus Publishing, LTD, 1994
9. Nazir Sabir, Expedition Organizer: Bodies Will Be Left On K2, Billings Gazette, August 19, 1995
10. Greg Child, The Last Ascent of Alison Hargreaves, Outside, November 1995
11. Charles S. Houston and Robert H. Bates, K2: The Savage Mountain, McGraw-Hill Book Company, Inc., 1954
12. Meaghan Miller, K2: Mountain of Death, 1995
13. Christian Brackman, The Curse of K2, The Denver Post, 1995
14. Xavier Eguskita, Spanish Version of the K2 Tragedy, based on the statements provided and corroborated by Jose Garces and Lorenzo Ortas, August 27, 1995
15. The Encyclopedia Americana, Encyclopedia Americana Corporation, 1952
16. Galen Rowell, The Yosemite, John Muir, Sierra Club Books, 1989
17. Gary Wisby, Flatlands Drive These Climbers Up a Wall, Chicago Sun Times, May 9, 1988
18. Dave Kingham, Slater Will Be On Annual Climb, The Wyoming Tribune-Eagle, December 25, 1976
19. United Press International, Teton Climbers Reach Summit,

The Wyoming Tribune-Eagle, January 1, 1977

20. Alison Osius, Fast Train, Climbing Magazine, November 1-December 15, 1995
21. John Sherman, Sherman Exposed: Slightly Censored Climbing Stories, The Mountaineers, 1999
22. Mark Schacter, Jumping Off Point: Cliffs, Towers, Spans Attract Sport Divers, Wall Street Journal, June 27, 1986
23. Dr. Brent Weigner, Polar Dreams
24. Royal Robbins, Basic Rockcraft, La Siesta Press, 1971
25. Geoff Shackelford, Golf at Mount Everest, geoffshackelford.com, April 21, 2009
26. Lennard Bickel, Mawson's Will, The Greatest Survival Story Ever Written, Stein and Day Publishers, 1977
27. Daniel Defoe, Robinson Crusoe, W. Taylor, London, 1719
28. Walter Isaacson, Einstein, His Life and Universe, Simon & Schuster Paperbacks, 2007
29. Wikipedia, El Capitan, Wikimedia Foundation, Inc, December 30,2010
30. El Capitan, www.extranomical.com, Extranomical Adventures, Inc., 2011
31. www.english.turkceilgi.com/death+zone
32. www.climbing.about.com/K2AbruzziSpur
33. www.stanford.edu/~clint/yos/elcapd.txt

11215737R00198

Made in the USA
Charleston, SC
08 February 2012